Family Torn Apart

Family Torn Apart

The Internment Story of the
Otokichi Muin Ozaki Family

Edited by Gail Honda

Japanese Cultural Center of Hawai'i

Honolulu

Printed in the United States of America
18 17 16 15 14 13   6 5 4 3 2 1

ISBN   978-0-9761493-1-6

Library of Congress Cataloging-in-Publication Data

Family torn apart : the internment story of the Otokichi Muin Ozaki
family / edited by Gail Honda.
       p. cm.
  Includes bibliographical references and index.
  ISBN 978-0-9761493-1-6 (pbk. : alk. paper)
  1. Ozaki, Otokichi Muin, 1904-1983. 2. Ozaki family. 3. Japanese
  Americans--Evacuation and relocation, 1942-1945. 4. Japanese
  Americans--Hawaii--Biography. I. Honda, Gail. II. Japanese Cultural
  Center of Hawaii.
  D769.8.A6F36 2012
  940.53'177309239560969--dc23   2011041287

The translated poems, "I bid farewell," "I look around," and "In the sudden downpour," are reprinted from *Poets Behind Barbed Wire* with the
permission of Jiro Nakano and Kay Yokoyama.

The translation of Shoichi Asami's poem, "Raging waves of fury," is used
with the permission of George and Emi Oshiro.

The sketch, "News Broadcasting," by George Hoshida is reprinted with
the permission of the Japanese American National Museum.

Layout by Shu and Suann Chen, FreelanceDreams LLC

Printed by Sheridan Books, Inc.

CONTENTS

FOREWORD

JAMES T. MCILWAIN

World War II was a catastrophe so vast that its impact on the personal lives of millions of individuals is scarcely visible in the grand narratives of victory and defeat. One must turn instead to memoir, biography or a book such as this, the story of one family's dislocation from their home in Hawai'i and their incarceration on the mainland of the United States. It represents the collective effort of a team of professionals, volunteers, and family members, who have selected, translated, organized, and provided commentary on material from the Otokichi Ozaki Collection of the Japanese Cultural Center of Hawai'i.

The voice of Otokichi Muin Ozaki, citizen of Japan, husband, father, language teacher, journalist, intellectual, and poet, is heard in transcripts of radio broadcasts he made after the war, broadcasts describing his experiences in internment camps run by the U.S. Army or the Department of Justice and, finally, reunited with his family, in the so-called relocation centers of Jerome in Arkansas and Tule Lake in California. His voice is also present in newsletters written in camp for fellow internees, in poems, and in a few personal letters to others, which found their way into the collection. Letters received from fellow internees speak of events in the camps, common concerns, friendships formed, and kindnesses rendered. Correspondence from his American-born wife, Hideko, portrays a family living for a time without the father and recounts the every-day concerns of a mother of four young children, who is coping with the privations of life in the relocation center at Jerome while keeping her distant husband informed about family and property in Hawai'i. In these letters Hideko's anxious devotion to her husband and children is palpable. Also perceptible here, if in muted form, is a delicate negotiation between a father who wished to return to Japan and a mother who did not. Another correspondent frequently represented is Ozaki's father, Tomoya, who emerges as a vigorous, generous, and sometimes amusing personality. Dependent on the kindness and hospitality of relatives in Hawaiʻi, he often illuminates the web of reciprocal obligations existing among four families bound to each other by marriage, custom, and necessity. These and a variety of other documents from the collection have been organized by editor Gail Honda into a fascinating account of the Ozaki family as it, like so many other families of Japanese ancestry, endured and survived the hard years of World War II.

Disillusioned by the indignities and injustices of wartime internment and the discriminatory laws that denied them full participation in American society, many men of the immigrant generation, including Otokichi Muin Ozaki, requested repatriation to Japan. This was doubtless a factor in the family's move from Jerome to Tule Lake, which had been converted to a segregation center for those classified as "disloyal" through a process distinguished by bureaucratic bungling and breathtaking arbitrariness. Over 4,000 people were shipped from Tule Lake to a devastated Japan after the war, a third of them minors, who were American citizens. We are fortunate that the Ozaki family was not among them. Were it not for their return to Hawaiʻi and Otokichi Muin Ozaki's continued participation in the life of its Japanese community, we would not have this book.

* * *

James T. McIlwain, emeritus professor at Brown University, has an abiding interest in the history of Americans of Japanese ancestry. During a pilgrimage to Tule Lake, he was introduced to the Ozaki story by Lily Ozaki Arasato, who gave him a copy of *Poets Behind Barbed Wire*, a collection of poems, which includes several by her father, Otokichi Muin Ozaki. He is grateful to Lily Ozaki Arasato for introducing him to her father's poetry.

MESSAGE FROM A DAUGHTER

LILY OZAKI ARASATO

This is a story of my family's trying experiences during World War II. We share it with you, as it is a human story that illuminates another unseen and unreported hardship caused by wars.

I am the youngest of four children of my parents, Otokichi and Hideko Ozaki. We lived in peaceful ʻAmauulu plantation camp near Hilo on the Big Island of Hawaiʻi.

On the evening of December 7, 1941, shortly after the bombing of Pearl Harbor, unbeknownst to us sleeping children, our father was unceremoniously arrested and imprisoned. He then expressed his thoughts in a short poem:

> I bid farewell
> To the faces of my sleeping children
> As I am taken prisoner
> Into the cold night rain.[1]

We would not see him for over two long years.

I must confess that I was too young to remember the details of our experiences recorded in these pages, but the letters, poems, and memoirs stir my emotions as I recall bits and pieces of my early days. Indeed, my mother's letters provided me with vivid pictures of my innocently growing up in concentration camps.

As I gained adulthood, my curiosity and interest in our internment experience intensified. I collected books and other writings concerning the internment of the Japanese during the war and made pilgrimages to Jerome and Tule Lake.

I am glad that we were able to settle back in our native Hawaiʻi. With the help of relatives and friends, we enjoyed a normal family life in Hawaiʻi. Our dad was able to utilize his talents in the media field and we children were able to get a good education.

During the war, the FBI concluded: "We do not see how this man [Ozaki] can ever become loyal to the United States of America, and we do not believe that his children will ever be brought up as Americans."[2] As it turned out, my brothers as adults were appointed to serve in positions of responsibility in the federal government: Earl served as head of the U.S. Department of Agriculture's Inspection Unit for Asia and resided in the U.S. Embassy Compound in Tokyo, and Carl served with the U.S. Army Signal Corps.

This is still a great country, and I am proud to be one of its citizens, but we must never again treat families in such a discriminatory, impersonal and dehumanizing manner. Hopefully, our past will make all of us better human beings.

* * *

This book was made possible by the dedicated efforts of many individuals. I wish to thank them all, especially my cousin Richard Hiromichi Kosaki and my friend James McIlwain.

PREFACE

This book is about the internment experience of a first-generation Japanese in Hawai'i, but it is first and foremost about friends and family. Internment of a population based on race is a blight on our history we hope never to see again, but an unexpected hardship such as this could happen to anyone. This book is about how one person coped with adversity, and how an entire community of friends and family rallied to support him and his family. In this sense, this book is about any and all of us.

This is the story of Otokichi Muin Ozaki's internment experience, but unlike other books on the firsthand experience of internees, most of the original sources included in this book are not written by him. The radio scripts and camp news are, yes, written by Ozaki. But the vast majority of the materials are letters written by family and friends responding to his correspondence. It is fortuitous that Ozaki was such a prolific writer, because the scores of letters written back to him provide a 360-degree view of internment rarely documented. Through these letters, a vast network of relationships, that spanned the Pacific between Ozaki in Mainland camps and his friends and family back in Hawai'i, is revealed in all its humanness, from the mundane to the heroic.

These letters also provide a unique glimpse into what life was like for those left behind in Hawai'i—the loss of the household head, the scarcity of foodstuffs, the enlistment of Nisei soldiers, the scrabble to make a living. Thanks to the generosity of the Ozaki family, we are privileged to witness the effect of war and internment on a family in all of its fascinating minutiac, including births and deaths, marriage, illness, finances, and friendships strong and weak.

Ozaki's story is the second in a trilogy of books about the internment experiences of first-generation Japanese in Hawai'i and involving the efforts of the Resource Center of the Japanese Cultural Center of Hawai'i. The first, *Life behind Barbed Wire: The World War II Internment Memoirs of a Hawai'i Issei*, is a translation by Kihei Hirai of *Tessaku Seikatsu*, a firsthand account by Yasutaro Soga, the editor of a Japanese language newspaper.[1] The account is erudite and factual, as bespeaks Soga's trained eye as a professional journalist. The third is another firsthand account, a soon-to-be-published translation by Tatsumi Hayashi of Kumaji Furuya's *Haisho Tenten*.[2] Of the three, Ozaki's story is the most homespun. It is a firsthand account, but rather than that of the internee himself, mostly of family and friends who provided emotional, financial, and in-kind support that would see Ozaki through his tribulation. Their writing is simple and conversational, allowing the reader to imagine the faces and personalities of the writers. What Ozaki did write that remains in the collection—his camp news, which he broadcast to internees while incarcerated, and his postwar radio scripts on internment—is often humorous, always forthright.

Indeed, a video of Ozaki filmed in 1978[3] captures the image of an ebullient man with an infectious smile and a luminous complexion un-marred by lines of worry and distress. It is the life of this man, intelligent and playful, and those of his close-knit family and abundant friends far-flung by the war, that I invite you to savor.

* * *

Notes on the Text

All documents in this book are Japanese language originals translated into English, unless otherwise noted.

Japanese American personal names, including those of the Issei, are given in the American order, family name last. Japanese names are rendered in the Japanese style, family name first.

The information that precedes each letter, which identifies the date and the author's and recipient's names and locations, is provided by the editor. In many of the original documents, people's names appeared in vari-ous ways, dates were incomplete, and place names were inferred from the identity of the author. Information that is bracketed does not appear in the original, but was arrived at by the translators, based on contextual readings of the documents.

Footnote information about Hawai'i internees is from the Japanese Cultural Center of Hawai'i database, "Hawai'i Japanese and Japanese Americans Detained During World War II"; or *Nippu Jiji*'s 1941 edition of its *Hawai nenkan*,[4] unless otherwise noted.

Three ellipses indicate trail offs used by the writers in the original documents; four ellipses indicate abridgement by the editor.

Information in parentheses is as it appears in the original documents; brackets enclose interpolations by the translators.

The translations retain the contemporaneous use of camp names and terminology as the writers used them. Thus, for example, what may be called an "incarceration center" today was referred to as a "relocation camp" in the documents of the time. The translators have attempted to retain this usage.

ACKNOWLEDGMENTS

Family Torn Apart: The Internment Story of the Otokichi Muin Ozaki Family is truly a collaborative work. Each person who contributed played a crucial role in its transformation from boxes of scattered notes to published book.

This book is possible thanks to the generosity of the Otokichi Muin Ozaki family. Eldest son, Earl Ozaki, kindly donated his father's papers—seven linear feet in total—to the Resource Center of the Japanese Cultural Center of Hawai'i (JCCH) prior to 1994. Youngest daughter, Lily Ozaki Arasato, played an active role throughout the process and shared family photos and memories of her father.

The Japanese Cultural Center of Hawai'i gratefully acknowledges the generous contributions of the following individuals and organization, without whose support this publication would not have been possible: Lily Ozaki Arasato, Kazuo and Ellen Kosaki, Richard and Mildred Kosaki, Russell and Gail Masui, James McIlwain, Dwight Nishida, Kazue Ozaki, George and Mabel Terada and the Hilo Nihonjin Gakko Endowment.

Thanks to the steadfast leadership of Jane Kurahara, who guided the book's creation from beginning to end, the Ozaki story has been told and is able to be shared. In the initial stages, she organized the papers and secured a grant from the Hawai'i Council for the Humanities to purchase supplies to preserve the documents. She was also able to bring Marie Dolores (Dolly) Strazar of the Hawai'i State Foundation on Culture and the Arts onto the project, who advised on organizing the collection into archival folders and boxes.

The Ozaki book committee provided thoughtful direction and guidance, as well as comments on earlier drafts of the manuscript. It was comprised of Brian Niiya, JCCH director of program development; Richard Hiromichi Kosaki, nephew of Otokichi Ozaki and vice chancellor emeritus for academic affairs at the University of Hawai'i at Manoa; James T. McIlwain, emeritus professor at Brown University; Dennis Ogawa, professor of American studies at the University of Hawai'i at Manoa; Lily Ozaki Arasato; and Jane Kurahara and Betsy Young, JCCH staff emeritae.

Tatsumi Hayashi, Kihei Hirai, Florence Sugimoto, and Shige Yoshi-take lent their bilingual expertise and talents to translate the documents. They worked assiduously to turn the notes, many in hard-to-decipher handwritten Japanese, into letters, poetry, and radio scripts accessible to an English-speaking audience. Poets Frances Kakugawa and Jean Toyama, professor emerita at the University of Hawai'i, rendered the translated poems more lyrically.

Once the final draft of the manuscript had been edited into book form, Shayna Coleon, copy editor, meticulously combed through the document to assure consistency in format and writing. Shu Zong and Suann Chen turned the word-processed manuscript pages into the beautiful layout you see before you. Sheila Chun, managing editor, applied her formidable organizational and editing skills to hunt down important pieces of information that add to the richness of the book and encouraged retranslations of certain documents to assure the highest possible quality of literary merit.

INTRODUCTION

"You had better take some heavy clothes with you. You may not be coming back for three or four days," said a policeman I had known, when he came to take me into custody at midnight on December 7. He did not tell me where I would be taken. Not knowing that three or four days would turn into three or four years, I stepped out of my house with just a jacket and a sweater . . . . We were turned over to the custody of the military authorities [at Kīlauea Military Camp]. That night I could not sleep at all, wrapped in a blanket and shivering with cold, listening to the sound of the falling rain. I wrote some *tanka* that night.

> Scattered among us
> Many a Nikkei
> Taken prisoner.
> Why?[1]

So began the tenure of Otokichi as an internee, a prisoner of war in America's concentration camps—in eight of them, in fact: Kīlauea Military Camp and Sand Island in Hawai'i, Angel Island in California, Fort Sill in Oklahoma, Camp Livingston in Louisiana, Santa Fe in New Mexico, Jerome in Arkansas, and Tule Lake in California.

Ozaki, who came to Hawai'i at the age of twelve, attended an English-language boarding school in Hilo, and completed his Japanese education at Hilo Dokuritsu Nihonjin Gakkō. He became the youngest charter member of Gin-u Shisha at the age of nineteen, taught at Dokuritsu Gakkō, married a *kibei*,* Hideko Kobara, and fathered four children. He also grew beautiful flowers, among them an anthurium that became known as "Ozaki Red."

---

* A person of Japanese ancestry born in the U.S., who goes to Japan to be educated, and then returns to the U.S.

Like others who were literate and educated, Ozaki became one of several individuals who functioned as agents for the Japanese Consulate in Hilo to service Japanese friends and neighbors. When war broke out on December 7, 1941, this made him a target for suspicion, and as indicated earlier, he was promptly picked up by the military authorities.

The Otokichi Muin Ozaki papers, a newly processed collection in the archives of the Resource Center of the Japanese Cultural Center of Hawai'i, is one of the first sizable collections of papers of a Hawai'i internee to be processed, much of it translated into English, and made available for research. A splendid amalgam of literary materials and historic records, this collection opens up many new possibilities for historical, sociological, literary, and other research into and education on Hawai'i's Japanese American community, and specifically, Hawai'i internees in the wartime camps.

The collection includes a wide range of materials either written or collected by Mr. Ozaki: correspondence, poetry, diary notes, radio broadcast scripts, newspaper articles, play scripts, song lyrics, photographs, as well as Mrs. Ozaki's letters from 1941 to 1943 and some family records and memorabilia. The predominant subject matter of the collection is Mr. Ozaki's internment experience; the collection represents various materials related to that experience, including some records of internment camp organization and operations, instructions, and lists of internees as well as what can be called internment camp news media. Mr. Ozaki appears to have written his radio scripts from notes he made during his incarceration.

With seven linear feet of materials that are primarily focused on the internment experience, there is an extensive range of topics that can be researched: specific details of internment operations, relationships among family members, treatment of Hawai'i's Japanese families during World War II, the details of separation of families, conditions in various camps, activities during internment, communication between camps, communication with "the outside world," gender roles, and gender-based differentiation of treatment.

Beyond strictly internment history, this collection also lends itself to an even wider range of topics for research; for example, general social and cultural history of America and Hawai'i in the 1940s and that history as it relates to a particular immigrant group in America and its territories. Aspects of lifestyle can be researched, e.g., what kind of clothing was worn, what personal items were desired or needed, what kind of food was eaten or desired to be eaten, what holidays were celebrated and how.

A quick perusal of some of the translated materials indicated some general characteristics of the 1940s lifestyle. For example, hair pomade or hair oil appeared to be important to the men. (And we are talking almost exclusively about men when we refer to early Hawaiʻi internees.) For uniquely Hawaiʻi touches in apparel, one will find aloha shirts in the lists of personal items that some Hawaiʻi internees chose to bring with them.

Since the collection also includes Ozaki's broadcast scripts and other materials that he produced or collected after his internment and return to Hawaiʻi, it can be researched for further details of Hawaiʻi history including the receptivity of Hawaiʻi Japanese to information about internment.

From a sociological point of view, a researcher can use data in this collection to estimate degrees of acculturation and/or assimilation by studying some of the lifestyle information that can be found. Lifestyle references can also possibly give some indication of the impact of the camp experience on further acculturation or assimilation that might have occurred. Because the experience of Japanese immigrants and Japanese Americans in Hawaiʻi was significantly different from the experience of Japanese immigrants and Japanese Americans on the Mainland, the internment camp experience could be studied for the impact it had in connecting two similar sets of people who had had different experiences. This may even yield some potential for comparison and contrast studies on that general topic of immigrant and ethnic sociology.

From yet another point of view, a literary one, this collection is important for the *tanka* poetry it contains and for the biodata, thought processes, and experiences of the poet, Muin Ozaki (Ozaki's pen name), himself. Scholars of literature should find this collection rich in resources. Furthermore, since Ozaki wrote drama scripts and prose pieces as well, the collection reflects an even wider range of literary materials. Linguists studying the Japanese language and immigration impacts on the language will also find these materials a rich trove, especially since the collection represents Ozaki's writing over a long span of time.

For researchers interested in the role of religion and philosophy in the internment experience, there is some information in Ozaki's internment notes, though it is not extensive. There is an occasional mention of the visit of a Buddhist functionary to a camp and references to the memorial services for those who died in camp. Nonetheless, the collection can be analyzed from the point of view of religion, philosophy, and psychology, especially if one focuses on the materials from the internment period. Both Ozaki's notes and his wife's letters can be analyzed for this purpose.

Standing out the most in a perusal of the entire collection is the overall impact of the internment experience on Mr. Ozaki and his thoughts about it. The materials reveal some of the contradictions that he felt internment represented and the inconsistencies of policies, the latter especially in the first months of America's being at war. (Patsy Sumie Saiki summarizes this very well in her 1982 book, *Ganbare! An Example of Japanese Spirit.*[2])

Hawai'i Japanese families had to endure the hardship of a far-flung separation of families as fathers were taken away to the Mainland. This was something that Mainland Japanese Americans did not have to endure quite as much since, in most cases, entire families were relocated. These differences in the impact of the internment pose another potential for research utilizing these Ozaki papers.

Humor is interspersed throughout the collection, lending the researcher a special view into the reality of POW and internment experience. Only with at least a little bit of humor could anyone endure life in an internment camp, especially without one's family. So, occasionally in Ozaki's portrayal of the experience, one will read a tongue-in-cheek rendition of an event that will include a reference like making sure to get enough to eat so that you can live until you are, perhaps, executed on the following day. Thus, just as one is reading through a piece of tongue-in-cheek humor, the reader is also faced with the fact that those incarcerated believed in the possibility that they could be facing execution. The reality of the experience for earlier POWs, such as Ozaki, was the almost unimaginable: not knowing whether they were facing death or not.

Bitterness, too, comes through to the reader. The bitterness seems to be balanced, however, in reference to the first months of America at war as Ozaki excuses the behavior of the American military as inexperienced and not having procedures and guidelines in place. Nonetheless, Ozaki does point out that some of the treatment he and his fellow internees received, especially at Sand Island, simply did not conform to the conventions for Prisoners of War.

Mrs. Ozaki's letters, written during the period when the family was separated from Ozaki, both in Hawai'i and on the Mainland in different camps, are also included in this collection. The completeness of this portion of the collection is noteworthy and useful as such to the researcher. The letters give the details of everyday life at home in Hawai'i and later, in camp, with the children and amidst a painful separation. The letters are laden with comments about the children's performance in school, their behavior, and their health. In the letters originating in Hawai'i, much is also said about the grandparents and their opinions in regard to Ozaki's family's possible repatriation to Japan (to which they were opposed) and what the family should do.

Mrs. Ozaki and the children had left Hawaiʻi in the hopes of reuniting with Ozaki in January of 1943. They were sent to Jerome, Arkansas, however, and Ozaki was in Livingston, Louisiana. The family was not reunited until fourteen or fifteen months later. The pain of separation is clearly conveyed in Mrs. Ozaki's letters; so, too, the dilemma of possible repatriation to Japan.

In conclusion, this newly available Otokichi Muin Ozaki Collection addresses the paucity of primary research materials, i.e., diaries, correspondence, and other firsthand written materials of Hawaiʻi internees who were incarcerated on the U.S. Mainland during World War II. It, therefore, represents a noteworthy addition of a wide range of historical materials for research and study of yet another aspect of the Japanese internment as well as the Japanese experience in Hawaiʻi and general local history.

The collection comprises a unique rendition of history by a literary man, Otokichi (Muin) Ozaki, described by Patsy Sumie Saiki as a "poet-philosopher-teacher."[3] It also includes Hideko Kobara Ozaki's record of her life and thoughts during the separation imposed by internment. The collection is, therefore, a uniquely rich and balanced one, a welcome addition to Hawaiʻi's archival resources.

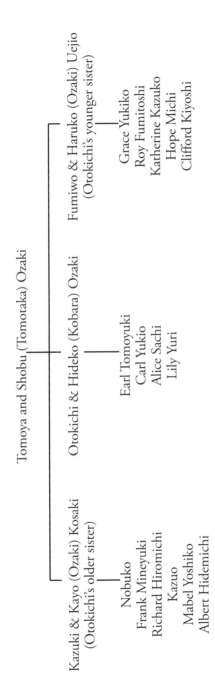

Otokichi Ozaki's Family Tree

Tomoya and Shobu (Tomotaka) Ozaki

Kazuki & Kayo (Ozaki) Kosaki (Otokichi's older sister)

Nobuko
Frank Mineyuki
Richard Hiromichi
Kazuo
Mabel Yoshiko
Albert Hidemichi

Otokichi & Hideko (Kobara) Ozaki

Earl Tomoyuki
Carl Yukio
Alice Sachi
Lily Yuri

Fumiwo & Haruko (Ozaki) Uejio (Otokichi's younger sister)

Grace Yukiko
Roy Fumitoshi
Katherine Kazuko
Hope Michi
Clifford Kiyoshi

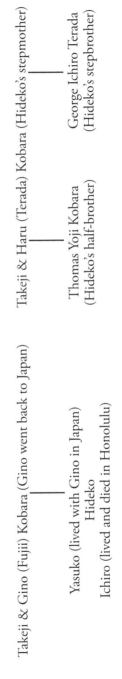

Hideko (Kobara) Ozaki's Family Tree

Takeji & Gino (Fujii) Kobara (Gino went back to Japan)

Yasuko (lived with Gino in Japan)
Hideko
Ichiro (lived and died in Honolulu)

Takeji & Haru (Terada) Kobara (Hideko's stepmother)

Thomas Yoji Kobara (Hideko's half-brother)

George Ichiro Terada (Hideko's stepbrother)

OTOKICHI OZAKI'S
INTERNMENT HISTORY

From	To	No. Of Days	Location
12-07-41	02-19-42	74	Kīlauea Military Camp
02-21-42	03-04-42	11	Honolulu Immigration Station
03-04-42	03-22-42	18	Sand Island Detention Camp
03-22-42	03-30-42	8	On board ship
03-30-42	04-09-42	10	Fort McDowell Internment Camp (Angel Island), California
04-09-42	05-30-42	51	Fort Sill Internment Camp, Oklahoma
05-30-42	06-02-43	368	Livingston Internment Camp, Louisiana
01-15-43			Hideko and children arrive at Jerome Incarceration Center, Arkansas
06-03-43	03-23-44	298	Santa Fe Internment Camp, New Mexico
03-23-44	05-08-44	46	Family reunited at Jerome Incarceration Center, Arkansas
05-08-44	12-02-45	573	Tule Lake Incarceration Center, California
12-02-45	12-10-45	8	In transit
12-10-45			Arrival in Honolulu

1,460 days/4 years[1]

FAMILY ROOTS:
JAPAN AND HAWAI'I

> They were so needy that they often wore hand-me-down
> clothes given to them by relatives and neighbors.
>
> —Nobuko Kosaki Fukuda, on her
> uncle Otokichi Ozaki's childhood in
> Japan

OTOKICHI MUIN OZAKI was born on November 5, 1904 in Ikegawa town, Agawa county, Kōchi prefecture, in the southern part of the island of Shikoku in Japan. He was the fifth son and ninth child of Tomoya and Shobu (Tomotaka) Ozaki. Tomoya, his father, struggled as a tenant farmer and owned no property. Their family had little beyond life's necessities. Tomoya was a man of many talents, but not financially successful because of the harsh economic conditions in Shikoku. In addition to farming, he dyed fabrics in Japan for *montsuki*.* He could sew, cook, do carpentry, and was a gardener for his sister, Fujiwara Ōyaku. Because she was a gentle, wise, and smart woman, people came to her for advice. Ōyaku lived next to the Tomotakas, which is how Tomoya Ozaki met Shobu Tomotaka.

They married and Shobu bore him ten children. Their first child was Haru (female, who died in infancy), followed by Seimi, Wakichi, Hakuma, Genkichi, Kikuju (female, who lived about ten years), Kaneo (female, later changed her name to Kayo), Itoe (female), Otokichi, and then Haruo (female, later changed her name to Haruko).† They were so needy that they often wore hand-me-down clothes given to them by relatives and neighbors.[1] Like many farmers at the time who sought a better life in another country, Tomoya left Japan for Hawai'i in 1907 or 1908. He left before Haruko was born, and helped to deliver all their children, except for Haruko, whom Shobu delivered by herself. Shobu joined him around 1912. They settled in the Puna district on the southern end of the Big Island of

---

*A formal kimono bearing the family crest.

†Ozaki's sister Kayo was actually given the name Kaneo at birth. But the name Kaneo is a masculine name, and thus she disliked it. She changed her name to Kayo in 1955, when she became a naturalized U.S. citizen. Because she so disliked her birth name, Kayo will be used in this book. Similarly, Ozaki's sister Haruko was given the masculine name Haruo at birth. She also disliked her name, and subsequently changed it.

Hawaiʻiˑ in a place called Kauʻeleau. Remaining behind were Otokichi and his sisters Kayo and Haruko, left in the care of their eldest brother, Seimi, and his family. Seimi later died from tuberculosis and did not live to see his twin daughters born. When Seimi died, the Ozaki siblings went to live with an uncle Tomotaka Heiji and his family. Later, Seimi's wife and their twin girls also died from tuberculosis.

Otokichi's childhood, in addition to being mired in poverty, was characterized by physical hardship. His leg became infected, when it was punctured by a crochet needle, and he had to spend a year and a half at home. With the help of a teacher, Yamanaka Haruka, he was able to keep up with his studies. Otokichi considered Yamanaka Haruka his mentor. She saw potential in him and encouraged him in his studies. After he received the Sixth Class Order of the Sacred Treasure[†] in 1977, he had his sister Haruko call Yamanaka Haruka on one of her many trips to Japan to thank Haruka for the support he received during his schooling in Japan.

Otokichi had always excelled in school and was awarded red ribbons yearly for being the top student (red was for the best; yellow for second best). With his injured leg, he could only sit in the Japanese style with one leg under him. His sister Haruko would sit next to him in the winter so that her *haori*[‡] would cover his stiff leg and keep it warm. Outdoors, she would tease him and call him "Otokichi *no chinba*"[§] and run away because he could not chase after her. Otokichi was a good brother and took care of his siblings. Haruko would tag along with him and his friend Masao. In the winter he would carry her metal sewing box to school so her hands would not get cold. The school was a long walk south over two mountain ridges.[2]

When Otokichi was twelve years old, his parents sent for him. Otokichi and his sisters were allowed to emigrate thanks to the so-called Gentlemen's Agreement of 1907-1908 between the U.S. and Japanese governments, before emigration was shut down completely in 1924. The agreement was a result of anti-Japanese agitation in San Francisco, so that the only Japanese allowed to immigrate, aside from certain classes of individuals, were spouses and minor children of bona fide U.S. residents.[3] In 1917, in the middle of the fourth grade, Otokichi left Ikegawa Elementary School and set forth

---

*The island that Ozaki lived on before he was interned is called the island of Hawaiʻi, the same name as the chain of islands. It is also referred to as the Big Island.

†Kun Rokutō Zuihōshō, an official decoration within the Japanese award system established in 1875. Bestowed by the emperor, upon recommendation of the cabinet. These awards are often given to Japanese American community leaders for their community service.

‡A short coat worn over a kimono.

§"Otokichi the cripple"

for Hawai'i. (His sister Kayo had arrived on January 4, 1916, and his sister Haruko followed on November 16, 1923).[4] Uncle Heiji took Ozaki to Kobe, his port of departure, and even in those early days, Otokichi's precociousness was evident. In Kobe, he played *go*, a sophisticated game of strategy similar to chess, with adult challengers, who were impressed with his skills.[5]

In April 1917, he arrived at the port of Hilo, a larger town north of Puna. Although in a brand new country and culture, he excelled in school, and progressed swiftly through the various grades: in July 1921, he graduated from Hilo Dokuritsu Nihonjin Gakkō;* in 1923, he graduated from the eighth grade at 'Ōla'a Grammar School† in Puna. He advanced to Hilo High School, which was quite a lot of education for a man of his generation,‡ but left in his second year in June 1924, possibly because he had to work to help support his family.

Ozaki began his career that same month as a salesman for the *Hawaii Mainichi*, a daily Japanese newspaper located in Hilo.§ In February 1927 he was promoted to assistant general manager and sales manager. Self-described in his personal history as "devoted to the development of the Japanese community as an employee of the only Japanese media in Hilo," Ozaki used his position at the daily to foster positive change. To wit, in May 1927, Yasusaku Kudo of Pāhoa town in the Puna district founded the Taiheiyō Kaihatsu Kaisha.¶ The company succeeded in getting a contract with the Olaa Sugar Company** to let the farmers grow sugar cane independently, rather than as laborers on the plantations. Ozaki was designated the person-in-charge of this project for the *Hawaii Mainichi*, and actively supported it by writing articles and holding symposia. Thanks to his and others' efforts, the number of independent farmers gradually in-

---

*Hilo Independent Japanese School, also known as Hilo Dokuritsu Nihongo Gakkō. In 1916, a group of parents broke from the Hilo Hongwanji Mission's Japanese school to establish Dokuritsu as a secular language school, independent of the Buddhist temple.

†Originally a three-room schoolhouse, it grew to include the intermediate grades and was later renamed Kea'au Elementary and Intermediate schools.

‡At the time, Hilo High was the only public high school on the Big Island. The territory of Hawai'i's Department of Public Instruction had established one high school on each of the four major islands, with the other three being McKinley High School on O'ahu, Hāmākuapoko High School on Maui, and Līhue High School on Kaua'i. – Trans.

§Established in 1913, the bilingual newspaper's last edition appeared on December 8, 1941.

¶Pacific Development Corporation

**Founded in 1899 by B.F. Dillingham, Lorrin A. Thurston, and William H. Shipman, the Olaa Sugar Company comprised some 16,000 acres in the Hilo area, and in the Pāhoa and Kapoho regions of the Puna district, making it one of the largest sugar plantations in Hawai'i. It embarked on a program in which small farmers purchased or leased the land they cultivated, while processing their sugar crop at the company's mill. The company was renamed the Puna Sugar Company in 1960. – Trans.

creased, and the project became "the foundation of economic development in Hawai'i."[6]

In July 1928, Ozaki resigned from the *Hawaii Mainichi* and was invited to teach at Dokuritsu Gakkō, where he was an alumnus. He switched career tracks and became a teacher because in 1924 President Calvin Coolidge signed the immigration bill into law,* which effectively ended Japanese immigration to the U.S. and stemmed the flow of Japanese teachers to Hawai'i.[7] At Dokuritsu Gakkō,† he stood out as a Japanese language teacher because, rather than use stories about figures from Japanese history, he brought into the classroom tales of American heroes, according to former student Bernice Hirai. Dr. Hirai recalled that he encouraged his female students to participate in the Girl Reserves after-school program (similar to Girl Scouts), unlike other Japanese teachers. He thus had a reputation of having a "very broad outlook and attitude."[8]

His outlook and attitude still resonate today with his former students. Shiho S. Nunes, a former student of Ozaki's who became a close family friend, recalls that Ozaki encouraged her at a young age to read classic English novels and took her and her brother to watch American movies: "He was always Ozaki Sensei to me. He was a teacher on the staff of the Dokuritsu Gakkō and already a reporter with connections to the Hilo and Honolulu Japanese language papers. He lived in the dormitory at the old Dokuritsu, taught Japanese, monitored the study hall required of boarding students. My father was the principal of the school, which in those days was on the corner of Ululani and Ponahawai streets in Hilo. My family lived in the dormitory until the war and the closure of the school.

"I remember standing with Ozaki Sensei next to the bookcase in the school office, listening to him talk about books. I was about ten years old, which places this around 1927. My father's desk was crammed into that small space with the desks of other teachers. In one corner was a small

---

*Known as the Japanese Exclusion Act, the 1924 Immigration Act used a quota system to limit the number of foreigners admitted into the U.S. and denied immigration to individuals ineligible for naturalization. In conjunction with an eighteenth century immigration law that allowed for the naturalization of only free whites and Africans, the 1924 Act essentially ended all Asian immigration for the next forty years. – Trans.

†For a description of the progressive nature of education at Hilo Dokuritsu, see Shiho S. Nunes and Sara Nunes-Atabaki, *The Shishu Ladies of Hilo: Japanese Embroidery in Hawai'i* (Honolulu: University of Hawai'i Press, 1999). According to Nunes, whose father, Yoshio Shinoda, served as principal during Ozaki's tenure, "Hilo Dokuritsu had an activist board and the backing of many of the more progressive families in town. They had a reputation as doers who rolled up their sleeves and got things done," Shishu, 37. On the eve of WWII, Dokuritsu had a student body of 775 and a teaching staff of fifteen, more than half of whom were Japanese American, making it the largest independent language school in the territory. – Trans.

bookcase with a set of encyclopedias and other books used by the staff, including Ozaki Sensei's personal collection of novels. *Les Miserables, The Three Musketeers, The Man in the Iron Mask, The Count of Monte Cristo*, a two-volume edition of *A Tale of Two Cities*, and (out of the blue) *A Girl of the Limberlost*, a novel written by the American naturalist Gene Stratton-Porter about a girl living on the edge of the Limberlost Swamp in Indiana.

"Ozaki Sensei was particularly fond of *Les Miserables*, by Victor Hugo, which was the first novel he started me on. I borrowed the book from the Hilo Library because his copy was in Japanese. In fact, most of his books were Japanese translations, though I recall that he was reading some in English. He told me the stories, encouraged me to read them, and by the time I was in intermediate school I had read them all. Now that I think back, they were all stories about outsiders who overcame huge obstacles, stories of endurance, fortitude and courage.

"He was a handsome man, somewhat formal, but very good with us children. He would take my big brother Minoru and me to the movies (admission ten cents) at either the Palace Theater on Hālaʻi Street or the Empire Theater directly across. (We preferred the Palace because of the pipe organ.) Ozaki Sensei always treated us, and our ten cents went for candy and peanuts. Thanks to him, we saw Janet Gaynor and Charles Farrell in *Seventh Heaven*, Ramon Novarro race a chariot in *Ben Hur*, Douglas Fairbanks in *The Iron Mask*, and other films."[9]

Nunes later writes in a letter to Ozaki's daughter, Lily Arasato: "Your dad's name Muin has always intrigued me. The modern dictionary [my daughter] Sue brought out was not helpful, but my father's old crumbling *Kenkyūsha Dictionary* yielded the following: *muin* = 'blank, free from writing or marks, having spaces to be filled in.' Now that is most interesting to me. In literature you learn about blank verses, an unrhymed, iambic pentameter verse that allows the poet considerable freedom. I can easily see your father taking advantage of every bit of freedom to express himself.'"*

"I never fully realized how important Ozaki Sensei was in my growing up years, until I really grew up. I have wished, though, that I could have, at some time in those busy years after the war was over, told him that. One of the great regrets of my life."[10]

---

*Shiho Nunes is referring to the word 無韻, also pronounced *muin*. Ozaki's pen name, Muin, is written with the characters 無音, which directly translated mean "without sound." Written as 無音, his pen name is a play on his given name, Otokichi 音吉 ("the lucky sound")—the character 音 being read "in" (the Chinese way) in his pen name and "oto" (the Japanese way) in his given name. This sort of play on words occurs in the pen names of Ozaki's poetry friends as well. – Trans.

Later, Ozaki was assigned to teach at Hilo Dokuritsu Chūjo Gakkō. The Hilo Independent Girls School came under the larger Hilo Dokuritsu administration and was founded to teach the Japanese language to daughters of Japanese families. A dedicated teacher, in 1933 he widened his influence on students in the Hilo area by volunteering to tutor students living on 'Amauulu Plantation near Hilo. Also in 1935, at the request of Higashi Hongwanji Mission, he opened classes on Sundays and organized the Ōtani Kondeidan* to "cultivate their aesthetic sentiments."[11]

'Amauulu Camp 1 in Hilo, where Ozaki lived during this time, was a sugar plantation where approximately 190 people made their home. The residents were mostly Japanese immigrants, but some were also Filipino and Portuguese. They worked in all areas of the plantation, as truck drivers and operators of heavy equipment, mechanics, mill workers, field workers, and office workers. According to one former resident,[12] most of the Portuguese laborers were the truck drivers and equipment operators, while fieldwork and some office jobs were given to the Japanese and Filipino workers. Few families could afford flush toilets, and bathhouses were communal facilities. Before 1935, most students in the camp attended school only through eighth grade because they had to work and help with the family finances. After 1935, some attended high school, and after the war, some attended college. Higher education was a luxury because children were needed to support the family. A few Nisei† children went to college, but only if their families could afford it, or if they were motivated to attend college. Some served in the military and attended college on the G.I. Bill. Most Sansei‡ children attended some post-high school institutions.

In 'Amauulu Camp, Ozaki volunteered his time to start a school where he provided help for students on their homework for both their English and Japanese classes. According to Elaine Hayashi Takato, a former student of his, Ozaki was very "straightforward." He spoke to his students in Japanese, and helped them with reading Japanese. "We respected him," said Takato, who was born in 'Amauulu in 1927. "When we had a question he was always there for us. We felt lucky to have him in 'Amauulu. All the kids respected Mr. Ozaki. He understood the plantation kids."[13] Elaine's

---

*The Higashi Hongwanji Mission, a Buddhist temple in Hilo's Waiākea Town, was established in 1928. A seventeenth century dispute among Shin-Jōdo Buddhist leaders in Japan split the sect into two branches, the Higashi (East) or Ōtani Hongwanji and the Nishi (West) or Honpa Hongwanji. The Ōtani Kondeidan, or the Vigorous Young Men of the Ōtani, was a club under the auspices of the temple. – Trans.

†A second generation Japanese American.

‡A third generation Japanese American.

sister, Patricia Hayashi Matsuda, knew Ozaki's children and was nine when Ozaki was arrested at the outbreak of war. She added, "Mr. Ozaki was no-nonsense."[14]

Herbert Segawa, a businessman and former state representative to the Hawai'i Legislature, describes his memories of Ozaki: "The Ozaki Sensei family lived in a wooden 10-x-12 plantation house, just below and next to the 'Amauulu Camp 1 gym. While every person or family who lived in a Hilo Sugar Co.-owned [plantation] house was an employee or retiree, the Ozaki family must have had special privileges to live there because neither the *sensei* nor his wife worked for the sugar company. I can only speculate that the sugar company felt that Ozaki Sensei would be a good influence on the camp people and allowed the family to live there.* Sensei would hold study periods every Friday night at the camp church and everyone who attended Dokuritsu Gakkō was required to attend—the *jinkoka* or younger children attended from 7:00 to 8:00 p.m., and the older *chūgakkō seito*[†] from 8:00 to 9:00 p.m. He would sit and do his studying while he made sure we were doing our homework and not playing around. I learned many of the moral values of *shūshin*,[‡] of respecting elders, filial piety, gratitude, honor, shame, etc., from Ozaki Sensei.

"I visited their home perhaps once or twice, and remember that the house was neatly painted and very orderly on the inside while the outside was the same maroon-stained camp house like everyone else's . . . . The Ozaki family kept pretty much to themselves and hardly mingled with camp people. The gym was always a gathering place for children but I rarely saw their children and never got to know them. While everyone else used the camp *furo*,[§] I did not see the Ozaki family at the camp *furo*, so I assumed that they had their own *furo*. They had plants and flowers around the small yard, but it was not until the 1950s when I had some interest in anthurium flowers that I heard that the Ozaki Red anthurium plant was developed by Ozaki Sensei.

"Ozaki Sensei was not very tall, had thick straight black hair combed to the right, wire rimless glasses, and always appeared well-dressed in a business suit . . . . He walked with a slight limp. He was a strict disci-

---

*Richard Hiromichi Kosaki, Ozaki's nephew, recalls that Ozaki's father worked in the sugar cane fields and, in fact, was given the task of caring for the sugar cane in an isolated patch of land that no one else wanted to cultivate. Richard Hiromichi Kosaki, e-mail correspondence to editor, February 27, 2009.

†Middle school students

‡A curriculum of moral education elucidated in the 1890 Imperial Rescript on Education and taught in grammar and middle schools in Japan, and in the Japanese language schools of Hawai'i.

§A bath; public baths were usually separated for women and men.

plinarian but had a friendly fatherly personality when talking to you. He was very much into *kendō** and coached the Dokuritsu Gakkō champion *kendō* team which competed against other Japanese school teams like Hilo Hongwanji, Kaumana, Yashijima,[†] and other countryside Japanese school teams, according to my older brother, Richard Segawa, who competed at a *yonkyū*[‡] rank and as *senpō*[§] of the team. Ozaki Sensei influenced me to take up *kendō* just before WWII broke out but the war ended my short *kendō* experience. I never saw Ozaki Sensei after the war started, and regret not having renewed acquaintance before his death."[15]

In addition to teaching, Ozaki was active with administrative duties, which further deepened his involvement in the community. These activities and others are the reason for his eventual arrest and subsequent internment at the outbreak of war in 1941. Among these activities, the main one that the FBI used as proof of his loyalty to Japan was his duties as a consular agent in the 'Amauulu area for the Japanese government. He was appointed as agent in 1937 and served until April 1941. Although he resigned as agent, he continued to assist Japanese residents in filing notices with the consulate, including notices of birth, death, marriage, and registration for military service and others, all of which were required by law in Japan.

In August 1928, Ozaki became a Big Island district member of the Hawaii Japanese Education Association,[¶] which represented 127 Japanese language teachers and their 6,843 students. As a member of the association, he worked to compile new textbooks and studied different teaching methods. From 1928 to 1930, he took on the responsibility of assisting the director and secretary of the Hilo Japanese Chamber of Commerce and

---

*A martial art based on Japanese sword fighting.

†Hilo Hongwanji Gakuen, the Japanese language school of the Hilo Hongwanji Mission, a Shin-Jōdo Buddhist temple built in the early 1900s. The temple and its language school supported a number of social organizations, including a kendō club, judo club, choir, and Boy Scouts troop. In 1938, the temple became the Honpa Hongwanji Hilo Betsuin. The Kaumana team was from the Kaumana Nihongo Gakkō. The Yashijima team was from Yashijima Nihongo Gakkō, known as Yashijima Nihonjin Shōgakkō when it was established in 1904. The school was located on Hilo's Waiākea peninsula, which was called Yashijima (Coconut Island) by its Japanese population. It was destroyed in May 1960, when a tsunami struck Hilo and obliterated Waiākea town. See Richard I. Nakamura and Gloria R. Kobayashi, *The History of the Waiakea Pirates Athletic Club and the Yashijima Story* (Waiakea Town). (Hilo: Waiakea Pirates Athletic Club, 1999). – Trans.

‡fourth

§leader

¶The Hawaii Japanese Education Association (Hawai Kyōikukai) was established in 1915 to unify the disparate language schools – Buddhist, Christian and secular – and to counter mounting criticism of the perceived anti-Americanism of Japanese language instruction. The association embarked on a revision of textbooks used in the language schools – heretofore largely imports published by Japan's Ministry of Education -- with the aim of bringing instruction more closely in line with conditions in Hawai'i. – Trans.

Industry.

Shortly after this, in 1932, Ozaki married Hideko Kobara, the daughter of Takeji and Gino Fujii Kobara. When Gino returned to Japan, Takeji married Haru Terada (Hideko's stepmother), who had a son, George Terada. Takeji and Haru later had a son, Thomas, Hideko's half-brother. Mr. Kobara was a successful restaurateur, the proprietor of Silver Surf Fountain in Waikīkī, and later the Blue Ocean Inn. Hideko was born in Hawai'i on August 1, 1912, when it was a territory of the United States. Thus, she was a United States citizen, as were the children she bore Ozaki, Earl Tomoyuki (b. 1933), Carl Yukio (b. 1935), Alice Sachi (b. 1938), and Lily Yuri (b. 1939). She was a Japanese schoolteacher in Hilo from 1932 to 1941, and from about 1950 worked at the Silver Surf Fountain until she retired in 1970.[16]

True to his description as a "Renaissance man,"[17] Ozaki experimented with cross-breeding flowers, and succeeded in developing a new hybrid of anthurium in 1935. Still popular among anthurium planters today, the Ozaki Red is a robust hybrid of the characteristic heart-shaped flower. The Ozaki Red is particularly known for its hardiness and profusion and was later introduced to Izu-Ōshima island in Japan.

Yet Ozaki's accomplishments were not limited to educational, administrative, and horticultural pursuits. He excelled in literary pursuits as well, and was an active member of Gin-u Shisha,* a *tanka* poetry club in Hilo, from 1924 to 1941. *Tanka* is an ancient form of poetry in Japan, characterized by syllabic units totaling thirty-one syllables in five lines in the following pattern: 5-7-5-7-7. Ozaki continued to write *tanka* during his internment, which are featured in later chapters of this book. He also continued his membership in *tanka* clubs, and even edited and published *tanka* collections following the war.

In addition, Ozaki tinkered with technology. His house in Hilo was strung up with antennas and wires so he could receive short wave radio broadcasts from Japan, through which he would receive the Dōmei News.† He was always wearing earphones and furiously writing things down as he translated the international Morse code. He would then take his translations to the Hilo radio station, where the news would be broadcast.[18] It was activities like this that were deemed suspicious by the FBI and eventually led to his arrest the night of the Pearl Harbor attack.

---

*Silvery Rain Poetry Society

†Established in 1936, the Dōmei Tsūshinsha (Dōmei News Agency) was Japan's only wartime news service until it was dissolved in 1945.

In recognition of all of his achievements, Ozaki received many commendations and commemorative gifts before the war. Ozaki was closely tied to the Japanese government during this time because of his participation in welcoming Japanese ships to the port of Hilo, as well as for his monetary contributions to the Japanese government. Unfortunately, these commendations and gifts were confiscated by the FBI at the outbreak of war.

FATHER'S ARREST AND DETENTION, 1941 – 1942

> In the atmosphere of wartime hysteria and exaggerated stories, we must have been seen as hated enemies who deserved to suffer as much as possible.
>
> —Otokichi Muin Ozaki, from a radio script documenting his internment at Sand Island

IN A **REPORT** to the FBI dated January 27, 1942, Agent Dale A. Curtis wrote:

"Ozaki, interned 12/7/41 by virtue of warrant of arrest issued by military authority. Hearing held on 1/9/42 before Board of officers and civilians, appointed by Military Governor, which Board recommended that Subject be interned for the duration of the war . . . . The report of the proceedings in the hearing of instant case revealed that after carefully considering the evidence presented before it, the Board finds:

1. That internee is a subject of Japan.

2. That internee is loyal to Japan and that his activities have been pro-Japanese.

In view of the foregoing facts the Board recommended, "that internee be interned for the duration and after the cessation of hostilities [and] that consideration be given to the subject of deportation of this individual. We do not see how this man can ever become loyal to the United States of America, and we do not believe that his children will ever be brought up as Americans."[1]

One of 391 persons of Japanese ancestry arrested in Hawai'i by December 7 and 8, 1941,[2] Ozaki was detained as part of the FBI's "custodial detention" program, which identified "dangerous" persons in Hawai'i to be held as hostages in case hostilities broke out between the United States and Japan. As far back as August 1939, FBI agent Robert L. Shivers was sent to Hawai'i to compile the list. He focused on perceived Issei* leaders,

*A first generation Japanese immigrant, usually one who arrived prior to World War II.

among them Japanese consular officials, Japanese language schoolteachers and principals, Buddhist and Shinto priests, prominent businesspeople, and "others of no particular affiliation but who by reason of their extreme nationalistic sentiments would be a danger to our security as well as others who have seen Japanese military service."[3]

Unlike on the U.S. Mainland where virtually everyone of Japanese descent, including women and children, was detained and interned, in Hawai'i only 608 Issei and Nisei were arrested through March 30, 1942. In the 1940s, there were approximately 157,905 persons of Japanese ancestry living in Hawai'i out of a total of 423,330, which represented 37.3 percent of Hawai'i's total population.[4] Thus to apprehend the entire Japanese population in Hawai'i, as was done on the Mainland, would have severely depopulated the islands and brought much of the economic activity to a halt.

On December 7, 1941, at 4:25 p.m., when the attack on Pearl Harbor was over, Hawai'i was placed under martial law by order of Territorial Governor Joseph B. Poindexter. The governor transferred his civilian powers to General Walter C. Short, head of the Hawai'i command. But even while the attack was unfolding, everyone on the FBI custodial detention list was ordered interned by the War Department. Ozaki was on the list. He had been thoroughly investigated by the FBI prior to his arrest, as evidenced by the November 1, 1941 report by FBI agent Dan M. Douglas. The FBI had interviewed not only Ozaki, but many people who knew him, including "Confidential Informants" referred to as HO 191 and HO 52. Ozaki's personal files, including letters, were searched for evidence of loyalty to Japan and espionage activities.

As a result, the night of December 7, 1941, FBI agents went to the Ozaki household in 'Amauulu and arrested him. He was taken first to Kīlauea Military Camp,* where he was detained until February 21, 1942. He was then shipped to the island of O'ahu, where he was kept at the Honolulu Immigration Station† for fourteen days before being moved to Sand Island Detention Camp.‡ There he remained until being transported to the

---

*Located within the Hawai'i Volcanoes National Park, it was established in 1916 as a Hawai'i National Guard training ground and recreation venue for the U.S. Army. All those arrested on the Big Island were initially detained at Kīlauea. – Trans.

†This Immigration and Naturalization Service site, located at the edge of Honolulu Harbor, was used for the temporary detention of Issei enemy aliens awaiting interrogation and internment proceedings. – Trans.

‡Run by the Hawaiian Military Government, the camp was located on the 500-acre island, near the entrance to Honolulu Harbor. The detention camp operated from December 8, 1941 to March 1, 1943. – Trans.

Mainland camps.

When he hosted a series of radio shows beginning in 1949, Ozaki reflected on his time spent interned, and often created themes around which to narrate his experiences. Several written and broadcast in 1949 and 1950 express a poignant, and even humorous, look at those early days in camp. These are included in this chapter, as is FBI agent Douglas' report, reproduced in part below.

The report shows the extent to which Ozaki was investigated. The investigation focuses on two of Ozaki's activities: first, his possession of short-wave radio equipment, which he uses to receive news briefs from Japan; and second, his duties as a consular agent for the Japanese government.

English original
FEDERAL BUREAU OF INVESTIGATION REPORT BY
DAN M. DOUGLAS[5]
Date: November 1, 1941
SYNOPSIS OF FACTS: OTOKICHI OZAKI, Amauulu
Camp 1, Hilo, Hawai, a Japanese language school teacher and
Consular Agent, is an alien, born 11/5/04 at Kochi-Ken, Japan,
and came to Hawaii 4/24/17 aboard the Nippon Maru. His wife
and four children were born in Hawaii and are American citizens
only. Duties of Consular Agents apparently consist of assisting
Japanese aliens and dual citizens, file certain notices with the
Consulate and also gathering census data concerning Japanese
residents and organizations in Hawaii for the Consulate. Evidence
to indicate these agents are under control of Consulate or that
they are considered as "officials" is very meager. Evidence shows
OZAKI is pro-Japanese and has sent money to Japanese armed
forces, but no evidence found that he is engaged in espionage, is
a potential saboteur, or is disseminating subversive propaganda,
except possibly by teaching school children under his direction the
Japanese culture and loyalty to ancestral country. Custodial detention memorandum submitted.
REFERENCE: Report of Special Agent DAN M. DOUGLAS,
Honolulu, dated May 5, 1941. Letter from Bureau dated September 25, 1941 (Bureau file #100-23301). Letter to Bureau dated
April 21, 1941.
DETAILS: At Hilo, Hawaii:
Modesto Savella, Phillipino mechanic, Hilo Motors, Ltd., Hilo,
Hawaii, advised that he formerly resided in Amauulu Camp 1 of
the Hilo Sugar Company and that OKOKICHO OZAKI resided
directly across the road from him. He stated that during his residence in Amauulu about seven months ago he seemed to get inter-

ference on his radio which consisted of telegraphic code. He stated that this usually happened about nine P.M. each evening, and that in an effort to learn the source of the trouble he was outside his house and heard the clicking of the telegraphic code coming from the house of Subject OZAKI. He stated that he quietly slipped around until he could see in the window of OZAKI'S house and he could see OZAKI sitting at a table before a radio set and wearing headphones. He stated that he did not see any sending key and that OZAKI seemed to be writing down the messages coming through.

Savella further advised that OZAKI has a very intricate system of radio aerials and that it is possible that he possesses a short wave sending set. S. stated that he is moved away from Amauulu about three months ago and that he does not know whether OZAKI is continuing his practice.

The writer and Antone Pacheco, Special Police Officer, surveilled the home of OZAKI between the hours of nine to eleven thirty P.M. on the nights of October 4 to 11, 1941, but nothing was seen nor heard to indicate that OZAKI was either sending or receiving any telegraphic code . . . .

Saburo Chiwa, translator of the Honolulu Office advised that he has known OZAKI for several years and was taught in Japanese school by him. He stated that OZAKI is an expert on the International Morse Code and was formerly engaged in receiving news dispatches sent over wireless by DOMKI, Japanese News Agency, and translating these dispatches from code into Japanese for the Hawaii Mainichi, Hilo Japanese Newspaper. Chiwa stated that OZAKI has a short wave receiving set in his home and that his receiving was all done at his home. He stated that he has not known him to have any radio sending equipment.

Chiwa further advised that OZAKI is a very shrewd man and has a wide fund of knowledge; that he is a strict Japanese language school teacher and pro-Japanese.

In view of the fact that a personal interview with Subject OZA-KI was necessary in connection with his activities as a Consular Agent, MR. R. J. STRATTON of the FCC was contacted and he advised that he would like to accompany the writer to the Subject's home and thus have an opportunity to look his home over in an effort to locate any radio sending equipment.

During the interview with OZAKI, MR. Stratton examined his radio equipment and found a short wave receiving set and a pair of earphones. He did not find any sending equipment and stated that there was no indication that OZAKI had such equipment. OZAKI explained as is set out above, that he was formerly employed with the Hawaii Mainichi in Hilo and used his short wave receiving set to take down news dispatches which came from news agencies in Japan in the international code, and still does so occasionally.

OZAKI further advised that he resides in Amauulu Camp 1 of the Hilo Sugar Company and is employed as a language school teacher at the Hilo Independent School. He stated that he was born in Kochi Ken, Japan in November 5, 1904 and came to Hawaii aboard the Nippon Maru, entering at the port of Honolulu on April 24, 1917. He produced his alien registration card which bore the number 2482357 . . . .

His immediate family consists of his wife and four children, all of whom are United States citizens, having been born in the Hawaiian Islands, and according to OZAKI, none are dual citizens. The members are as follows:

1. HIDEKO OZAKI, wife
2. EARL TOMOYUKI OZAKI, son, age 8
3. CARL YUKIO OZAKI, son, age 6
4. ALICE SAIHI OZAKI, daughter, age 4
5. LILY YURI OZAKI, daughter, age 2

OZAKI was previously interviewed by the writer regarding his Consular Agent duties and as set out in reference report, he stated that he was appointed as an Agent in 1937 and served until April, 1941. It will be observed that in April, 1941, about ten consular agents on the Island of Hawaii were interviewed for the purpose of furnishing the Department with information as to the activities of Consular Agents, for an opinion as to prosecution. After having interviewed some two or three the word immediately was passed around among the Agents that an investigation was being made. This caused alarm particularly among those who were also Japanese language teachers, due probably to the fact that pressure has been brought on the Japanese to discontinue to language schools because they are considered by the American community as a barrier to the Americanization of the young island born Japanese.

Therefore, when interviewed originally, OZAKI stated that he had resigned as Consular agent, and when questioned as to the reason therefore, he stated that he had received instructions from MR. Hideji Kimura,* President of the Hawaii Central Educational Association, to return his letter of appointment as agent to the Japanese Consul in Honolulu, and resign this position. His letter of appointment was therefore not available. He stated that Kimura told him that in view of the tense international situation it would be best that the language school teachers not be consular agents to avoid suspicion . . . .

---

*Principal of the Honomū Japanese Language School, he too was interned. Internee information is from the JCCH internee database, "Hawai'i Japanese and Japanese Americans Detained During World War II." – Trans.

OZAKI further stated that he does not consider it an honor to be appointed such an agent and that he accepted more from a sense of duty to the other Japanese and his native country. He stated that he can refuse such appointment and that he can resign at any time he desires, with no stigma attached. He stated that he receives no compensation whatever from the consul or the Japanese government proper, nor does he receive a fee from those he assists. He added, however, that he often receives gifts of food and clothing, particularly around Christmas, as tokens of gratitude for his assistance to them. He did deny that the consul has any control over him whatever, other than the control the Japanese government exercises over all of its citizens, and stated that he does not know the consul personally.

OZAKI denied that he in any manner taught anything to the Japanese children in his school other than the Japanese language and obedience to parents and to the law of the country where they reside. He stated that many years ago when the schools were first founded, that all the fundamentals of a Japanese education were taught, including loyalty to the Emperor of Japan, but that such has now disappeared, particularly in those schools where the teachers are not also Buddhist Ministers. In schools where the teacher is also a minister of the Buddhist faith, OZAKI stated that the teachers teach as much as they can get away with relative to a Japanese education. He stated that this is natural inasmuch as such teachers come into Hawaii as Ministers and then go into teaching for the express purpose of making good Japanese of the children. He stated that these teachers are fresh from Japan, and only stay in Hawaii for a few years and then return, whereupon he is replaced by a Buddhist priest, who also is fresh from Japan and full of Japanese Nationalism. On the other hand, he stated that those teachers who are teachers in the independent language schools have been in Hawaii most of their lives, and are for the most part Americanized and teach their children to be so . . . .

OZAKI was asked to produce any letters or other papers relative to his association with the consul, and he produced all of his personal files, which he allowed to be examined by Saburo Chiwa, translator of the Honolulu Office. From these files several letters were found which indicate that OZAKI takes an active part in Japanese affairs, makes donations to the Japanese Navy, and that he is a loyal subject of the Japanese Emperor. Nothing was found to indicate he is engaged in espionage or is a potential saboteur, but possibly that he is engaged in verbal propaganda in a small way among his own race.

These papers were taken with the permission of OZAKI and will be photostated; one copy of each paper will be forwarded to

the Bureau with copies of this report and one copy will be retained in the Honolulu file. The translations of the papers are as follows:
Exhibit A:

In a letter of appreciation sent by Tomoji Matsumura, Chairman of the Reception Committee when the Japanese Training Squadron visited Hilo, to OZAKI, who was designated a member of the General Affairs Committee, and dated November 1, 1939, M. thanks OZAKI in the following manner:

"That we were able to accord the squadron full satisfaction of a sincere welcome through the cooperation of the people of this island, when the Japanese Training Squadron visited here in October, 1939, is the result of your self-sacrificing efforts, and I wish to express here what little appreciation it is my privilege to express."
Exhibit B:

Translation of a letter of appreciation issued by Hitsumasa Yonai, Navy Minister in Japan, to OZAKI, and dated July, 1939.

"We are deeply grateful to you for the donation towards accomplishing the aim of completion of national defense on the occasion of the present incident, and this is to express our appreciation."
Exhibit C:

Receipt issued by one Ishibuchi, naval officer in charge of the national defense donations in the Paymaster's Department of the Ministry of the Navy, to OTOKICHI OZAKI, under date of May 3, 1939, acknowledging receipt of the sum of ten dollars ($10.00) as donation from OZAKI towards perfection of national defense. Receipt #22860-5030 . . . .

Among OZAKI'S papers were three books containing carbon copies of letters he had written. These were examined and two were found which might be of some significance to this investigation. These were in bound volumes and were not removed for photostating but were translated as follows:

In a letter sent by OZAKI to a party named Haruko (female) and dated May 5, 1941, he writes:

"I pray that you will grasp the magnificent spirit from within the beauty of the spiritual unity of Japan in the present crisis.". . . .

MISS Annette Hammersland, Head Nurse, Hilo Sugar Company, advised that she gets around to all the homes on the plantation and that she is acquainted with Subject OZAKI. She stated that about a year ago she walked into his house and found him wearing a pair of earphones and listening to a broadcast in code, which he was writing down. She stated that he told her that HITLER is a great man and that she considers him very pro-Japanese. She stated that she has experienced non-cooperation from him relative to the community activities of the camp during Christmas, and that he is not liked by the younger Japanese of the camp . . . .

* * *

Based on the evidence such as the above, on the eve of the attack on Pearl Harbor, an official decision was made by John Edgar Hoover, Director of the FBI, United States Department of Justice, in Washington, D.C. In a memorandum to a Mr. L. M. C. Smith, Chief of the Special Defense Unit, written on December 6, 1941, Hoover declared that Ozaki should be arrested in the "event of a national emergency." The memo declared:

English original
MEMORANDUM FROM JOHN EDGAR HOOVER TO
L.M.C. SMITH[6]
Date: December 6, 1941

"There is transmitted herewith a dossier showing the information presently available in the files of this Bureau with respect to Otokichi Ozaki whose address is Amauulu Camp #1, Hilo Hawaii.

It is recommended that this individual be considered for custodial detention in the event of a national emergency. The information contained on the attached dossier constitutes the basis for appropriate consideration in this regard.

It should be understood, of course, that additional information may be received from time to time supplementing that already available in the Bureau's files, and as such data are received they will be made available to you that the dossier in your possession may be supplemented thereby.

It will be greatly appreciated if you will advise this Bureau at your earliest convenience as to the decision reached in this case. Very truly yours, John Edgar Hoover, Director."

* * *

When Ozaki returned to Honolulu following his internment, he worked in the media and was asked to speak about his internment experiences on a series of radio shows. These shows, which were broadcast around 1949 and 1950, were first scripted by Ozaki before being used as notes for the live broadcasts. In the scripts, he provides details of his arrest and experiences being incarcerated in Hawai'i. No correspondence between Ozaki and others during his internment in Hawai'i camps is archived so the only record of his stay during this time exists in radio scripts.

These are excerpted here.

RADIO SCRIPT

Memories of Four Years Behind Barbed Wire: Body Searches[7]

"You had better take some heavy clothes with you. You may not be coming back for three or four days," said a policeman I had known, when he came to take me into custody at midnight on December 7. He did not tell me where I would be taken. Not knowing that three or four days would turn into three or four years, I stepped out of my house with just a jacket and a sweater.

Through the headlights, I could see raindrops falling on a blue car. The town was under a total blackout. All of this created a grave atmosphere. Armed soldiers patrolled the streets of Hilo. With rain falling on their helmets, they peered through our open car window to see who was inside. After going to two or three places to pick up a few people who happened to be my acquaintances, our car stopped at a public school campus. I saw people going back and forth in the dark, and it occurred to me that they were hauling in people like me. It seemed they had started in the daytime. There, I underwent the first body search. This search involved patting down my clothes. Knife-like objects and materials written in Japanese were taken away. The only things I was allowed to carry with me were my wallet, keys, a handkerchief and a sweater.

As I sat on the seat of the paddy wagon, man after man came aboard in the darkness. I gave my name to them and discovered that all of them were close acquaintances I had frequently seen in Hilo. The van headed for the Kīlauea Volcano area and stopped at a place which seemed to be a military barracks. We were turned over to the custody of the military authorities there. That night I could not sleep at all, wrapped in a blanket and shivering with cold, listening to the sound of the falling rain.

I wrote some *tanka* that night.

A silent farewell	子の寝顔
For sleeping children	別れて出ずる
Into the dark cold I go	闇寒く
The rain gently falling.	しょうしょうと雨の
	降り出でにけり

I look around	闇に慣れて
The hushed darkness	見廻す中に
In which I am settling –	聞き慣れし
I hear a familiar voice	人声のありて
And feel comforted, for now[8]	先ず落ち着きぬ
Scattered among us	何の故に
Many a Nikkei*	囚われ来しぞ
Taken prisoner.	その中の
Why?	日系市民の
	あまた交じる

I groped in the dark to find my assigned bed. As I sat down, I could sense that dozens of people were already sitting on their beds. In the darkness, some gave their names. Others responded, "Oh, you too. XXX is here, too." I felt comfortable at last, finding my old friends from the small town of Hilo. At the time, I noticed that some Nikkei were there too. At first I wondered why they had been taken into custody. Then I presumed that it was due to prejudice against the Japanese, and the thought saddened me.

The next morning, December 8, we went through a second search, and even though it was raining, we were ordered to line up in front of the barracks. Dozens of armed soldiers surrounded us, and their guns glittered ominously in the rain. It flashed across my mind that they were preparing to execute us. We were ordered to walk. So we started walking in the cold rain through the barracks, fearing that we would be killed. Everyone looked so worn out, for we had been anxious and restless all through the night. I must have been a sorry sight, too; after all, I am just an ordinary man having had little mental training for a situation such as this.

We were ordered into a building, the windows of which were covered with black paper. It smelled of food. My God, we had come to the mess hall! I suddenly felt so hungry. I thought, "If they are going to kill us, I may as well have my fill." My brazenness surprised me. Perhaps it was this attitude that sustained me during the whole four-year period, or it could be that I am simpleminded. At any rate, I consider myself fortunate that I retained my health and objectivity, while maintaining a positive outlook.

Now, let's get back to tonight's subject.

Sometime later, I learned that the authorities conducted body searches in Honolulu also, going so far as cutting coat collars to see if anything was hidden inside. We, on the Big Island, were spared such an experience. But when we arrived at the Immigration

---

*A Japanese American.

Detention Station in Honolulu, they checked our belongings at the holding area of a building and crowded us into a room on the second floor. We were detained there for two weeks.

Then they moved us to Sand Island [Detention Camp] and put us in an office space by the main gate. They ordered us to line up according to our age. Then they called us one by one into a small room. They ordered us to strip naked and checked us thoroughly. All of our belongings were confiscated, and we were let out another door. At the time, I had a handkerchief, a towel, an overcoat, a hat, and a pair of *zōri.** Most of us carried similar items. After that, we were assigned to a tent.

After a while, we were ordered to line up in an open area in front of the mess hall. Captain [Eifler],† chief of the internment camp, briefed us on the dos and don'ts of camp life. He repeatedly told us not to carry any metal products. On July 27, 1929, members of the League of Nations convened in Geneva and signed an international agreement covering the treatment of prisoners of war, but I suppose someone who had been hurriedly chosen to be camp commander could not have been expected to know these rules. In the atmosphere of wartime hysteria and exaggerated stories, we must have been seen as hated enemies who deserved to suffer as much as possible. In all, I experienced internment in five different camps, but I have never been treated as unreasonably as I was at Sand Island. At every other camp, I was able to spend some time without stress. At Tule Lake my problems with camp authorities were of a different kind, but my experience at Sand Island was clearly the worst.

Right after we joined the Sand Island Camp, I heard about an incident involving a priest, the Rev. O.‡ On December 14, 1941, he was found to possess a knife-like article that had been made from a belt buckle. With several guards pointing their guns at him, he was made to strip and stand naked. All the other internees were ordered to line up in the yard and take off all their clothes. Guards searched their clothing. In the meantime, other guards searched their belongings inside the tents and confiscated every item, including fountain pens and pencils. I heard that all of the internees

---

*Japanese slippers

†The original text reads "Captain Ai," a phonetic abbreviation for Carl F. Eifler (1906-2002), who commanded the Sand Island camp in the aftermath of the Pearl Harbor attack. Shortly thereafter, he was named to head a Far Eastern covert operations unit under the Office of Strategic Services, the precursor to the Central Intelligence Agency. See his biography by Thomas N. Moon, *The Deadliest Colonel* (New York: Vantage Press, 1975). – Trans.

‡Yasutaro Soga identifies the priest as Rev. Ryoshin Okano in his description of this event in *Life Behind Barbed Wire: The World War II Internment Memoirs of a Hawai'i Issei* (Honolulu: University of Hawaii Press, 2008), 30-31. Okano was a Buddhist priest from Pearl City on the island of O'ahu, who was repatriated in 1943. – Trans.

shivered with fear at that time. I think it was quite unreasonable for the guards to have made them stand naked in the strong wind blowing down from Nu'uanu. Unfortunately, internees could not protest against such inhumane treatment.

There is a movie entitled *Three Came Home* that will be shown shortly. This is a story of a Japanese [colonel], played by Sesshu Hayakawa,* who treated American [prisoners of war] compassionately and humanely. I understand that the original story was written by one of the former American [prisoners].† If a novelist were to write about our life at Sand Island Camp, it might be a historical document showing another side of the fairness and justice of which Americans are so proud . . . .

A few days after we joined the camp, an emergency call was issued for us to gather in the yard. We were told that a tube of after-shave cream was missing from the bathing facilities in the German section of the camp. The captain told us, "As you know, that tube containing after-shave cream is made of metal, and any metal is considered a weapon. We will continue to search until we find it."

Several soldiers conducted body searches while we stood in the cold wind, barefooted, our socks and shoes off to the side. But we were lucky enough not to have had to stand naked. In the tent, another soldier searched our belongings. Rain started to fall and it hit our cheeks. The captain who was watching the search looked quite arrogant. We began to feel the cold air coming from below. Many internees were more than sixty years old, and for them this was too cruel. Who in the world would hide or steal shaving cream? Our group consisted mainly of people who were business and community leaders. The search ended in vain. Suddenly, a soldier came running to the captain. He looked very serious and it seemed he was going to report something important. I wondered if someone in our group had been found carrying the [tube]. We all watched from a distance to see what he was going to report.

RADIO SCRIPT
Memories of Four Years Behind Barbed Wire: Body Searches, Part Two[9]

---

*An actor in Japan and Hollywood, he also was known as Sessue Hayakawa (1889-1973) and played the role of the POW camp commander. Hayakawa was a silent movie era matinee idol best known for his Academy Award-nominated role in the 1957 movie *The Bridge on the River Kwai.* – Trans.

†Agnes Newton Keith, an award-winning American writer, who had been living with her family in Borneo at the time of the Japanese invasion. Held captive with her young son for more than three years in a series of Japanese prisoner of war camps, Keith later wrote about her experiences in a best selling book, *Three Came Home.* The book was made into a Hollywood movie in 1950. – Trans.

Today I am going to continue last week's episode about body searches.

Although they searched us thoroughly, they could not find the tube of shaving cream. But a soldier did come to report what he had found in our tent: an old nail in Mr. T's overcoat and a bill hidden in the necktie belonging to a man from Maui. No disciplinary action was taken that day, but since we had been forced to stand in the rain, several elderly and sick internees caught colds.

According to Mr. T, he had used the nail to pick his ears while he was at Kīlauea Camp and most likely had left it in his coat. I thought they should have found it when they first searched us at the entrance to Sand Island Camp. We listened to our spokesman as he translated the officer's decision. He said, "According to military regulations, these two must be tried. We must select attorneys, prosecutors and jurors. Mr. Ozaki, I want you to be a juror." Our spokesman seemed puzzled over the appointments. I had never been in a courtroom, and I was in no position to judge the guilt or innocence of the two men, but I had little choice.

The next morning, the trial began in the designated tent in our section [of camp]. I cannot remember what I said, but the jury convicted both men based on their apologies. Since they admitted that they were guilty, the trial was nothing more than a formality. The officer, who served as the judge, sentenced the two men to forfeit their next ration of cigarettes and candy. It was our impression that this nonsensical act had been a part of Captain [Eifler's] strategy to flaunt his authority, and we laughed over such a cheap trick.

Mr. T remained with our group until his return to Japan at the end of the war. During our confinement, whenever the conversation turned to life at Sand Island, Mr. T invariably said he had never felt more miserable than at that trial before his fellow internees.

RADIO SCRIPT
Life Behind Barbed Wire: Body Searches[10]

Thinking that the only way to escape the life behind barbed wire was to return to Japan, one of our fellow internees, Mr. [Shoichi] Asami, editor-in-chief of the *Nippu Jiji*,* joined the group going home. He and I had been in the same barrack at Camp Livingston [Louisiana] for a year.† During periods of idleness, he

---

*The bilingual newspaper ran from 1906 to 1942. Under the leadership of its owner, Yasutaro Soga, the *Nippu Jiji* became the largest Japanese language newspaper outside of Japan prior to World War II. With the internment of Soga and Asami, the newspaper resumed publication under a new name, *The Hawaii Times*, until its demise in 1985. – Trans.

†Asami was with Ozaki in the Livingston Internment Camp from June 1942 to June 1943. –

made up his own lyrics to popular Japanese songs, expressing his feelings at the time. He wrote ten such lyrics, here is one example:*

Cold night in Camp McCoy[†]	夜が冷たいマコイのキャンプ
Am I caged bird on a journey	籠の鳥かよおいらの旅は
Gazing at the moon	バープワイヤに月を見る
Through the barbed wire?	

The moon is bright,	月はさゆれど心は曇る
my heart clouded	ガード銃剣、命をかけて
Guards carry bayonets	渡る流転の旅の空
And I stake my life	
On this aimless journey	
beneath the sky.	

A Hawaiian paradise—	布哇楽園昔の夢よ
yesterday's dream.	父をうばわれ夫と別れ
Robbed of father, torn from husband,	泣いて月見る妻や子が
Wife and children view the moon	
through tears.	

Months of wandering a thorny road	流転幾月茨の道を
Even this uncertain journey will end	越えてゆくてを定めぬ旅も
In the Land of the Rising Sun,	末は日の本父母の国
Homeland of Father and Mother.	

Returning to his father and mother's homeland, tragically, on April 1, 1945, off the Taiwan coast in the raging waves[‡] of the China Sea—this sad memory is the last I have of him.[§]

I would like to use this opportunity to pay homage to the spirit

---

Trans.

   *These lyrics are based on the song, "Tabigasa Dōchū" (Journey of a Wanderer), popularized by Shoji Tarō in 1935. – Trans.

   †McCoy Internment Camp, Wisconsin, where Asami was held from March 9 to May 25, 1942. – Trans.

   ‡"raging waves" (*kyōran no dotō* 狂乱の怒濤) is a reference to a poem Asami wrote in 1922:
Raging waves of fury,
If you should take me away
To the bottom of the sea,
So be it.

   Translation courtesy of George and Emi Oshiro. The original Japanese poem appears in Yasutaro Soga's memoir, *Gojūnenkan no hawai kaikō* (Osaka: Osaka kōsoku insatsu kabushiki kaisha, 1953), 683. – Trans.

   §Shoichi Asami's poem of 1922 which refers to "raging waves" "tak[ing him] away" is a sad and ironic note that Ozaki captured in this radio script. On April 1, 1945, en route from Singapore to Japan on the exchange ship *Awa Maru*, Asami and his third son, Ryozo, lost their lives when the *Awa Maru* was sunk by an American battleship. – Ed.

of my departed friend and to dedicate this story of one man's personal experience to all of my fellow internees.

RADIO SCRIPT
Life Behind Barbed Wire[11]

Today's episode of our life behind barbed wire goes back to the days on the Big Island. I begin my story in chronological order.

It was February 4, 1942. The camp we were detained in was located at Kīlauea Volcano. Although the camp belonged to the U.S. Army, its facilities were spare. One after the other, we had been sent to these barracks on the morning of December 8, and with each passing day, all of us 112 Hawai'i internees were feeling increasingly insecure. Investigative hearings were held, but they were superficial. Every day a few people were summoned under heavy guard to Hilo, where they would be taken to the second floor of the post office building.

A voice announced, "An order has been issued to those of you who are to be transferred from this camp. I do not know where you are bound. Now I will read the names on the list. Those whose names I call should get ready to depart as quickly as possible." He started calling names in alphabetical order. When I heard my name, I thought that the day had finally come. It was very gusty over the volcano area in February, and an *'ōhi'a'* tree in the yard was shaking in the wind. In the yard, stuck into three or four mountains of sand were signs that read, "For air raids."[†] Several armed and helmeted soldiers stood there, as usual. Thirty-six names were on the list. "Do you understand what I said? For those of you whose names were called, I have prepared a list of personal belongings that you will be allowed to take with you." Suddenly, the quiet room became noisy. Ever since December 7, we had been living together in this camp. I felt very lonely as I realized that thirty-six out of 112 of us would be the first group to leave, and we did not even know where we would be going. I sat on my bed and began reading the sheet of paper that had just been handed to me.

---

*A native Hawaiian tree commonly found in the volcano area of the Big Island. – Trans.
†Sand was often used to smother fires caused by air raid attacks. – Trans.

Overcoat	x1	Hat	x1	Handkerchief	x6
Shoes	x2	Socks	x6	Gloves	x2
Pajama	x1	Bathrobe	x1	Slacks	x2
Shirts	x2	Money	no more than $25		

Only the minimum amount of daily necessities is allowed. Possession of watches and mirrors is prohibited.

Judging by the number of shoes and gloves that we were allowed to take, I assumed that we would be going to a cold and distant place. I heard the voice say, "If you want to write to your families, do so now."

I hurriedly wrote a short letter to my wife. "We have received an order. A total of thirty-six people will leave here today or tomorrow. We have no idea where we will be going. I assume we will be moving to a cold place. Take care of yourself. I ask you to look after our children. Do not act disgracefully at any time. My best to the people of ['Amauulu] camp."

Thoughts and images flashed across my mind – the pitiful state of a fatherless family, the daily struggle for survival, the faces of my elderly mother and my young children. The Japanese government could neglect the existence of Japanese living abroad like us, as it launched its war to build the Great East Asian Commonwealth and make others aware of the Japanese race. I had no idea how long the war would last.

Sixty-some days had passed since the night of December 7, when I said goodbye to my children sleeping in their beds and was brought to this camp. I had thought I would be released after the investigation proved that I was not a hostile person. I realized that was wishful thinking and I was ordered to move to the other camp. At the time, we managed to maintain a reasonable level of existence, as our families sent some items in to us. Those who were to remain in the camp consoled us by offering us canned Japanese foods that we perhaps would not be able to eat hereafter. "Please eat a lot. We may be joining you later. Until then, stay healthy," they told us. We wished them well and asked them to take care of our families if they were to be released from camp. With great emotion, we shook hands.

Rumor spread that we were leaving around two in the afternoon. We packed our belongings in a hurry. Items that we did not need or could not take with us were packed separately so that they could be shipped to our homes. Then we waited for an order for our departure, sitting on our beds with our shoes on. Two o'clock, three o'clock, four o'clock . . .Time passed. Someone said that we would be leaving at night, because they had to keep our movement confidential. Our tension was fading. Five o'clock, six o'clock, seven o'clock . . . Still no orders. In the barrack, under the blackout, I could hear the sound of the wind and rain. We groped in the dark, taking our pajamas from our bags. And thinking, "What the heck!" we lay down in bed without taking off our shoes. I tried to sleep, but I could hear people whispering to each other in our usually quiet barrack. I was awakened several times, and when I heard someone walking on the sand outside, I thought he was coming to give us our orders. But there were no orders that night. I fell asleep somehow and the sun soon rose. It was the morning of February 5. The day ended with us still waiting for our orders. We had no idea what had happened. We wondered if the transfer had been canceled. We packed our belongings in the morning and took out our pajamas from our bags at night.

Then on February 14, a new order was issued. It canceled the previous orders and called for 106 people to be transferred instead, with only thirteen to remain at camp.* It also was announced that our families would be allowed to visit us on the afternoon of Sunday, February 15. Thus, our trip to nowhere was to begin.

RADIO SCRIPT
Impressions of Kīlauea Volcano Camp[12]

February 15, 1942 was the day we had to part from our families. Since the night of December 7, we had been feeling insecure, and now 119 of us had been given transfer orders, leaving thirteen of our group behind [at Kīlauea Camp]. Our baggage was limited to the bare minimum of personal belongings. My limited ability to express myself prevents me from adequately describing the situation on that day.

We were allowed to meet for two hours with family members, whom we had not seen for the past seventy days. We were not sure when we would be able to see one another again. Our crowded barrack was filled with people. Exchanging notes was prohibited, but families were allowed to write down what their husbands and fathers said. I had my wife copy in conversational style poems I had written that described the happenings of the past seventy days.

Today I shall read some of these poems that are reminiscent of those bygone days.

------

*The numbers of transferees and those remaining in camp are inconsistent in Ozaki's various accounts of this incident. This is understandable, as Ozaki is recollecting the incident years after it happened. – Ed.

Singapore has finally fallen.	シンガポール
On our reunion	遂に落ちしと
After a long separation	先ず妻は
My wife's first words.	語り始めぬ
	最初の言葉

At that time, the war had expanded to the South Pacific. Because we had no knowledge of what was happening, the first question we always asked newcomers was about the most current situation. Her first words about Singapore falling to the Japanese Army indicate our frame of mind at that time.

A care package	差し入れの
Wrapped in newspaper which	物を包みし
I stretch out to smooth away the creases	新聞紙
I devour the latest news.	皺をのばしつつ
	むさぼりて読む

Whenever my family made care packages, they intentionally wrapped them in newspapers. The newspapers may have been old, but I smoothed out the creases and read the articles word by word. My wife, together with our four children, had come to see me for the first time in seventy-some days.

One by one	かわるがわる
I carry my children	抱き上げて
"Look at Daddy," I say	トウチャンの眼を
Each turns shyly away.	ご覧と云えば
	子ははにかみにけり

When a car stops,	自動車の
Yuri runs out to see	止まれば
If daddy's come back	父の帰りかと
But she returns so sad.	出て見ると云う
	由利は悲しき

My wife described the situation in Hilo since December 7, and I was surprised to learn how things had changed. She had heard that the military ship scheduled to take us [to Honolulu] had been sunk by a Japanese submarine lurking off the shore of Maui. For this reason, the departure of the first group of thirty-six had been cancelled. I was shocked to learn that a young man we had known died as a victim of that incident. My wife said, "The Mainland might be a safer place than Hawai'i, but crossing the Pacific . . ." She became silent.

Now that I have been officially branded as a Japanese citizen, and the decision has been made to have me sent to the Mainland as an enemy alien, I feel a kind of relief – a feeling that I am now free to live my life without restraint. Since the age of eleven, when my father sent for me and I arrived [in Hawai'i] as an immigrant's son, I have never been back to Japan. I married a Nisei woman and became the father of four children who are American citizens. Upon reflection, I can swear that I have done nothing underhanded or deceptive. I think my life has centered on the desire to repay a debt of gratitude.

At my hearing I was asked, "If Japanese forces were to come ashore, will you fight against them?" What a silly question, I thought. Then I recalled a poem from Gin-u Shisha, written by a fellow poet. Basically he said, "America is my son's country. He must defend it with his life."

There is a saying that a greater cause can destroy one's parents. In Japanese history, there are many cases in which parents and their children have faced off as enemies and have fought one another for a greater cause. This is the bane of the samurai. As long as one has been adopted as an American, it is only proper that he sacrifice his life for his country. For its part, Japan would surely applaud such an attitude.

The war in the Pacific [has] many incongruences and inconsistencies. Americans could never understand our deeply instilled values of *bushidō,** such as *giri,*† and *ninjō.*‡ They have indiscriminately labeled all Japanese as dangerous spies and have confined people who have for many years lived and worked for the betterment of Hawai'i. On the West Coast, they have forcibly removed hundreds of thousands of Japanese from their homes. These actions have given America, a country priding itself on its [ideas of] freedom, justice and fair play, a black eye. The director of the FBI at the time declared that there had not been a single case of sabotage committed by the Japanese in Hawai'i.

There is an instance of a father undergoing interrogation and having to say goodbye to his newly enlisted son, who was eager to fight for his country. Later, in another instance, a Nisei soldier

---

*Lit., "the way of the warrior." A moral code of conduct embraced by the samurai, it included such values as loyalty to one's lord, devotion to duty, and adherence to personal ethics. – Trans.
†duty
‡humanity

was on the lower deck of a ship traveling from Hilo to Honolulu. Also aboard [on the upper deck] was his father, classified as an enemy alien and guarded by an MP, on his way to be interned. The two were not allowed to speak to each other.* Is this what America is about? It made me reconsider the greatness of America, where I had been raised over the decades. I wonder how the highly decorated boys of the 100th Battalion and the 442nd Regimental Combat Team felt while fighting under the American flag.

In still another instance much later, while I was at Jerome Camp in Arkansas, young soldiers from Hawai'i undergoing difficult training at Camp Shelby,† not far from us, visited us regularly on weekends. A letter sent by Mr. K, one of my [former] students, explains their mental attitude. Dated March 12, 1944, Mr. K writes, "I am sorry to be writing so late, especially after your generous hospitality and your parting gift." His syntax is poor and some of his *kanji*‡ incorrect, but the fact that he wrote in Japanese is touching. He continues, "I hope everyone is well. I am fine in spite of the extremes in the weather. During the long year after leaving Hawai'i, I have struggled through basic training and experienced the changing seasons. We have been recognized as good soldiers, the reason being that we not only have American blood but also samurai blood flowing through our veins. The fact that we Nisei are Americans, yet Japanese, is not forgotten. Right now I am checking my weapons. It will not be long before we leave Mississippi. I would like to write more, but I shall end here with a prayer for your health and happiness. Good bye."

The impressive letterhead reads, "United States Army" and "Camp Shelby, Mississippi." Soon after this, Mr. K left for the war front in Europe. Though wanting in the use of proper language and writing, here was a Japanese soldier, one who embodied the goodness of the Japanese. This son and the parents who brought up this young man . . . §

I had been branded as an enemy alien, yet I owed a debt of gratitude [to America for nurturing me], but now I felt I was free of my obligation.

"Even though you have lived in Hawai'i for many years and have devoted yourself to the United States, we do not believe you. You are a Japanese." So the U.S. government clearly declared. We left Kīlauea Camp and sailed out on the rough Pacific Ocean. It

---

*Ozaki also describes this scene with a poem in an undated radio broadcast. See "Memories of the Internment Camp," p. 73 - Trans

†Located in south Mississippi, this military training site provided basic training for Nisei recruits of the 442nd Regimental Combat Team and 100th Battalion. – Trans.

‡Chinese characters used in combination with the Japanese phonetic writing systems.

§Ozaki's use of three ellipses is intended to convey his feelings of admiration for the young Nisei soldier as well as the Issei parents who raised him. – Trans.

was February 21, 1942.

* * *

Ozaki's time spent at Kīlauea Military Camp was his most prolific in terms of writing poetry about his internment experience, at least based on the *tanka* existing in the files. According to Shige Yoshitake, who translated the poems[*] (Frances Kakugawa gave the translated *tanka* poetic renderings[†]): "There are about 119 poems, about twenty-two are partially unreadable because of the fold crease in the paper, or caused by a tear in the paper. Also, about fifty percent appear to be duplicates of the poems previously examined. These appear to be among the earliest of the writings. However, 'check marks' at the top of certain lines indicate that at a later date there were copies made and that they were 'classified in some fashion.' There are no definite dates of his actual writing, but the events mentioned indicate that these were written while he was at Kīlauea Military Camp (Volcano) before his transfer to O'ahu. Ozaki writes of the evening of his arrest, one week of sleeping on the same unwashed sheet, ten days of no communication with those of the investigation team, receiving a hair clipper on the twentieth (of December), arrival of new internees ten days later, eating *mochi*[‡] on the third (of January)."[13]

Of the 119 poems, twenty- seven have been completely translated and poetically rendered. These are printed here for the first time.[14]

My compensation For helping older residents Is internment.	在留民に 代わりて世話を せし事の そのつぐないの 囚われにして
The evening chill of the volcano Becomes harsher and harsher. Sleeping becomes difficult. I can only wait for daybreak.	しんしんと せまる火山の 夜の冷えに まんじりとせず 明けを待ちおり

---

*See "Interview with Shige Yoshitake, Translator of Otokichi Muin Ozaki's poetry: July 20, 2007," Appendix D.

†Frances Kakugawa, a native of Kapoho on the Big Island, is a published poet and educator.

‡rice cakes

He'll be home tomorrow,
My wife assures the children.
He'll be home tomorrow,
As each lonely day goes by.

あす帰る
あす帰ると
子等に言いきかせ
妻も淋しく
日を送りけむ

There is nothing special to say,
Yet a word or two
Eases my anxiety,
My wife writes.

別に用は
なけれど何か
言いやらば
安心せんと
書ける手紙ぞ

The arrival of a hair clipper
Turns the day into a barber's day.
The big grin on each of the faces
Is like the smile of a child.

バリカンの
着きし一日は
髪かりて
子供の如く
喜びあえり

The slashing rain stings my face.
Each breath turns white,
This cold morning in military camp.

横なぐりに
たたきつける雨は
顔に痛し
吐く息白き
営所の朝

A single evening primrose
Blooms laden with morning dew,
One morning in military camp.

月見草
一輪咲きし
霧雨に
濡れていたりぬ
営所の朝

After my evening meal,
A walk on the lawn of the camp,
An upward glance at the sky
Reveals a lone shining star.

夕食の
帰りを歩む
営庭に
見上ぐれば星の
一つ光れる

Twenty or so Christmas lights
Glow in the mess hall,
Allowing but a wee feeling
Of the jolly season.

食堂に
二十あまり
電気つけられぬ
クリスマス来ぬと
ほのかんじつつ

The much awaited Christmas season
Comes and goes
As we pray for good fortune.

僥倖を
祈りてまちし
クリスマスの
ついに来たりて
過ぎにける哉

* * *

After documenting his stay at Kīlauea Military Camp, Ozaki turns to scripts that revolved around a theme, like Japanese language, beards, eating utensils, numbers, and cigarettes. These scripts provide a glimpse into Ozaki's sense of humor, and his probing, analytical mind.

RADIO SCRIPT
Internees and the Japanese Language[15]
   This week, I am going to cover the topic of internees and the Japanese language.
   For about a month after we were sent to Kīlauea Camp, we were not allowed to possess Japanese books or any written materials in Japanese. Later we were allowed to read several Japanese books sent by our families, but only after the books had been censored.
   My family sent me a book by Kubota Utsubo entitled *Tanka Shiken.*[*] I read the entire book several times. I usually read it in the morning, wrapping myself with a blanket, as it was still cold. However, because of a change in regulations – something that occurred frequently—we were ordered to turn in all Japanese reading materials. All of our books, except one or two Japanese Bibles, were confiscated. About the only Japanese reading material to make it all the way from the Big Island to Fort Sill was the book *Seimei no Jissō,*[†] written by Hiroshi Tahara, a well-known [Japanese language] teacher from Pāpaʻikou on the Big Island. Speaking of Mr. Tahara, who was once renowned throughout Hawaiʻi, he became seriously ill during his internment and was confined to bed. He passed away on August 31, 1945 at the Santa Fe Camp. I would like to cover his story someday.
   At any rate, how empty were our lives without Japanese books. Yet, when I arrived at Fort Sill, Oklahoma and met internees from the Mainland, I discovered that they had been allowed to keep many things. They had many books – a far cry from the restric-

---

[*] *Tanka Shiken* (My Thoughts on *Tanka* Poems) by Kubota Michiharu Utsubo (1877-1967), a poet, author, and scholar of Japanese literary classics. – Trans.
[†] *The Facts of Life*

tions we had faced, having been denied even hair oil for several months. I often imposed on Yoshisuke Hatanaka, who had once lived in Hilo, by going to his tent to borrow books and other things.

We were only allowed to write letters in English in the early days. At the time, I had difficulty writing in English, as I had already forgotten how. Nevertheless, I wrote letters in English to my family and did so with great pain for my fellow internees. English also was a must for the letters from our families. Of course, we spoke only in Japanese amongst ourselves, but we had to avoid doing so when there were soldiers nearby. On the morning of December 8, when we went to the mess hall in [Kīlauea] camp, we were told that no Japanese was to be spoken and no finger pointing would be allowed.

RADIO SCRIPT
Memories of Four Years Behind Barbed Wire: Internees and Beards[16]

In February 1942 we were notified that we were leaving Kīlauea Camp. We were told not to carry any watches, metal products, or mirrors, regardless of their size. So I arranged to have the authorities send my wristwatch home, and I received a receipt for it. This watch was a gift from my friends at Gin-u Shisha, a *tanka* poetry club in Hilo, of which I was a permanent secretary. I also left my small two-to-three-inch mirror behind so it could be sent home. I wrapped some of my clothes around them and wondered what my family's reaction would be when they uncovered them. Several years later, I asked my family if they had received the items and learned that only the watch had been delivered.

I had heard that initially fountain pens also were not allowed among our personal effects. [The Kīlauea authorities] inquired with Hilo military headquarters and were told that although they contained metal parts, eye glasses and fountain pens were the exception [and would be allowed]. When our group arrived in Honolulu, I saw detainees from other islands boldly ("boldly" may sound odd) displaying their watches and mirrors. How we envied them. We realized then that there was no consistency among the authorities of the different islands regarding the way detainees were treated. When we landed at Sand Island in Honolulu, we were stripped of our clothes, and all of our personal belongings were confiscated.

A detainee who was transferred to the Mainland on the first ship had left behind a sundial that he had devised to compute time based on the position of the North Star.* Without our watches, it was the only timepiece we had to rely on for the day's schedule. From morning until night, our activities were determined by the hour and the minute – reveille at this time, roll call at that time, barrack inspection at such-and-such time. When the toilet facility was to be inspected, it was off-limits until the work was completed.

As time went by we adapted to life without our watches. One day, my friend in the same tent absentmindedly asked me, "I wonder what time it is."

"Ask the sun," I answered.

"I think it's around noon," he said.

"Judging by my stomach, I agree," I replied.

After thinking about it, I would say that watches and mirrors were not really necessary for the kind of life we had.

As for mirrors, when I first saw my face in the mirror, it was on the tenth day of our confinement at the Honolulu Immigration Station. "Are you me?" I asked the unshaven face in the mirror. It reminded me of a character from one of Mr. Chikuma's† *rakugo*.‡ The point was that since razor blades were considered lethal weapons, why bother to shave? Simply let your beard grow. I've never heard of anyone dying because he did not shave. I even thought that a beard might be something to remember our confinement by.

There were numerous types of beards—General Nogi-style,§ commander-style, Kumaso-style,¶ Manchurian mounted bandit-style, mountain robber-style, court noble-style, etc. Some people looked dignified, others pathetic. Mr. Izuno,** a school principal

---

*The original text reads 北斗星 *hokuto-sei*, the characters for the Big Dipper. Ozaki meant to write 北極星 *hokkyoku-sei* (the North Star). – Trans.

†Masayuki Chikuma of Honolulu, manager of the Toyo Theater. – Trans.

‡A short comic form of theatre performed by a single person on stage.

§Nogi Maresuke (1849-1912), a military figure who quelled an anti-government rebellion in the years shortly after the fall of the Tokugawa and commanded armies in the Sino-Japanese and Russo-Japanese wars. When he and his wife committed ritual suicide upon the death of the Meiji Emperor, Nogi became revered as a symbol of loyalty and sacrifice. – Trans.

¶A tribe of early inhabitants thought to be from the southern Kyūshū area. The ancient chronicles of early Japan include tales of a Kumaso rebellion waged against the Yamato court. – Trans.

**Tokio Izuno of Pāhoa on the Big Island, a Japanese language school principal. – Trans.

in Pāhoa, grew a General Nogi style beard. He really looked like General Nogi, so people called him "Mr. Nogi" throughout the internment period. Someone told another, "Hey, stop growing a beard. When you see your family, your son will tell your wife there's a guy with a beard at the door."

Such casual comments made in jest triggered anew thoughts we were trying to suppress – of our families, our empty lives, and our uncertain future. But I told myself that we are at war, and I thought of the bearded soldiers fighting and risking their lives for their country in the muddy trenches.

* * *

Ozaki wrote more poems documenting his transition from Kīlauea Military Camp to Sand Island in Honolulu. Uncertainty and the thought of truly leaving family behind are more pronounced in his poetry of this time.[17]

The days of imprisonment	監禁も
Approach two months	二月となりぬ
The coolness	冷気せまる
Of the volcano evening	火山の夕べ
Brings winter rains.	雨降り出でぬ
When will the day come	何時の日に
That I may see	帰り来るべき
My home in the middle	吾が家ぞ
Of the green leaves	キビの緑の
Of the sugar cane?	中に並らべる
The street lined	ハイビスカスの
With hibiscus plants. Oh.	並木の道よ
When will I return	いつの日に
To see them again,	帰り来て又
The flowers in bloom?	花を見るべき
Word comes	砂島に
For the move	移動すと云う
To Sand Island.	その声に
I am not moved	どうにでもなれと
One way or the other.	心動かず

The full moon comes   二回目の
The second time around.   満月は又
Will I get to see   巡り来ぬ
The moon   三度目の月を
Its third time around?   見るはいづこぞ

When will I see   何時の日に
My children again?   再び子等と
I am overcome   会うことぞ
As I hug each child   かわるがわるに
One at a time.   抱き上げつつ

The bitterness in my heart   胸にありし
Will not melt.   かたまりとけぬ
My first words with my wife   三月ぶりに
In three long months   妻と語りて
Do not change my feelings.   思うことなし

We don   救命具
Our life preservers   つけてデッキに
And line the deck.   並びつつ
Our ship gets ready   ヒロの港を
To leave Hilo Harbor.   出でゆかんとす

I put my faith   一切を
In heaven today,   天に任せて
As we prepare   吾等今日
To leave   ホノルルの港を
Honolulu Harbor.   出で行かんとす

My elderly roommate   同室の
Wonders aloud,   翁は語る
"Will that day come   いつの日か
When I may have a bowl   晴れて味噌汁の
Of tasty *miso* soup?"   味わう日ありやと

Get up, go to sleep.   起きて寝て
Get up, have my meals,   食ひて一日も
For five days, repeatedly.   又暮れぬ
Another day is soon   かくて五日は
To pass by.   過ぎにける哉

After the roll call,　　　　　「ありがとう」と
The guard says,　　　　　　点呼の後に
"Thank you"　　　　　　　日本語で
In Japanese,　　　　　　　兵はあいきょうを
Wearing a big smile.　　　　ふりまける哉

Lying on the grass,　　　　草にねて
I looked up at the sky.　　　空を仰げば
The clear blue sky　　　　変りなき
Continues endlessly　　　　青空なりき
This Sunday afternoon.　　　日曜の午後

Mistakenly taken in　　　　同姓の
For another　　　　　　　間違ひもおかし
With identical name,　　　　ひかれ来し
One can only stare beyond　　男ぼんやり
In disbelief.　　　　　　　外をみていたり

A fellow internee,　　　　囚れに
A medical doctor,　　　　　医師もありて
Checks my blood pressure.　　血圧も
Pronounces it　　　　　　順調なりと
Normal.　　　　　　　　計りてくれぬ

Food has become　　　　　食う事より
Our only pleasure.　　　　　外に楽しみの
There is nothing　　　　　なき身なり
To look forward to　　　　ただそれのみを
Except our three meals.　　　楽しみとせり

The sound of footsteps　　　濡砂を
In the wet sand　　　　　ふむ音のして
Signals　　　　　　　　巡り来る
The approaching sentry　　　歩哨の剣の
And his shining bayonet.　　　キラリ光れる

* * *

If life in Kīlauea Military Camp was difficult, life at the Honolulu Immigration Station and Sand Island on Oʻahu was even more taxing. Accommodations were more uncomfortable, and leaving the "comfort" of the Big Island for the more impersonal treatment on Oʻahu was almost unbearable. In the following radio scripts, Ozaki discusses the themes of chopsticks and eating, numbers, and cigarettes.

RADIO SCRIPT
Memories of Four Years Behind Barbed Wire[18]

I think back to the time that I spoke to the children about chopsticks. By children I mean the students I taught at the language school. The Japanese need only a pair of chopsticks when eating. An American needs a fork, a spoon and a knife. When I said that silverware looked like weapons in contrast to a non-threatening pair of sticks, the children burst out laughing.

During our three-month confinement at Kīlauea Camp, there was strict control over the distribution of forks and knives. With bayonet at the ready, a helmeted soldier with beady blue eyes checked everyone's utensils. If we failed to show him our spoons and forks, or if either one was missing, the soldier detained us while a thorough investigation was conducted.

One evening, aboard ship from Hilo to Honolulu, we went down to the dining room for our meal and found just a spoon at each setting. Knives and forks were apparently weapons, so perhaps the officials were afraid we might use them to incite a riot and had ordered their removal. The sight of an adult eating with just a spoon, looking like a baby, was enough to make me burst out laughing. There were to be several more months of this kind of life.

The next thirteen days, from the night of February 21 to March 4, were spent within the cocoon-like enclosure of the Immigration Station. The officials were very strict about meals. If we left even one slice of bread, food restrictions were imposed. Fresh vegetables were seldom served: instead we had soggy cooked beans nearly every day. The food was served in an egg-shaped military-issue container, or mess kit, made of aluminum. It could be used as a pot, and all the food was thrown into it. At mealtime the door to our room was unlocked, and we went downstairs, then took the mess kit to the serving line, where the soldier on kitchen duty served us. We were then sent out to the backyard of the building, where we sat on the grass or squatted to eat our meal, since there were no benches. Of course, MPs stood by every three-to-six feet, glowering at us and ready to pull the trigger at a any moment.

From the time of my arrest, we were [rarely] served rice. If there ever was any, it was half-cooked or runny like paste and did not taste at all like rice. Our diet of rice, *miso* soup,* and *tsukemono*† of years past was suddenly replaced by sticky food cooked in oil. Somehow I never felt as though I had eaten, and it was a problem for me in the beginning.

A month after my arrest, food from the outside was allowed, and we were so happy that we shed tears of joy when we received sushi, *tsukemono*, and rice with *umeboshi*‡ in the center. [In the camps] we used the word "*shaba*"§ for the outside world, but even Hawai'i, in the middle of the Pacific, depends on the Mainland for its food supplies, and day by day as the war expanded, families were faced with a serious problem. In spite of this and the burden of carrying on without their husbands and fathers, our families managed to send us food, so it should not be a surprise to anyone that we became teary-eyed.

When our Mainland departure became official, our families sent us *tsukemono* and all kinds of precious Japanese canned goods, which we were loath to consume, so we hoarded them in our suitcases. For nearly two months, from the time we left Kīlauea Camp until we reached Fort Sill in Oklahoma, we were separated from our suitcases. When they were finally handed back to us, we were shocked to find that all the locks had been broken and the suitcases forced open, apparently to inspect the contents. All the food we had packed was gone.

Let me return to the [topic of] meals at the Immigration Station. Besides having a minimum of utensils, we had so few drinking cups that we had to share them. After the first group hurriedly ate – no, drank down – their food, they rinsed their utensils two or three times in tepid water, then passed them on to the next group. These utensils were still greasy, and touching them sickened me. The so-called coffee had no sweetness, and sometimes there was not enough for everyone. Two of us shared an aluminum drinking cup. We picked the side we would drink from, which led to the forging of friendships among us.

Eating outdoors was fine when it was sunny, but when it rained, we sought shelter under the eaves of the building. The MP would point his gun at us and yell, "Get outta here!" So we hur-

---

*soup seasoned with soybean paste
†pickles
‡salted plum
§The term *shaba* is used by prisoners to refer to the outside world. To be shut off from *shaba* is to be considered an unwanted member of human society, an outcast. The WWII internees often used the term to connote their status, when writing about the world outside the barbed wire. – Trans.

riedly drank down our food in the rain.

There was a tall, young banyan tree, perhaps fourteen feet high. When it rained, the internees would seek shelter under the tree, and there we would eat as raindrops fell from the leaves onto our eating utensils. Did we really need to be treated like criminals? One of us laughed cheerfully, "Look at us like this, chased into the backyard, squatting on the ground like beggars asking for hand-outs. We're worse off than dogs and cats."

I laughed it off cheerfully and looked up at the sky. "Cheer-fully" sounds out of place here, but the others and I were in a grin-and-bear-it frame of mind. "Wind, rain. What's the differ-ence?" was our attitude. It was only for a short while, three times a day, that we were outdoors for our meals, and we were able to look at the sky and get our fill of fresh air, so the rain did not really matter.

Apparently the Immigration Station was the headquarters for the military police. Out in the yard, trenches had been dug and mounds of fresh dirt piled up. In the empty lot outside the fence, one side had been cleared and plowed, and beans, potatoes and other vegetables planted, possibly because of a food supply problem. I began watching the bean plants grow while having my meals outdoors. Soon I was concentrating more on the plants than on my dirty eating utensils. I was really enjoying the experience of watching these plants.

My friend Mr. K once asked, "What's so interesting out there?"

I replied, "Look at that bean plant. It's grown a few inches since the day we were thrown into this place. It has the determination to survive. The least we can do is keep ourselves in good health and survive like the bean plant."

Mr. K said nothing and stared at the bean plant.

From then on, the bean plant became a great comfort to Mr. K and me. At times when I sank into despair and became edgy like an abrasive *sasara*,* the plant's climbing vines brightened my spirits and raised my hopes.

In the sudden downpour,	にわか雨に
A voice whips, "Get outa here!"	軒下によれば
As we take cover under the eaves.	ゲラウエヤと
Herded into a small yard,	雨の小庭に
We eat – in the rain.[19]	追はれたうぶ

---

*A bamboo whisk used to clean pots. Thin strips of bamboo are tied at the base to form a handle and the loose ends are used as a brush. Also, a musical instrument of similar appearance. – Trans.

Even the bean vine	のびてゆく
Is glad to be alive	豆のつるにも
Stretching its tendrils up	生きし事の
Into the morning air.	喜んで深し
	朝の大気に

I don't think they are well written, but I fondly recall these poems as reflecting our feelings of those days.

RADIO SCRIPT

Monologue on Cigarettes[20]

We spent fourteen days at the Honolulu Immigration Station after being transferred from Hilo on February 21, 1942. During that period, we could not get any daily necessities, and we slept as we were on a bare mattress, with only a blanket and no sheet or pillow. It goes without saying that cigarettes were a precious item. Relatives in Honolulu had sent the cigarettes to us, and we passed each one around among seven or eight of us. It was a pathetic sight.

When we were transferred to Sand Island, we joined thirty or more Honolulu detainees who remained behind [after the first group had left for the Mainland], and we asked them for some cigarettes. In time, a sympathetic camp official arranged to have us purchase cigarettes, deducting the expense from our individual maximum savings retained by the authorities—the large sum of fifty dollars. Until then, however, Mr. Miyata of Honolulu, saying that he did not smoke, distributed cigarettes sent by his family. I cannot forget the sight of him standing at the dining room exit after lunch, passing out his cigarettes. Although I have always had a take-it-or-leave-it attitude about cigarettes (I'm not kidding), at that time, our desperate craving for a puff was shameful.

Here I must insert the story of a *"hidane otoko."* As you know, there were very strict rules about what we could have in our possession – no watches, no pens, no mirrors, not even a pin. About the only metal item allowed was a belt buckle. Matches were out of the question. The only place where we could get a light was at our battalion chief's tent. That is where the *"hidane otoko"* appeared early each morning, lit a piece of string, and went from tent to tent, battling the Nu'uanu wind to offer a light for our cigarettes. This gentleman ended up taking care of us like this for four years, working in silence and doing menial tasks for our benefit. He had the respect of everyone and was affectionately called

---

*Lit., a man with a fire light.

"kimoiri don." He was none other than Mr. Saichiro Kubota of
Kaua'i, a schoolteacher.†

RADIO SCRIPT
Life on Sand Island[21]

It has been seven and a half years since [this event occurred
in] 1942. The place is the detention camp on Sand Island at the
entrance to Honolulu Harbor. On March 3, Girls' Day, internees
numbering 106 from the Big Island and more than eighty from
Kaua'i and Maui were sent here to Sand Island. Pearl Harbor, the
scene of the December 7 attack, is right before our eyes. We can
feel the tension in the air. There are canvas folding cots and two
or three blankets in each of the tents that we ourselves had put
up over the sand. We have no change of clothes, not even a towel.
From the day we were brought here, it has truly been a miserable
life. We have no idea when we will receive our baggage—our entire fortune—that had been hurriedly packed by our families when
we left Kīlauea Camp. I have one overcoat and two handkerchiefs
with me.

About a couple of weeks before our arrival, the first group of
170-plus detainees had left for the Mainland and were on their
way by train to wintry Wisconsin. The rest, about thirty men,
including a good friend, Mr. Ryou Adachi,‡ had been left behind
at Sand Island. As the old-timers [of the camp], these men looked
after us, and we were grateful and happy.

Several times each day, we lined up for roll call in the open area
outside our tents. We were told that metal objects were dangerous weapons, and we were not allowed to have even a nail in our
possession. Of course, we had already undergone several physical
examinations, and all of our personal belongings had been taken
from us, so we had absolutely nothing. Life without a watch,
without warmth, without reading matter, without even a pencil
and paper. How long would this continue, anyway? One could not
help but become edgy. Honolulu was within eyesight, but barbed
wire separated us, and we had no idea what was happening there.

As residents of the city where the war began, Honolulu
detainees were treated harshly, according to the old-timers. Our
hearts went out to them when one man said, "My friends, our
hands have been picks, hoes and shovels." What he meant was that
although there was nothing to do, we were expected to do some-

---

*A man who looks after others.

†Kubota was a Japanese language teacher from Waimea, Kaua'i. – Trans.

‡Tokuji Adachi was a Japanese language school principal from Honolulu. Ryou was his pen
name. – Trans.

thing – even pull the grass around our tents where there was none. The authorities were particular, to the point of being ridiculous, about censorship, sanitation, and cleanliness. [Yet] they seemed to be unconcerned about our health.

Then on March 9, toward evening, as the strong winds blowing down from Nu'uanu begin to beat against our tents, the silence is suddenly broken by a call to assemble. We each put on our one-and-only coat and line up as usual in front of the mess hall. An Army vehicle marked with a red cross comes to a stop in front of the hastily converted hospital barrack, and a body wrapped in white cloth is brought out. In the deep and heavy silence, a *kiawe*[*] tree swaying in the wind casts a long, dark shadow on the ground.

Just thirty to forty minutes earlier, Mr. Hisahiko Kokubo of Kaua'i[†] had been chatting with others. After dinner he had returned to his tent and was sitting on his cot when he suffered a heart attack and died. With no emergency equipment available in the tent, the three doctors—fellow detainees from Honolulu, Maui and the island of Hawai'i – had done what they could, but Mr. Kokubo became the first casualty among us. Of course, no one can be sure that he will be alive tomorrow. Neither can we predict that Sand Island will not become a battleground at any moment, since we are so close to Pearl Harbor and surrounded by pillboxes and barbed wire fencing.

Explosions reverberate against a sky dotted with flickering early morning stars, while at Pearl Harbor the dissipating black smoke reveals the sight of military ships. My thoughts suddenly turn to my family. Worried and anxious –fearful even of the sound of the wind – families no doubt pray for the safe return of their husbands and fathers, their breadwinners and heads of households. We have been here one week, but have been given nothing – not even a toothbrush or soap. We have merely existed day to day, as clouds of dust beat against our tents. Even a healthy young man forced to live under such extreme conditions would not last very long.

As the army vehicle silently passes by, we put our hands to-gether in prayer as a farewell gesture. I wonder what will happen to Mr. Kokubo's body. I can imagine how shocked and grief-stricken his family will be. Without benefit of a wake service or the reading of the [Buddhist] Sutra, it is a lonely send-off, eased by a wreath of magenta bougainvillea flowers that has been placed on the casket.

With wind adding to the cold, the vehicle's taillight sways from side to side, like the spirit of the deceased, as it fades in the sea breeze. The gates of our compound, secured with layers of barbed

---

*Hawaiian: mesquite
†Kokubo was a storekeeper from Waimea. – Trans.

wire, open one after the other and the vehicle finally disappears. All of our pent-up emotions give way, like the ground crumbling underfoot, leaving behind an indescribable emptiness. Without a word, we sadly return to our tents. For a pioneer, who devoted his life to the advancement of his fellow countrymen, to be rewarded at the age of sixty-four with a lonely death behind barbed wire is too tragic a fate.

That night, unable to fall asleep, I step outside the tent and look up at the stars twinkling in the sky, as if laughing at man's wretched state. Earth continues to spin, carrying its two billion inhabitants who behave like crazed people. Tomorrow will follow today. Our tent squeaks under the slanting Nu'uanu winds, and I feel like saying a prayer.

Three days later, forty-six ministers of various faiths, who were confined in camp, gathered to offer prayers to the departed. So ended the life of the first of us to be sacrificed.

RADIO SCRIPT

Internees and Numbers[22]

On February 21, 1942, we were thrust into bunk beds at the Honolulu Immigration Station with nothing but the clothes on our backs and a rationed blanket. On the eighth day, each and every one of us was allowed two minutes to shave and take a shower. Of course, we were not allowed to keep safety razors, since they were considered dangerous weapons. From the day we arrived, we had not expected to be able to shave. Our hair had become dry and our beards had grown sparsely. The room we were in was too small for eighty of us, yet the first group of 162 Honolulu internees had been detained here. Unable to move freely, they suffered great distress.

Now, then, the problem was how to shower and shave in two minutes. I had not had a chance to bathe for the past ten days, so one minute was spent scrubbing down my body. I used the other minute to scrape my mustache and beard with a dull safety razor. I became nostalgic as I soaped my body, and I wanted to shower for as long as I could.

"Hurry up! We'll catch cold," shouted someone who was

waiting [outside]. Washing away the grime, I felt as though I had removed a layer of skin.

Just as I was feeling lighter, it was time to prepare for a free trip to the Mainland. One by one our names were called in alphabetical order, for we were to receive a series of inoculations. A foot-long identification card stamped "1068" was hung around my neck and several pictures were taken of me from various angles. Here I was identified as "No. 1068." To be exact, my identification number was "ISN-HJ-1068-CI." "ISN" stands for "internee," and "HJ" is for "Japanese in Hawai'i." Those who lived on the Big Island were given numbers beginning with "1000," and so I was the sixty-eighth internee from there. Finally, "CI" stands for "civilian internee. As long as I have a name, I can feel confident, but when it is changed to a number – well, no good can come of it.

The ID numbers for O'ahu began with "1." I was told that they were assigned in alphabetical order according to the FBI list, so the first number went to Ensign Kazuo Sakamaki,* but he was the first military prisoner of war and not a civilian. There must have been an internee from Honolulu whose name began with "A," who was given the number "1" in the civilian category. That would explain why Mr. [Shoichi] Asami, former editor-in-chief of the *Nippu Jiji* [newspaper], was assigned the number "2" . . . .

In addition to the number "1068," I was assigned another number when we arrived at the Immigration Station on Angel Island[†] in San Francisco. An eight-by-twelve inch denim ID tag with the number "336" was pinned on the back of the collar of my coat. We were warned by the officer-in-charge that without these ID tags, we would not be allowed in the dining hall. For the first few days, it was odd to see these big tags on the backs of the internees. Although I could not see mine, I could clearly see the tag of someone in front of me.

"Hey, No. 287, you look good with your ID!" We teased one another in this way.

The day came when we were taken by boat to an inland location, crossing San Francisco Bay and passing under the Oakland Bay Bridge. We disembarked at a pier with a sign that read, "Oakland." It was the night of April 6, 1942, when 167 of us boarded

---

*The sole survivor of an Imperial Navy midget submarine that ran aground during the attack on Pearl Harbor, Kazuo Sakamaki (1918-99) was the first Japanese prisoner of war. Sakamaki was held at Sand Island until his transfer to the Mainland, where he was imprisoned for the duration of the war. See Yasutaro Soga, *Life Behind Barbed Wire: The World War II Internment Memoirs of a Hawai'i Issei* (Honolulu: University of Hawai'i Press, 2008), 50-51. – Trans.

†A 740-acre island in the middle of the San Francisco Bay. On it is located the U.S. Army's Fort McDowell, which served during the war as a processing center for internees and prisoners of war from Hawai'i and other western areas, such as Alaska. From here internees and POWs were sent to permanent inland camps. – Trans.

a Southern Pacific Line train that had been waiting for us. We had on the same shirts with our ID tag numbers pinned on our backs. On the afternoon of April 9, after traveling 2,000 miles, we reached a station in Lawton, near Fort Sill, Oklahoma. I wrote a poem at the time:

The destination	行く先も
Closer and closer	近まりにけむ
ID tag removed from my back	昔につけし
How light I feel!	番号ものけぬ
	軽くなりたる

Before noon of that day, MPs came to remove our ID tags. I said goodbye to my No. 336, and somehow I felt lighter. Then it was on to Fort Sill and life in a desert tent, of which I have many memories.

Soon after we arrived, we prepared for a medical check. Under the sun, temperatures rose to almost 100 degrees, as we stood for several hours waiting our turn. The extremes in temperature were so great that some of us went out of our minds. Our names were called, ten at a time, and we were taken into a makeshift clinic, where we were stripped naked. When told to hold out my chest, I thought I was to be inoculated. Instead, the number "111" was written in red ink across my entire chest. An overwhelming sense of anger came over me. Large numerals written directly on my skin in red as though I am an animal – how can a civilized country like America do such a thing? It made me feel very sad.

That night I took a shower and tried to scrub off the numbers with soap, but they did not come off easily. I still recall that one of my fellow internees complained about [the Americans'] uncivilized acts, saying they had treated us like cattle or horses.

After two years of moving from one camp to another, I joined my family at the Jerome Center in Arkansas. There our family was assigned the number "H-50," which meant the fiftieth family from Hawai'i.

My life as an internee—when I had to write "ISN-HJ-1068-CI" on every letter I wrote—it all seems like a dream now.

* * *

Ozaki's stay at Sand Island marked his last period of detention in Hawai'i before being shipped to the Mainland to Angel Island off San Francisco. He then went to Fort Sill in Oklahoma, to Livingston in Louisiana, to Santa Fe in New Mexico, to the Jerome Incarceration Center in

Arkansas, and to his last camp in Tule Lake, California. The next chapter will chronicle camp life on the Mainland, seen primarily from the eyes of Ozaki: everyday life, activities of internees, and impressions of life by internees.

FATHER'S LONG JOURNEY IN MAINLAND CAMPS, 1942 – 1944

> The unbearable monotony of a life without variation
> seems to slowly warp our minds.
> —Otokichi Ozaki, from a radio script
> on Mainland camps

THE FIRST TWO years of living in Mainland camps, 1942 to 1944, were the most difficult for the Hawai'i internees. Not only were they leaving their friends and families behind with no knowledge of what was going to happen to them, or even whether they would be allowed to live, they first had to contend with having their freedoms and symbols of a free life taken away. As Ozaki indicates in his radio scripts broadcast after the war, when they first arrived in San Francisco, they were stripped and all of their belongings were confiscated. They later discovered that expensive watches were missing from their bags. When they reported this, the soldiers added insult to injury by treating the internees themselves like the thieves and searching their beds and personal effects.

Life in Mainland camps was unbearably monotonous. In one radio script, Ozaki mentioned that, "If we continue to live like this for another two or three years, we will become living corpses. Everyone's eyes are beginning to look like those of dead fish . . . . Someone has called us 'defecating machines,' which is absolutely correct. Are we not becoming like leaking balloons – ambitionless, lethargic and apathetic?"

Nevertheless, camp itself was highly structured with well-defined roles and jobs for each of the internees. They took on the responsibilities of priests of various religions, sports directors, administrators, educational instructors, cooks, and laundrymen. They also had a say in camp operations, as they were allowed to petition for better conditions, to have their families join them, and even to be released. Possessions were strictly regulated, as the amount of money they could carry was limited, and the articles permitted were specified.

Then there was the first killing the internees experienced in camp: Kanesaburo Oshima from Kona either was confused or tried to escape (various accounts interpret his actions differently) and started to climb up the inner wire fence. He made it to the top and jumped to the other side. A guard ordered him to stop and chased him with a pistol, firing a few shots that missed. When Mr. Oshima, apparently confused, kept running and tried to scale the second fence, another guard shot him in the back of the head and he died on the spot.

Mr. Oshima's death both shocked and outraged the internees. They held an elaborate funeral for him, and mourned their comrade's life. Thinking of their own families back in Hawai'i, they grieved for Mr. Oshima's wife and eleven children in Kona. They were deeply angered at the thought of their innocent, unarmed friend, who was ruthlessly killed. As Mr. Oshima's body was being transported from the funeral attended by over 700, the internees saw the soldiers carrying in a machine gun, brought "in case of a riot." This was the ultimate offense to their sense of justice.

While life in Mainland camps was occasionally rattled by incidents such as this, most of it was dull and grinding. As indicated in the letters included in this chapter between internees in Mainland camps, they tried to make their lives more comfortable with small creature comforts such as Japanese pickles, poetry and calligraphy clubs, recreational games such as baseball, soccer, and tennis, and even unexpected delights such as making a soy sauce-based wild duck soup when four migratory birds fell like manna from heaven onto the roofs of their barracks.

The following radio scripts, reports, camp news, and letters bring to life the grief, affronts, and occasional bright spots of life in the first two years of Mainland camp life.

In an undated radio script, Ozaki recalls life on the ship across the Pacific.

RADIO SCRIPT
Memories of Four Years Behind Barbed Wire: Internees and Beards[1]
Aboard a ship crossing the Pacific Ocean to the Mainland, we were kept in a hold of wire fencing that was lit twenty-four hours a day. At that time, wristwatches were our only source of entertainment. Those of us from the Big Island had no watches, but we were fortunate to have in our quarter two men from other islands who did. Thus we could at least find out the time of day. As we proceeded across the Pacific, however, time adjustments had to be made – from Hawai'i time to Pacific Ocean time, then to San Francisco (Pacific) time, and then Texas (Central) time. We

became totally confused.

When we reported to the [Angel Island] Immigration Station in San Francisco, soldiers ordered us to remove our clothing, searched our belongings, and took them all away. A week later, when we were about to be transferred and our belongings returned to us, three watches were found to be missing. All of them were expensive (more than $100) gold-plated watches. We had our representative file a complaint right away. We were asked, "Do you remember the faces of the soldiers who conducted the search?" and "When did this take place?" The result was that we were body-searched, then hustled out into the backyard while our government-issued duffle bags – our entire fortunes – were inspected. Even the mattresses on our beds were turned over in the thorough search for the watches.

Our belongings had been taken away, yet we were treated as though we were the thieves. There was no reason at all for us to have been suspected of stealing. Things were going the wrong way. It should have been the other way around. Shocked by the turn of events, the owners of the watches bowed and apologized to the rest of us for the problem they had caused. For me the incident was more comical than infuriating. With tongue-in-cheek, I said to my friend Mr. K, "The watches probably turned into drinking money, and by now the thieving soldiers are having a good time. I've heard of Chinese soldiers stealing from prisoners, but I guess they're not the only ones." In the end, the watches never turned up among our belongings.

Later when we arrived at Fort Sill, Oklahoma, the suitcases we had left two months earlier at Kīlauea Camp were delivered to us. All of them had been forced open, the locks broken, with most of the contents missing. At that time I still remembered what I had packed, so I promptly made out a list and submitted it to the authorities. My continued efforts to negotiate some form of compensation were in vain. I still have a copy of the twenty-three-page typed list of items, which were valued at a few thousand dollars.

* * *

One of the many strengths of the Ozaki archives is the collection of materials on camp organization and operations. From these materials, a wealth of knowledge can be gleaned about how the internees lived in the Mainland camps. The bulk of these documents consists of lists: of internees at a specific camp, of internees from Hawai'i, of internees about to be transferred to a different camp, of internees about to be repatriated to Japan, of names of workers and officers and their positions at various camps, and of internees being released and the funds owed them.

As the documents indicate, life in Mainland camps was highly organized, with the internees themselves serving as barracks leaders, and holding various functional and administrative jobs around the camp. For example, one document on Fort Missoula, Montana, provides statistics on the religious background of the internees and a list of jobs held by the internees. It provides a snapshot of life as it was organized in camp:

English original
DOCUMENT FROM THE OFFICE OF JAPANESE DETAINEES, FORT MISSOULA, MONTANA[2]
Date: December 23, 1943

Office of Japanese Detainees
Fort Missoula, Montana
December 23, 1943
Information requested by Mr. Kashima
1. Statistics:

Total Japanese as of August 14, 1943	424
Total Japanese received since August 14, 1943	18
Released or paroled	9
Transferred	1
Death	1
Repatriated	47
Present Population	384

2. Spokesman:

Full Name	Takaichi Saiki[*]
Present Address	P.O. Box 1539
Profession	Bank Official
Former Occupation	Assistant Manager, Bank of Hawaii, Hilo Branch
Last Residence	1896 Kalanianaole Ave., Hilo, Hawaii

3. Other Agents Entrusted with Representation

Totaro Matsui[†]	Executive Secretary

4. Japanese in Charge of:

Work	Sawajiro Ozaki[‡]
Education	Hideyuki Serizawa[§]

---

[*]Assistant general manager of Bank of Hawaii in Hilo. Internee information is from the JCCH internee database, "Hawaiʻi Japanese and Japanese Americans Detained During World War II." – Trans.

[†]From Honolulu, president of Pacific Bank.

[‡]From Honolulu, president of Smith Auto Supply.

[§]From Honolulu, principal of the Tōyō Gakuen Japanese language school.

General Welfare		Takaichi Saiki
		Totaro Matsui
		Katsuji Onishi
		Taijiro Tochio
		Kinzo Sayegusa*
Canteen		Kinzo Sayegusa
Administration of Funds		Katsuji Onishi

5. Number of Japanese Employed in:

Kitchen	28 (4 regularly, 12 each bi-weekly)
Dish Washing	20 (daily by turn without compensation)
Tailor Shop	1
Firemen	6
Poultrymen	5
Laundry	8
CCC Camp Janitors	2
Coal Detail	8
Utility-men	7 (as needed)
Movie Operators	2 (twice a week)
Officers Mess	9
Farming	4
Warehouse	5

Religious Services:

Christian	Catholic	Every Sunday
	Protestant	Every Sunday and Bible Study twice weekly
Buddhist		Every Sunday and Lectures by different Sects weekdays
Shinto		None

A. Statistics:

Christian	Catholic	8
	Protestant	40
Buddhist		318
Shinto		18

B. Numbers of:

Buddhist Priests	19
Shinto	7
Christian	2

Another document from the U.S. Department of Justice Immigra-

---

*From Honolulu, president of Yonekura Shōkai.

tion and Naturalization Service in Missoula, Montana, October 18, 1943, shows that the Office of Japanese Internees comprised a host of men serving as officers, administrators, skilled laborers, managers, and instructors.[3]

The following posts were listed:

General Welfare Committee	Saiki, Takaichi
	Matsui, Totaro
	Onishi, Katsuji
	Tochio, Taijiro
	Sayegusa, Kinzo
Mayor (Spokesman)	Saiki, Takaichi
Executive Secretary	Matsui, Totaro
Assistant Secretary	Sasaki, Yoshinobu[*]
Treasurer	Onishi, Katsuji
Auditor	Tochio, Taijiro
Clerk	Kashima, Ryuichi[†]
	Morita, Takeshi
	Kurotobi, Isamu
Janitor & Errand Boy	Hamamoto, Shoyu
	Takahashi, Rien[‡]
Canteen:	
Manager	Sayegusa, Kinzo
Buyer	Tokioka, Setsugo
Clerk	Okada, Saichiro
	Furuya, Kumaji[§]
	Nakamura, Yukio
	Takutake, Shikaichi
Post Office:	
Chief	Konno, Ichiro[¶]
	Yamamoto, Hiroshi
Detail Supervisor	Ozaki, Sawajiro
Supply Dept.:	
Chief	Kiyosaki, Masato
	Horiuchi, Mitsutaka[**]
	Watanabe, Kenzo
First Aid	Kimura, Akio[††]
	Kohatsu, Yukihide[‡‡]
	Taira, Yojo[§§]

---

[*]A Japanese language teacher from Honolulu.
[†]A Japanese language teacher from Kaʻaʻawa on Oʻahu.
[‡]A Buddhist priest and Japanese language school teacher from Honolulu.
[§]From Honolulu, the manager of Fuji Furniture Store. His internment memoir, *Haisho Tenten*, was published in 1964.
[¶]An employee of the *Nippu Jiji*, from Waipahu, Oʻahu.
[**]A store clerk from Lahaina, Maui.
[††]A physician from Honolulu.
[‡‡]A physician from Honolulu.
[§§]From Pāʻia, Maui.

Janitor #3	Wada, Ichiro*
News Dept.	Arai, Kazuo
	Murakami, Minoru†
	Watanabe, Ittetsu Tadao‡
Barber	Tomita, Kazuo§
	Takahashi, Kakichi
	Gondo, Seitaro
Plumber	Shigemoto, Osuke¶
Recreation Director	Koba, Tsuneyoshi
A. Soft-Ball Manager	Obata, Soichi**
Asst. Manager	Takehara, Renichi
B. Tennis Manager	Koba, Tsuneyoshi
C. Judo Manager	Kabashima, Suijo††
D. Golf Manager	Sakimizuru, Atsuo‡‡
E. Movie	Kimura, Muneo§§
	Takizawa, Kichiro
Education Director	Kubota, Soichiro¶¶
A. English Class Instructor	Himeno, Masa Hilo***
	Hisatake, Itsuo†††
B. Commercial Class	Sokabe, Miyuki‡‡‡
Instructor	
C. Shakuhachi Class	
(Flageolet) Instructor	Mikami, Shuji§§§
D. Art Class Instructor	Ikeno, Masao¶¶¶
E. Kendo Instructor	Mikami, Shuji
F. Librarian	Hisatake, Itsuo
Religion	
Christianity	Maeda, Kametaro****
Buddhism	Sarashina, Shinri††††
Hospital Pharmacist	Tsutsumoto, Nobuichi, with pay
Chief Cook	Nagai, Sekitaro "
Steward	Takeuchi, Taro "

---

*From Hana, Maui.

†An employee of the *Nippu Jiji* in Hilo.

‡A salesman from Maui.

§A storekeeper from Waipahu, Oʻahu.

¶A contractor from Honolulu.

**From Honolulu, manager of the *Nippu Jiji*.

††A Buddhist priest from Honolulu.

‡‡A hatter from Hilo.

§§From Honolulu, manager of Nichibei Enterprises.

¶¶A misspelling of Saichiro Kubota, a Japanese language teacher from Waimea, Kauaʻi.

***A misspelling of Masahiro Himeno, a Christian minister from Honolulu.

†††A misspelling of Itsuei Hisatake, a Japanese language teacher from Pāʻauhau on the island of Hawaiʻi.

‡‡‡An accounting instructor from Honolulu.

§§§A storekeeper from Honolulu.

¶¶¶A Japanese language school principal from Kailua, ʻOahu.

****A Christian minister from Honolulu.

††††A Buddhist priest from Honolulu.

	Yoda, Ichisuke*	"
Tailor	Sonoda, Santaro†	"
Inside Detail	Shinoda, Masaichiro‡	"
Laundry	Kochi, Hotoku	"
Fire Dept. Chief	Arita, Tamaki§	"
Outside Mess Chief	Abe, Yazaemon	"
Poultry Chief	Oi, Joei¶	"

It is clear that internees were allowed to voice their concerns and raise questions regarding their treatment. On December 17, 1943, two meetings were held in Missoula between a group of internee representatives, led by spokesman Takaichi Saiki, and Captain A.R. Martin, the consul of Spain. The internees voiced their concerns regarding repatriation and reunion with their families, as well as expressed their complaints and wishes regarding the camp. As shown in the meeting report below, the Consul's responses were terse and perfunctory and not at all satisfactory. Most responses were refusals or deflections, to be considered at a later date.

REPORT OF INTERNEE MEETING WITH CONSUL
OF SPAIN, CAPT. A. R. MARTIN, FORT MISSOULA,
MONTANA[4]
Date: December 17, 1943

Report by the Meeting Committee
Of its Meetings with
Mr. A.R. Martin, Consul of Spain**

Date and Time: December 17, 1943. Two meetings were held; one in the morning and one in the afternoon.††

Committee Members:

Mainland: Iwao Matsushita
                                       Katsuji Onishi

---

*A misspelling of Kichisuke Yoda, a Japanese language school principal from Wahiawa, Kaua'i.
†From Waipahu, O'ahu.
‡A salesman from Hilo.
§A plumber from Honolulu.
¶A Buddhist priest from Honolulu.
**As a neutral third party, Spain oversaw Japanese interests in the United States, including those of the Issei in the camps. – Trans.
††The meetings were held in the internee barracks at 10:30 a.m. and 2:30 p.m. See *Correspondence to the Hon. Consul of Spain, Capt. A.R. Martin*, Missoula Montana, December 16, 1943, AR1, B10, F1. – Trans.

Hawaii:	Minoru Murakami
	Tetsuji Kurokawa*
Peru:	Taijiro Tochio
	Masao Mochizuki
Spokesman's Office:	Spokesman [Takaichi] Saiki
	Secretary [Totaro] Matsui

The meetings were held between the Consul of Spain and the internee representatives only. The two State Department officials, the official from the INS, and Mr. Fraser, the camp commander,[†] who accompanied the Consul, did not attend.

NOTES OF THE MEETINGS

(Made from notes written and compiled by the committee members. The Consul was also questioned on some points.)

Questions posed by the Consul (concerning living conditions at the center):
1. How is the food situation? Are you served tofu?
    Answer: On the whole, we have no complaints, but we strenuously request more Japanese food be available.
2. How do you feel about the number of people in the barracks?
    Answer: Since quite a large number of people have been either repatriated or paroled, in general, the overcrowding has been resolved, with the exception of two or three barracks.
3. What improvements have been made since I last visited?
    Answer: Nothing in particular.
4. Compared to other camps and relocation centers, I believe this center is much better in all aspects. You are lucky. The conditions in some other relocation centers are incomparably more miserable.
5. Is the clothing ration adequate?
    Answer: Satisfactory.

Questions posed to the Consul:
                    I. Repatriation
A. Questions concerning the second exchange ship
    1. Why were some internees forced to repatriate against their

---

*General manager of Marine Products Co. in Honolulu.
†Bert H. Fraser was officer-in-charge of the Fort Missoula Internment Camp. – Trans.

will? (For example, Mr. Agena and Mr. Kakiuchi.)*

Answer: I did not know about this. (In the afternoon meeting, the Consul reported as follows: Mr. Fraser received instructions [regarding who was to be repatriated] through a cable from the State Department.)

2. Some internees were not allowed to board the ship and were left behind.† What was the reason for this?

Answer: Simply because there was no room for them.

3. Was the list of repatriates made by the Japanese Government?

Answer: Yes.

4. Some internees were not allowed to bring their families [from Hawai'i] with them and were forced to sign an agreement indicating their desire to repatriate alone.‡ What was the reason for this?

Answer: This is the first time I am hearing of this. If you give me their names, I will check on it and report back to you.

B. Questions concerning the third exchange ship

1. Is the third exchange ship scheduled to sail? If so, when?

Answer: Possibly. I believe consideration will be given following receipt of this report. As soon as possible, send a list of those wishing to be repatriated on the third exchange ship.

2. How will you select those to be repatriated? Will you go by the old list or the new list?

Answer: The Japanese government makes the selection by itself. It will compile a new list.

3. Some repatriates, who are scheduled to leave on the exchange ship, have left family behind in Hawaii. Will those families be sent to the Mainland before the exchange ship departs?

Answer: Send us the names and details of the families. I will do my best to see that your wishes are fulfilled.

4. Is priority to board the ship given to the sick and the elderly?

Answer: I have no idea.

5. We hope that priority is given to internees [over

---

*Both from Panama. See *Correspondence to the Hon. Consul of Spain, Capt. A.R. Martin* – Trans.

†Tokuji Onodera, a reporter with the *Hawaii Hōchi* in Honolulu, and Wataru Takamoto, a businessman from Hilo, were internees known to have been removed from the second exchange ship. JCCH Internee Database. – Trans.

‡*Correspondence to the Hon. Consul of Spain, Capt. A.R. Martin* lists the following individuals; information about these internees is from the JCCH Internee Database: Seiichi Ohata, physician from Pā'ia, Maui; Eiichi Kishida, principal of a Japanese language school in Honolulu; Motoichi Kobayashi, storekeeper from Kahului, Maui; Eishu Asato, manager of the Honolulu Hotel; Tokuji Baba, innkeeper from Honolulu; Masayuki Kodama, Konkokyo priest from Honolulu; Shigeru Kuwahara, farmer from Pāhoa on the Big Island; Shozo Kawakami, storekeeper from Honolulu; Shintaro Miyagawa, druggist from Honolulu; Honi Ohye, Buddhist priest from Waimea, Kaua'i; Iwataro Shitanishi, laborer from Kekaha, Kaua'i. – Trans.

non-internees].

Answer: That is solely the decision of the Japanese government.

II. Reunion with Families

Please discuss the following two issues with Mr. Fraser, commander of this camp, Mr. Kelly of the INS in Philadelphia, and Mr. Ennis in the Department of Justice in Washington so that we may live together with our families:*

(1) Transfer internees to the Family Camp; or

(2) Reinvestigate and transfer us to relocations centers or free zones.

Please emphasize that it is against American humanitarianism to keep us separated from our families, as we have been for more than two years now.

Please point out the following: Whereas those in the Santa Fe Internment Camp now enjoy living with their families after having been reinvestigated, we in this camp have been forgotten.

As for those from Peru and Hawai'i who have requested reunion with their families, please arrange for this as soon as possible.†

Answer: Please send the list of those who wish to live with their families. I have been doing my best, but construction material for family units is in short supply, and construction is behind schedule. I will contact Mrs. Halsey, a welfare officer who once visited here, and I will continue to do my best.

III. Complaints, requests, etc., regarding this camp

1. Hospital patients complain about the attitude of the doctors who are treating them. We request rectification of this. Meals are not suitable for Japanese taste. Doctors are unkind.

Answer: Protests based on emotion, not facts, are not effective. Show me concrete examples. (We explained in detail the cases of Mr. Utsumi and Mr. Ikeno.)

2. Please negotiate to employ at least one Japanese doctor and two nurses in the hospital.

Answer (in the afternoon meeting): According to Mr. Fraser,

---

*Willard F. Kelly was assistant INS commissioner for alien control; Edward J. Ennis was director of the Justice Department's Alien Enemy Control Unit. – Trans.

†The internees were requesting that their families be brought to the Mainland, so that they could be reunited. Those from Hawai'i making this request included Gendo Okawa, a Buddhist priest from Waipahu, O'ahu; Totaro Matsui; Minoru Murakami; and Daizo Sumida, a businessman from Honolulu. See *Correspondence to the Hon. Consul of Spain, Capt. A.R. Martin.* – Trans.

camp commander, the hospital is in the hands of the Management Control Committee, and neither the camp commander nor the head doctor has any authority over this issue. The Japanese committee members asked the Consul to have the camp administration take necessary action to alleviate this situation and to include this matter in its report to the Japanese government.

3. Please ask the authorities to provide us with a special barrack with appropriate medical equipment and nurses for convalescents and the elderly. They do not require hospitalization, but they do need to rest quietly.

Answer (in the afternoon): Mr. Fraser has promised to provide this within two or three weeks.

4. We ask for regular physical check-ups of all residents.

Answer (in the afternoon): The camp commander has promised to provide this twice a year.

5. Please ask the authorities to provide us with an adequate supply of good Japanese food.

Answer (in the afternoon): The authorities reported that 150 gallons of *shōyu* would arrive within a few days and a tofu-making facility has been completed.

6. We are dissatisfied with the way the accounting section handles things. It is in need of substantial improvement.

Answer: Protests based on emotion, not facts, are not effective. This is difficult to respond to, but I will call the camp administration's attention to the issue. (In connection to this, we handed him a copy of our strongly worded protest, which we had submitted to the camp commander in late August.)

7. The accounting section holds on to the deposit receipts, when we deposit our cash. Thus, we have no evidence of our deposits. We ask that either this system be abolished or that a monthly statement be issued to every depositor.

Answer (in the afternoon): I have been told that the camp administration will consider issuing deposit passbooks or statements.

8. Postal service for packages to Hawaii has been suspended. Please allow us to send packages at least once a month.

Answer: This was instituted according to orders from Washington, and the camp can do nothing about it.

9. We ask for an increase in the restricted amount of weekly outgoing mail.

Answer (in the afternoon): The answer is the same as that regarding the previous issue. This is according to regulations from Washington and beyond the control of the camp commander.

10. Please immediately deliver, without inspection, those publica-

tions that have been approved. This includes newspapers, magazines and books sent directly from the publishers.

> Answer (in the afternoon): There are also regulations requiring the examination of publications.

We asked him to further negotiate with the authorities regarding the last three items (8, 9, and 10).

11. At Santa Fe and Kooskia* camps, internees are allowed to visit their families and friends on the outside (in special cases such as serious illness). They are also gradually being allowed to make group visits. However, at this camp, a similar request was turned down, and no one was accorded this opportunity. Why?

> Answer: I will discuss this with Mr. Fraser, camp commander. (No response, as of now.)

12. Privately owned table lamps and their cords have yet to be returned to their owners. Internees are troubled when they read books at night. Please return lamps and cords to their owners, as was done in other camps.

> Answer: I understand. I will negotiate for this. (No response, as of now.)

13. We had hoped to have a meeting room (for visitors from the outside).

> Answer: I will negotiate for this, too.

14. We demand a soft diet suitable for convalescents and the elderly. (We have twice delivered a copy of our demands to the authorities.)

IV. Miscellaneous

1. Request from Hawaii internees: Yokohama Specie Bank in Honolulu allows only citizen depositors, not internees, to make withdrawals. Please negotiate with the bank so that internees can make withdrawals.

> Answer: I will investigate this.

2. Question from internees from Peru:

> a. When will be able to return to Peru?
>
> Answer: I know nothing about this.
>
> b. We were asked to sign receipts for the money that had been taken from us in Panama and for our $9.50 allowance – ten cents per day for ninety-five days—but we have not yet received the cash. Please arrange a transfer of the funds, and pay us as soon as possible.

---

*Located in north central Idaho. Kooskia internees were part of a volunteer labor force recruited from among incarcerated Issei, who worked to build the Lewis and Clark Highway linking Idaho and Missoula, Montana. – Trans.

Answer: I will discuss this with Mr. Fraser so that appropriate
action can be taken.

3. Some internees feel that it is difficult to make withdrawals from
Sumitomo Bank in Seattle. We hope you will take appropriate
action.

Answer: We will report to you after the Federal Reserve Bank
investigates this.

4. How can we recover personal belongings that have been confiscated or lost?

Answer: If you send us a detailed list, we will take appropriate
action.

5. We would like to know the actual facts of the Tule Lake
incident.

Answer: I have not visited there, and I do not know the details.
I think the newspapers have exaggerated in their reporting
of this incident. It is certain that no one was killed, although
some internees were detained. The camp is now under military
control.

6. The two suitcases left by the late Mr. Gosaku Masuda, who
died at Fort Livingston Center on December 16, 1942, have not
yet been returned to his family. Please investigate this matter.

Answer: I will investigate this immediately.

7. There are some who wish to move to Tule Lake Camp. We
would like to know the procedures for this.

Answer: You have to negotiate with the INS. As I understand
it, the camp is only for those who wish to return to Japan.

The above is a summary of the two meetings, which lasted for
a total of two-and-a-half hours. We gave to the Consul all our
complaints, protests and demands in writing (one original and
three copies), asked him to report this document in its entirety to
the Japanese government, and also asked him to begin negotiat-
ing immediately with the U.S. authorities concerning matters
that need attention. (The documents to be mailed are now under
preparation.)

* * *

If an internee was allowed to repatriate to Japan, there were many restrictions on what could and could not be taken out of the country. The following is a memorandum distributed to those internees who were about
to be repatriated:[5]

English original
THE FOLLOWING ARTICLES INDICATED ARE THOSE
THAT THE JAPANESE MAY AND MAY NOT TAKE WITH
THEM TO JAPAN

a. <u>Money</u>. Every adult Japanese is allowed to take $300 out
of the United States. A Japanese under 21 years of age traveling
independently or as the head of a family will also be permitted to
take $300.

b. <u>Baggage</u>. Japanese are allowed to take with them their personal effects, limited to three suitcases of stateroom baggage and
30 cubic feet of hold baggage. Paper cartons or baskets that may
be crushed and broken are not permitted. Children between the
ages of 5 and 10 years may take with them 15 cubic feet of hold
baggage and children under 5 are permitted to take 7.2 cubic feet
of hold baggage.

c. The Japanese may take with them the following types of
articles: In general Japanese repatriates are to be permitted to
take those personal and used household effects which are used in
normal life and which persons who are traveling are permitted to
take under the export control regulations of the U.S. Government.
Thus Japanese repatriates may take clothing of all types, robes,
household linen, silverware, blankets, kitchen utensils, antiques,
art objects, collapsible baby carriages and similar articles in normal
household use. Excessive quantities of clothing are also prohibited,
but the interpretation of this restriction should be liberal in view
of the fact that the repatriates will require a variety of clothing as
the exchange vessels will traverse three climatical zones and they
will need a sufficient quantity of clothing as the voyage will cover
approximately 90 days and laundry facilities will be insufficient.
The Japanese will be permitted to retain their passports for identification purposes. Following the examination, Customs officers
will stamp in this passport the date, place of examination and the
detention number of the prohibited articles seized.

d. Japanese repatriates are prohibited taking the following
articles: Household furniture, garden tools, electrical appliances,
sewing machines, radios, mechanical equipment, typewriters,
other than portable typewriters, camera, photographic equipment,
binoculars, firearms and other weapons, rationed food stuffs, gold
objects except personal jewelry, professional instruments except
doctor's instruments which are usually included among the doctor's personal effects and are of a nature carried by general practi-
tioners. Food stuffs, toilet articles, tobacco products, medicine and
drugs, which are in excess of the amounts carried by travelers, may
not be included in the category of personal effects. <u>Photographs,</u>
<u>printed matter, sketches, except portraits, documents or papers</u>

<u>of any kind except Japanese passports are prohibited. American</u>
<u>passports are prohibited.</u>

* * *

Internees were allowed to petition to be released, citing primarily their character, as in the following letter by Charles Hasebe,[*] interned at Missoula, Montana. It is dated March 14, 1944.[6]

English original
Commanding General
Office of the Military Governor
Honolulu, Territory of Hawaii

Sir:

I, Charles Ichitaro Hasebe, a Japanese national from Territory of Hawaii, now interned at Fort Missoula, Montana, hereby respectfully submit a petition requesting for a release or parole from this internment, for your kind consideration.

I wish to reiterate that I was originally admitted into the Territory of Hawaii in December 1899 and have been living continuously for the past 44 years as a permanent resident. I have declared my desire not to be repatriated to Japan. I have never engaged in any activities subversive or un-American but wanted and continue to be a respectful and good law-abiding resident. My business at Leilehua, Oahu for the past 28 years, was solely connected with Schofield Barracks and its personnels where I still have many friends.[†]

I am married to a citizen of Japanese ancestry and have six children all born in Hawaii. Three of my daughters are married to Americans, ex-service men, all of them are in Hawaii. I also have a daughter who is now serving as nurse registered with the American Red Cross, at Queens Hospital, Honolulu.

As to my character and responsibility, I beg to refer to the following gentlemen:

Honorable James Coke, former Supreme Court Justice, Territory of Hawaii.

Honorable William H. Heen, Senator, Territory of Hawaii.

Honorable David Trask, Senator, Territory of Hawaii.

---

[*]Tatsuo Charles Ichitaro Hasebe, a storekeeper and restaurateur. - Trans.

[†]Hasebe operated a restaurant in the Wahiawā area of central Oʻahu, which was also known as Leilehua. Military personnel from Schofield Barracks, a U.S. Army post in Wahiawā, were frequent customers of Hasebe's restaurant. In the 1930s, the population at Schofield numbered some 14,000, making it the second largest city in the territory. – Trans.

Honorable Ex-Mayor Crane, City and County of Honolulu.

As to my behavior in this internment, I wish to refer to Mr. Bert H. Fraser Officer in Charge and Mr. Raymond H. Thomason, Liaison Officer at Fort Missoula, Montana.

Therefore, upon your due consideration of the above mentioned facts, I sincerely beg of you to review my case and kindly grant me an early release or parole me from internment.

Very respectfully yours,
Charles I. Hasebe
ISN-HJ-15-CI

* * *

As indicated in the desire to be released from internment camp expressed in Charles Hasebe's letter, life in Mainland camps was difficult. It was difficult enough being separated from home, family, and friends for an undetermined period of time and the uncertainty as to whether one was even going to be allowed to live, but the conditions under which the internees had to live was for some unbearably harsh. In a couple of radio scripts, Ozaki describes life in camp and the inability of one prisoner to cope.

RADIO SCRIPT

Life Behind Barbed Wire[7]

Good morning, everyone. Today I change the subject to our daily lives at the Fort Sill Internment Camp that was near Lawton,* Oklahoma. The following notes were written on a canvas mat in the camp on May 14, 1942.

"We are living in an area surrounded by barbed wire, bayonets, and machine guns, because the U.S. Army wants to protect us from outside dangers." So said a gentleman, one of the leaders of the Mainland group who joined us shortly after we had settled here. Hearing him, I thought about our life at Sand Island in Honolulu: a month with no change of clothing, no mirrors, no watches or pens or writing paper; a life in which a missing spoon resulted in our standing barefoot at attention outside our tents for several hours; a ridiculous kind of life where the discovery of a used nail in someone's overcoat led to a trial, and I as a juror helped convict the defendant. There also was that toilet hell of a

---

*The original text reads "Newton," but Ozaki meant Lawton, the city adjacent to Fort Sill. – Trans.

life aboard the USS *Grant* military ship as we sailed out of Honolulu, when we were cooped up like caged birds in the crowded hold and not allowed to go to the bathroom.

No, there were a number of things that kept me from agreeing with the gentleman. The spiteful guards glaring at us as though they would shoot us at any minute; the barbed wire surrounding us, one enclosure after the next; the soldiers watching us from every angle; machine guns positioned at each corner on the high towers and manned by soldiers twenty-four hours a day.

Here at Fort Sill, Oklahoma, where glittering heat waves rise and peak as far as the eye can see, the jumbled sound of machines and hammers can be heard, triggered apparently by the sudden need for more barracks. There is not a tree to be seen. Tents stand in rows. The heat. As though the wind is dead.

Just as a breeze brings cooling relief, dust clouds cover the entire desert in a spectacular display and a sandstorm sweeps over the land. Everything disappears in a dense, shroud-like fog. When I lick my lips, I can feel the particles of sand. In time, the sandstorm moves on and crisscrossing flashes of lightning race across the entire sky like a whip rope. All day long, plumes of thick smoke and soot rise from eight chimneys above the kitchen and bathing facilities, pushing their way into our tents.

No soap rations. No toothpaste. No hair oil for the past two months. Even my one-and-only suitcase, containing my entire fortune, and my bag – I have not seen them since February, March, April, May. What money we had was taken from us, so we have none. Inside the barbed wire fence, there is nothing we can buy anyway.

We become irritable. Eat. Sleep. Wake up. Eat. Sleep. Wake up. A life cut off from everything in the world. The unbearable monotony of a life without variation seems to slowly warp our minds. The crazy weather and the tent life—one cannot help but begin to lose one's mind. I once heard a story of Russian convicts who were ordered to draw water from a well and pour it into barrels day after day. Eventually they went insane from the monotonous work.

Six months of this kind of life, in which we are not permitted to do anything and are not provided with anything—given nothing to read to tell us about the world – I feel we are becoming addlebrained and our thinking ability is diminished.

Koran Murakami* tells us that if we continue to live like this for another two or three years, we will become living corpses. Everyone's eyes are beginning to look like those of dead fish. Mr.

---

*The pen name for Minoru Murakami, an employee of the *Nippu Jiji* in Hilo. – Trans.

Shiotani, known as "the Volcano saint"* and with whom I share the tent, says to me, "While you were lying on your cot, looking at the ceiling, all you did was blink your eyes."

I replied, "If my eyes blink, I'm still OK."

I suddenly recalled the article, *Futatsu no Hawai*"† by Sawada Ken, which I read when I was living on the outside. Mr. Sawada maintains that paradise must be somewhere in the heavens and cannot possibly be here on earth. He writes, "It is said that Hawai'i is the paradise of the Pacific, but the native Hawaiian population was wiped out, and who can be sure that those living there, languishing under boredom, will not suffer the same fate? When I landed at Honolulu Harbor for the first time, I saw a police officer holding an umbrella and directing traffic. The eyes of the pedestrians were like those of a dead fish, unmoving and focused only on the officer."

In this world, a community of people who simply eat and sleep cannot be expected to survive. Someone has called us "defecating machines," which is absolutely correct. Are we not becoming like leaking balloons – ambitionless, lethargic and apathetic?

It was the morning of May 12, 1942.

"Someone seems to have been shot." We rushed out of our tents and raced toward the main gate. The sun was already high in the sky and the wind was beginning to blow from the north. "It seems to be Mr. Oshima."‡ Our group of 176 men from Hawai'i had been divided into several companies.

As I hurried to where others were gathering, I recalled that earlier, someone in Company Three had been looking for Mr. Oshima. Then it struck me. "This must be serious," I thought. I had not noticed it earlier, but outside the wire fence, soldiers had already lined up ten feet apart, with their guns aimed at us and the safety latches off. At every corner of the guard towers, machine guns were exposed, and the mouths of their huge barrels, loaded with belts of ammunition, were focused on the confines of the enclosure.

"Disperse! Do not congregate! Go back to your tents or you will be shot!" someone screamed like a crazed person. The scene looked like a ruined spider web, as the crowd near the east gate scattered instantly.

Soldiers were running, their faces tense. I quickly headed for

---

*Motoi Shiotani, a Japanese language school teacher from the town of Volcano on the Big Island. – Trans.

† *Two Hawai'is*

‡Kanesaburo Oshima, an automotive service station owner from Kealakekua, Kona on the Big Island. – Trans.

the main gate, thought better of it, and returned to my tent.

RADIO SCRIPT
The Death of Mr. Oshima[8]

Good morning, everyone. Today's story is again about the death of Mr. Oshima.

It happened in the Fort Sill, Oklahoma desert where sandstorms blew. We, 167 internees from Hawai'i, arrived in San Francisco on March 20, 1942. We spent six days at Angel Island in the middle of San Francisco Bay. We then boarded an old-fashioned train that took us south through California and past Arizona, New Mexico, and Texas. On April 9 we entered Lawton, Oklahoma, where we took our duffle bags off the train. Fort Sill was a place where the weather seemed to change from one extreme to the other. At night and in the early morning, it was very cold, so we had to light a stove located in the middle of our tent. During the day, the temperature would suddenly shoot up. You can imagine how hot it was, when you listen to the following: One day, I placed on my head a handkerchief that I had just washed a minute earlier in the washroom barrack about 200 feet from our tent. By the time I got back to our tent, it was already half dry. You can understand how this kind of weather would drive us to exasperation.

"Do not assemble. Return to your tents or you will be shot!" We rushed back to our tent and waited anxiously for our commander to come back.

As mentioned in a previous episode, the authorities had ordered us, the Hawai'i internee group, to form a battalion. The battalion was made up of several companies with a commander for each. Every company held meetings. Our battalion was commanded by Mr. Takaichi Saiki of Hilo. With him was lieutenant commander Minoru Murakami. They negotiated various matters with the authorities. As the commander and his assistant, Mr. Saiki and Mr. Murakami acted on our behalf throughout our four-year internment. Two days after we settled at Fort Sill, our countrymen from Panama arrived. Then several days later, about 350 Mainland internees transferred from other camps, making our total number about 700. Around that time, the first group was sent to snowy Camp McCoy in Wisconsin. Everyone in our tent was quiet and in low spirits. At lunchtime, in the mess hall, a kind of emptiness pressed down on us.

Mr. Murakami stood up and informed us of Mr. Oshima's accident. "At about seven o'clock this morning, Mr. Oshima clambered up the barbed wire fence on the left side of the main entrance to the compound. Surprised fellow internees tried to pull him down, but he was too fast. He jumped down on the other side of the ten-foot high inner fence. A guard on duty standing nearby ordered him to stop, but he ran southward. The guard gave chase, pistol in hand. Seeing this, fellow internees ran along their side of the fence shouting, 'Please don't shoot! He's gone crazy!' The guard seemed to hesitate for a second, then fired two or three shots, none of which hit Mr. Oshima. Startled by the gunshots, Mr. Oshima, ran to the end of the fence, reaching the foot of a guard tower, where machine guns were positioned. He scaled one of the barbed wire posts at the bottom of the tower. When he reached the platform jutting out about three feet, he hesitated, and at that moment, a pursuing guard fired a shot. It pierced the back of Mr. Oshima's head and exited his forehead. He fell backward, having died instantly. I feel so sorry for him."

Mr. Murakami's voice broke, and a long, deep silence fell over us.

Who in his right mind would attempt an escape in the middle of the day? Why now, after enduring months of hardship and coming all the way to the Mainland? Where would he go and for what reason? It was Oklahoma's weather and the life here that seduced Mr. Kanesaburo Oshima into wanting to take his life.

Mr. Murakami went on. "Let us not forget Mr. Oshima's death. Regulations prohibit us from approaching the barbed wire fencing, but shooting a man just for climbing over the fence is not justified. What sane person would even attempt to escape through the main gate in broad daylight? We have every intention of having the Spanish consul, who represents the Japanese government, make restitution to Mr. Oshima's family. We are determined to pursue this course and will not be deterred by any splendid funeral arranged by the authorities."

A sense of moral indignation welled up in our hearts. Nothing is more transient than human life. Who can be sure he will be alive tomorrow? Mr. Oshima was fifty-eight years old when he died. He had lived in Kona for forty years. He owned and operated a barbershop, an ice shop, and a car dealership. The father of eleven children, he had been arrested as an agent of the Japanese Consulate. He had given us haircuts and was especially kind to me. Because both of our family names began with "O," we found ourselves in each other's company.

On the ship from Hilo, we shared a cabin together with the elderly Mr. Gentaro Ota of Kohala.* Again on the USS *Grant*, a ship that took us across the Pacific, we shared bunk beds in that

---

*Ota was a Japanese language teacher from Hālawa in the Kohala district of the Big Island. – Trans.

toilet hell of the ship's hold. I was seasick all the time, but he thoughtfully brought back food for me from the dining room. I still remember our serious discussions aboard the ship from Hilo on the evening of February 21, 1942.

I said to Mr. Oshima and Mr. Ota, "We have no way of knowing what lies ahead or how long we will be living like this. Let's all help each other and work in harmony, and take good care of ourselves. Since our last names begin with 'O,' we will probably continue to be together, so I will count on your help."

"You're right, you're right," elderly Mr. Ota agreed with a smile.

But now, Mr. Oshima is gone. Under crimson Kona skies, as the evening sun sinks into the ocean, his wife and eleven children will no doubt be shedding tears of grief and sorrow over the loss of their husband and father.

The following day, May 13, more than 700 internees from Hawai'i, Panama, and the U.S. Mainland lined up and paid their final respects to the late Mr. Oshima, as his coffin was carried away in a funeral coach. Another funeral was held at the same time and in the same place for Mr. Ochi from Panama, who had been ill when he died a week before Mr. Oshima.

Smoke from the burning incense stung our eyes. On behalf of all the internees, Mr. Yahei Taoka of Nihon Yūsen Co., Ltd. gave the memorial tribute. "I speak to the spirit of Mr. Kanesaburo Oshima. Seven hundred of your fellow countrymen have gathered here to pay our final respects to you. Our hearts are filled with sadness when we recall your friendly face. The grief and sorrow of your beloved wife, your eleven children and your friends must be beyond bounds. We are greatly impressed with your record of hard work and service to the Japanese community. Your death as a victim of the war between the United States and Japan will not be easily forgotten. We pray that your soul may rest in peace. May 13, 1942. Yahei Taoka, spokesman for the Japanese at Fort Sill Internment Camp." As the funeral coach approached the main gate, escorted by the members of the Hawai'i battalion, the iron gate opened and the coach passed through alone.

"Look, there's a machine gun," my friend said. I looked and saw soldiers making an obvious display of removing a number of these guns from the area inside the inner fence. "They brought them in case of a riot." An indescribable feeling of anger surged through my heart. A non-resisting civilian was killed simply because he had climbed over the barbed-wire fencing and had managed to get twenty or thirty feet beyond the first enclosure. It seems to me that there is no need for a guard to "shoot to kill" for a violation of this kind.

Let us commit to memory this incident: the pitiful death of

a fellow countryman whose life was shattered when his blood stained the distant desert sands of the Oklahoma plain as the glowing evening sun sank beyond the horizon.

* * *

Some aspects of life in the camps were unbearable, while others were inconveniences and annoyances. Take the censoring of letters, for example. In another radio script, Ozaki gives us a sense of the frustration that occurred when precious letters from outside the camp arrived, only to find that scissors had been taken to the stationery:

RADIO SCRIPT

Internees and the Japanese Language[9]

We were wondering about what had become of the first group of internees who had been sent to snowy Wisconsin a month before [we had been sent to Fort Sill]. On May 7 at noontime, Mr. Minoru Murakami, our battalion lieutenant commander, who now lives in Hilo as publisher of the popular magazine Hawai Engei,* shouted in a strident tone, "Gentlemen! Look at this letter written in Japanese. Mr. M,† a former resident of Honolulu, received this from Mr. S,‡ who is now in Wisconsin. Take special note of this (pointing)." Everyone looked.

"You will notice there are windows here and there. You may think that Mr. S, presuming that Fort Sill is in the desert and that we suffer from the heat, cut out these windows to give us more ventilation. But this is not the case. Actually, it was the President of the United States who personally examined this letter (which I doubt) and apparently cut out sections that he considered inappropriate. Since this refreshingly airy letter was sent to give us the latest news, let me read it to you." Mr. Murakami licked on a lemon [to clear his throat].

For the next four years, Mr. Murakami made live broadcasts like this, injecting humor and wit, and creating a source of encouragement and entertainment for us. As he read in a clear voice the letter written in Japanese, we listened intently with the feeling that it had been sent to each of us. Written six months after the start of the war, graphically describing the life of Honolulu internees at

---

Hawai'i Gardening

†In the original script, Ozaki has crossed out the name "Miyata" and replaced it with "Mr. M." – Trans.

‡Ozaki has crossed out the name "Shigenaga" and replaced it with "Mr. S." This is likely Kakuro Shigenaga, a bar owner from Honolulu. – Trans.

Camp McCoy in the wintry state of Wisconsin, Mr. S's letter was of historic significance to us. Mr. Murakami began reading the letter in his unique way.

By the way, I would like the listeners to know that the Xs that appear in the following sentences represent the letters and figures that were deleted by the authorities.

"Greetings and salutations. Since our tearful Shiobara Tasuke farewell at Sand Island,* we have been negligent in our correspondence, but all of us here are overjoyed to learn from your previous letter that everyone in Group XXX (Group 2)† crossed the ocean in good health and that you are doing well. We too are thinking of our wives and family members.

"There is no hierarchy here. Buddhist and Shinto priests live with farmers. To relieve our boredom, we play *hanafuda*‡ and poker, and we share small talk day and night. What I enjoy most is to listen to the nightly news reports broadcast by men standing on a platform, who act like radio announcers and shout in a strident tone. First, Mr. XXX *Nippu* broadcasts news about the war, then Dr. XXX gives us news about the situation in the South Pacific. This doctor has problems with his Japanese, and his direct translations from the editorials of XXX newspapers and magazines is something to hear. When Mr. XXX *Nippu* reads letters from Hawai'i and from men at your camp, he does it in an entertaining manner. We listened with great interest to the latest letter sent by one of you. I say 'broadcast,' but in reality no microphone is used. I understand the weather there is bad. Please tell us about it."

Mr. Murakami lowered his voice and said, "I should explain that Mr. XXX *Nippu* is Mr. Asami, who was the editor-in-chief of the *Nippu Jiji* newspaper. Dr. XXX is presumably Dr. Takahashi."§

At Fort Sill it was quite hot in the mess hall at noontime. I happened to glance outside and saw a guard with a bayonet on his shoulder standing about twenty feet away, staring at us with suspicion. In the distance I could hear the roar of guns being fired in the midst of war exercises. "Say," I whispered to my friend Mr.

---

*A reference to the popular Meiji-era comic tale *Shiobara Tasuke ichidaiki* (The Life of Shiobara Tasuke). Based on the real life rags-to-riches story of charcoal merchant Shiobaraya Tasuke (1743-1816), it tells the story of the heir to a samurai family, reduced to scratching out a living as a farmer, who resolves to leave his hometown to seek his fortune in Edo. Upon his departure he bids farewell to his faithful horse. Made famous through kabuki and *naniwa-bushi* (narrative ballad) performances, the story became a best-selling book. By the 1890s, moral education textbooks contained variations of the well-known tale. See J. Scott Miller, "Early Voice Recordings of Japanese Storytelling," *Oral Tradition*, 11/2 (1996): 301-19, http://journal.oraltradition.org/files/articles/11ii/10_miller.pdf. - Trans.

†Ozaki has inserted "(Group 2)" alongside the Xs, suggesting that this would have been what the original letter contained. – Trans.

‡Japanese playing cards

§Tokue Takahashi, a physician from Honolulu, was repatriated in 1943. – Trans.

K, "that opening greeting—what an excellent job."

Until next Sunday, good bye, everyone.

RADIO SCRIPT

Memories of the Internment Camp[10]

Aboard our ship sailing out of Hilo Harbor on February 21 were many Nikkei soldiers on their way to active duty. An acquaintance of mine was under guard as an enemy alien about to be sent to a place unknown. On the lower deck was his son, an American soldier, who must have known that his father would be on the same ship. They were not allowed to speak to each other. What an incongruous situation. All they could do was look at each other, perhaps for the last time.

I described the scene with a poem:

Together on a ship	兵となりて
The son off to war	下のデッキに
And the father,	子は乗れり
An enemy alien,	父なる人は
Off to prison.	囚われにして

Later, many Nikkei sons volunteered for military service and distinguished themselves in the war as members of the 100th Battalion and the 442nd Regiment. In one particular case, a father was living behind barbed wire when his son, who was fighting in New Guinea, was killed in action. The young man's memorial service took place in the internment camp with an American flag lowered to half-mast.

When I think about this past war and its incongruities, I cannot help but feel disheartened.

* * *

Rounding out the picture of Mainland camp life is a series of letters received by Ozaki from friends in other Mainland camps. In them, his friends write of everyday activities, of the rhythms of life in camp. Sometimes there was little news if any, but just the gesture of writing and keeping in touch was enough to brighten the day of the receiver. Ozaki's friends were scattered all over the Mainland camps. The following provides a glimpse through first-hand accounts.

Date: May 1, 1943[11]
From: David M. Marutani,* Lordsburg Internment Camp, New
Mexico
To: Otokichi Ozaki, Livingston Internment Camp, Louisiana

How are you doing, Mr. Ozaki? I am in good health, and every
day I do the same kind of work, which is to handle the mail service for Company Eight. I do it happily, along with an old friend
of mine from Kona.

When I am free, I practice calligraphy and the Kanze style of
Noh chanting. I am also a member of the Sakyū Poetry Society
and meet with other members once every two weeks.

Recently a gentleman from your camp came here to care for his
ailing brother. He brought us the latest news from your camp. We
all seem to be doing more or less the same things.

Date: June 24, 1943[12]
From: Shoichi Asami, Crystal City Internment Camp, Texas
To: Otokichi Ozaki, Santa Fe Internment Camp

On June 22, I received your letter of June 19. I learned through
a canteen bulletin that you have gone to Santa Fe and have
received hospitable treatment. I understand that the younger ones
are with you, too. I often think of you.

Since coming here, I have been in good health. Since a large
number of women also gather when we broadcast the latest news, I
try to do my best. However, because my wife also comes to listen,
I cannot say anything offensive, but I try to make everyone laugh.
Your letters have become material for my news.

My wife and children are in good health. My children are
studying very hard. From the time I lived on the outside, I have
had the habit of moving from place to place. Having found a cool
and comfortable house here, we moved in a few days ago and now
have a parlor, a kitchen and three rooms all to ourselves.

Unlike in the military camp,† we seven or eight families had
to move furniture and even iceboxes by ourselves. People in the
neighborhood helped us, but everything is still a mess.

I hope there will be a small family of about three next door. It
would be nice to have "Mr. *Omoshirokunai*" or "Mr. *Dodai*"‡ move

---

*David Matsuo Marutani, a mechanic from Hilo. – Trans.
†Crystal City was administered by the U.S. Department of Justice, while Livingston, where
Ozaki and Asami spent a year incarcerated together, came under the purview of the Army. For more
on the different types of camps and their administration, see Tetsuden Kashima, *Judgment without
Trial* (Seattle: University of Washington Press, 2003). – Trans.
‡These are nicknames of specific internees, who were no doubt well known to both Asami and

in there.

This place is very comfortable. We are enjoying the atmosphere of the outside world. Although we are mature, our conjugal love is substantial. Houses are being built one after the other. At any rate, you should come here.

I understand that the Oiwake school* has begun. Please give my best to my teachers and schoolmates. I've sung only once here at the variety show and have not yet had a chance to sing Oiwake. Looking up at the sky and shedding tears does not fit my present lifestyle. When you come here, I have to try again with your help.

Now I must work on my yard. I plan to plant lawn grass. I shall try to forget about repatriation and settle down here.[†]

Please give my best regards to the Old Man [Yasutaro Soga] and the other staff of the [*Nippu Jiji*] company.[‡]

Date: August 4, 1943[13]
From: Kametaro Maeda,[§] Fort Missoula Internment Camp, Montana
To: Otokichi Ozaki, Santa Fe Internment Camp, New Mexico

I deeply appreciate the kindness shown me during my stay at the previous camp. I understand that everyone there is in good health and that the scenery is the best, which makes me envious. This is not such a bad place either, and there is unanimous agreement among us that we made a good move by coming here. I guess you have the same impression.[¶]

"So many countries, so many customs," the saying goes. Let me tell you about a bizarre incident. Last Sunday, between midnight and dawn, I heard the quacking of migratory birds as they flew across the sky. Just before daybreak, there was a sudden gust of wind, and it was as though the birds had landed on the roof. As usual, I awoke at six o'clock, and when I stepped outside, I saw a

---

Ozaki. It is likely that the nicknames refer to the men's habit of using the conversational expressions "*omoshirokunai*" ("not very interesting") and "*dodai*" ("absolutely" or "from the beginning," as the case may be). – Trans.

*Also Oiwake-*bushi*, a style of folk song that originated in the melancholy songs of the packhorse drivers of the Shinano-Oiwake region, today Karuizawa, Nagano Prefecture. – Trans.

†Another sad and ironic note is struck in this letter from Asami to Ozaki. Asami did indeed repatriate and was en route to Japan on April 1, 1945 when his ship, the *Awa Maru*, was sunk by an American battleship. See Ozaki's Radio Script on pp. 23-24 – Ed.

‡Yasutaro Keiho Soga (1873-1957), owner and president of the *Nippu Jiji* newspaper, of which Asami was editor-in-chief. Soga's account of his internment experience, *Tessaku Seikatsu*, was published in 1948 and later translated into English. See Yasutaro Soga, *Life behind Barbed Wire: The World War II Internment Memoirs of a Hawai'i Issei*, translated by Kihei Hirai (Honolulu: University of Hawaii Press, 2008). – Trans.

§Kametaro Maeda, a Christian minister from Honolulu. – Trans.

¶This is a facetious reference to Ozaki's displeasure with the conditions at Santa Fe. – Trans.

dead wild duck on the ground. When I went for a walk, I found another, and then another, until I had collected four wild ducks. People came rushing to Barrack 27. Someone else had also found a dead duck, and the total number came to five. We eventually found five more. That night, our entire group of forty men from Hilo, Maui and Honolulu enjoyed, for the very first time in our lives, wild duck soup seasoned with shoyu and *Aji-no-moto*.*

We go fishing twice a week and catch a lot of fish.
3732 4649†

* * *

While few letters of Ozaki's remain for reproduction in this book, we are fortunate that he kept not only his radio scripts, but articles he wrote for the *Camp Santa Fe News* in 1943. In the following articles, all of which he wrote in July 1943, he reflects on people and activities in camp, and especially on the relationships between the internees and their loved ones at home. Especially poignant are the gifts sent from home to the internees and their significance, as seen by Ozaki.

What the FBI Checks Is Beyond Imagination[14]

The actions of the FBI are really reckless and often harebrained. The wife of Preacher I from Barrack 66 of the Jerome Camp related an incident in a letter to me.

A few days ago she was asked to report to the office. Thinking that she was finally going to be allowed to live with her dear husband, she went there in high spirits. To her dismay, she was greeted by an FBI agent, who began by asking her if she was related to Prince Chichibu.‡

She was too shocked to speak. What blasphemy, to invoke the name of the august royal family in an attempt to catch her off guard. It made her realize how appalling the methods used by the American intelligence network were.

Of course, Mrs. I was on edge throughout the investigation, but apparently decided that the FBI had mistaken her for royalty because she looked so refined. I cannot be certain, but I imagine that as soon as she returned to her barrack, she took out a mirror to look at her own noble face.

---

*The brand name for the flavor enhancer monosodium glutamate.
†These numbers, when read in Japanese, are homophonous with the expression, *Minna-san ni, yoroshiku*, "Best regards to you all." – Trans.
‡Chichibu no Miya Yasuhito Shinnō (1902-53), brother of then Emperor Hirohito. – Trans.

At any rate, she wrote a letter to her husband suggesting that under the circumstances, he would do well hereafter to respect his noble wife a little bit more.

Japanese American Combat Team Welcomes Nikkei USO Group[15]

Miss Etsuko Hirama, daughter of Mr. Teruzo Hirama,* a barber at Barrack 56 in the Jerome Camp, sent the following news dispatch: A Japanese American regimental combat team organized mainly of Nikkei from Hawai'i lives in Camp Shelby in Mississippi. A group of eighty-three young and pretty Nikkei girls from Jerome traveled nine hours by bus to socialize with them and cheer them up. They were warmly welcomed.

In her letter, Etsuko mentions how deeply moved she was to see the joy on the soldiers' faces, to see the boys she knew from back home and to meet the sons of other internees. Sometime later, last Saturday to be exact, a baseball team of Nikkei soldiers visited Jerome to play against the camp team. Admission was fifty cents for the two games. There was a huge crowd in attendance. All the girls were there to give them a big welcome.

Sincerity Can Get You Somewhere—A Man Is Paroled[16]

Many children wait for the return of their fathers, all the while being discriminated against as children of internees. However, recently an increasing number of fathers are being reunited with their families.

One of them is Mr. Eizo Miyahara of Barrack 60, whose family lives at the Rohwer Center [in Arkansas]. Knowing that their father had spent thirty years as a law-abiding resident of the United States, his children were confident that he would rejoin them, and they prayed morning and night for his return. One day Mr. Miyahara sent his children flower and cucumber seeds, telling them that he would be with them by the time the cucumber plant bore fruit. Later he received the following sweet letter from his thoughtful daughter Sachiko:

Dear Father,
Thank you very much for your loving letter and beautiful postcard dated June 26. I am glad that you are fine. We are too, so you need not worry. Father, you said that when the seeds you sent grow and the

---

*Teruzo Hirama of Honolulu, proprietor of Island Barber Supply, was later repatriated along with his family. – Trans.

plant bears fruit, you might be able to join us. Well, the seeds sprouted, buds appeared and bloomed, and the cucumbers are getting larger everyday. As we watch them grow, we have prayed and prayed for your return, but we have received no news.

Today I am sending you some [pickled] cucumbers. I packed them, feeling quite sure that you will be pleased. Mother said that I could pick the first cucumber, and as I picked it off the dew-covered vine, I said to her, "Father should be coming home by now." She began to cry silently, although up to now she has never shown a sad face to us. I guess she has been trying to be strong for our sake.

Father, please keep well. God will surely protect you. I will graduate from school on July 30. I shall pray to God that you will be at the graduation ceremony. Please take care of yourself!

Touched by his daughter's letter, he cried several times as he read it, and then read it again. By a strange coincidence, on the day that the fruit of his daughter's tender loving care arrived, he received a notice of parole from the office. He dispatched a cable saying that he had received a parole notice on July 5 and that he would be joining them soon. Although it is not clear when he will be able to leave, how happy Sachiko must be.

On Father's Day, Cake and Beautiful Flowers
Arrive from Children in Hawai'i[17]

Upon returning to my barrack after breakfast, I found three beautiful, bright red, fresh gladioli on the news desk. Taken aback, I blinked a few times. They were real, so I presumed there had been a mistake, until a barrack friend said the flowers were from Postmaster Matsuo Marutani in Barrack 57.* I began to wonder if Mr. Marutani had forgotten who he was – one of us one hundred million loyal subjects of the Emperor – and had left [camp] for [the city of] Santa Fe last night after climbing over the barbed wire fence. I must have Dr. Mori† examine the postmaster, I thought, and hurried to Barrack 57. The postmaster was out, but on his table was a note bearing the letterhead of the [American] Red Cross. After some detective work, I learned the source of the flowers. The letter reads:

---

*See his letter signed David M. Marutani, Ch. 3, p. 74 - Trans.
†Motokazu Mori, a surgeon from Honolulu. – Trans.

*To: Mr. Matsuo Marutani, American Red Cross, Santa Fe Chapter**
Through the American Red Cross in Hawai'i, I received a request
from your daughter, Alice, to send you a Father's Day cake with the
enclosed card, "From your children." To my regret, I could not send
it in time for Father's Day, because I received this request on July 10.
However, I am sure you will be pleased when you receive it.

Beatrice Chauvenet, Executive Secretary

Last night Mr. Marutani was apparently called to the administration office, where the cake and the flowers were handed to him. Thanks to Mr. Marutani, the spot of red added a brightness to the otherwise dull newsroom, which was staffed only by men. My heart also is warmed by the thoughtfulness of children who care about their father and try to comfort him from faraway Hawai'i.

An internee poet composed the following poem:

Even in far away Hawai'i	この空は
My dear wife and children	遠くハワイに
Are looking at the same	続く空
Sky I see.	いとし妻子の
	仰ぎ見る空

I am reminded of the families who performed *kagezen*, setting a meal for an absent father and praying for his well being and safe return. With his children's photo before him, Mr. Marutani became thoroughly absorbed in nostalgia and was overcome by his children's loving Father's Day gift . . . .

Barbers Defy the No-Striking Law[18]

The most troublesome thing for an internee is the hair on his head. It is rumored that nine barbers went on strike this morning against the orders of Mr. Lewis, and this will likely become a hot topic of discussion in Congress, given that the law banning strikes has passed.

However, according to a barber, it is not the barbers, but the hair cutting implements—the hair clippers themselves—that have gone on strike. Currently, five barbers in the morning and four barbers in the afternoon service customers. In the morning hours alone, barbers cut the hair of about 150 people a day. There are four working clippers, but only one belongs to the shop, and it was donated by the group on the second ship from Hawai'i. The

---

*This English translation is based on Ozaki's Japanese translation of the original letter, which was written in English. – Trans.

others are the barbers' personal clippers. Besides these, there are
two additional clippers, which were sent for repair and have been
out for a long time.

There should be two or three hair clippers for general use somewhere in the camp, and if they were made available, the barbers
would be back in business tomorrow. It is said that this subject has
been brought up at the barrack managers' meeting as a matter af-
fecting the welfare of the internees. Sooner or later, it is hoped that
a good solution will be found.

Money Circulates, Boosts Hawai'i Lifestyle[19]

We received a report on daily life in Hawai'i from Mrs. "Santa
Claus" Takata, wife of Mr. Takata, owner of Takata Store in Kohala, now of Barrack 56.*

*Presently there is an abundance of food supplies – clothing too. But
prices have really gone up. Cotton is becoming scarce; now most of the
fabric is rayon. It is a problem for working people, who have no choice
but to wear rayon.*

*Recently life here has become very urbane. Geta[†] and zōri are
things of the past, and even I wear shoes every day. Because soldiers
come to our shop, we cannot be flip-flopping around any more. These
days the elderly wear Western-style shoes, too. Even if we want to, we
do not see [any] people in kimono. Yesterday I attended the funeral
of Fukuda-san and noticed that all the women were wearing black
dresses. Mrs. Enjo Kobayashi[‡] served as the officiating priest.*

*These days everyone alters their kimono into dresses, and all the
dressmakers are quite busy. The sewing fee is about $7 or $8 in Honolulu and $3.50 for cotton fabric. Some charge at least $10, but people
are becoming so well off, that they don't seem to care about prices.
Shops are open until eight o'clock at night.*

This is the time of military rule in Hawai'i, and everything
Japanese, including geta and zōri, must disappear. How the world
is changing.

---

*Keizo Takata from the town of Hāwī in the Kohala district on the northwest coast of the Big
Island. Mrs. "Santa Claus" Takata is a humorous reference to Mrs. Takata's generosity and the likelihood that she sent goods from the store to camp, which Mr. Takata then shared with the other
internees. – Trans.

†Japanese wooden clogs

‡Enjo Kobayashi, a Buddhist priest from Hāwī on the Big Island, was confined in the Fort Missoula Internment Camp. – Trans.

Second Exchange Ship Likely[20]

Since the departure of the first exchange ship for Japan, the possibility of a second exchange ship had been mentioned from time to time, but it has now become a reality.* A few days ago, the Spanish consul reportedly visited the camp and provided the authorities with a [repatriation] list of sixty-five people, half of whom are from Hawai'i. This afternoon, the list was forwarded from the camp authorities (an adobe house) to Mr. Kondo of the [Japanese] office. The news sparked excitement among the internees, as they gathered in a huge crowd around the list and searched for their names. Those who found themselves listed were pleased. Those who were not listed were disappointed.

The list was compiled by the U.S. State Department after checking with those individuals who expressed their desire to return to Japan. It has yet to be approved by the Japanese government, but approval is likely.

The list is comprised of sixty-five names, with fourteen people from Barrack 56 alone. They are:†

Fujishiro Utanosuke
Suzuki Katsu
Hamamura Kyoichi
Akegarasu Takeo
Toyama Takinosuke
Suetomi Koten
Tofukuji Koshiro
Matsuda Ishichi
Tanaka Yaroku
Asaeda Horyu

---

*The Swedish ocean liner the MS *Gripsholm* served as an International Red Cross exchange ship, departing New York harbor on June 18, 1942 with 1,065 passengers. It stopped in Rio de Janiero and picked up an additional 417 passengers from various Latin American countries, before meeting up with the *Asama Maru* along the African east coast. There the exchange of passengers occurred – Japanese nationals and family members, many of whom were U.S. citizens or citizens of Latin American countries, in exchange for Americans who had been in Japan. The *Gripsholm* made a second trip, sailing out of New York on September 2, 1943, this time with 1,340 exchange passengers. See Tetsuden Kashima, *Judgement Without Trial: Japanese American Imprisonment during World War II* (Seattle: University of Washington Press, 2003), p. 280fn75. – Trans.

†Internee biographical information is from the JCCH Internee Database. Fujishiro Utanosuke, a Christian minister from Lahaina, Maui; Suzuki Katsu and Hamamura Kyoichi, storekeepers from Honolulu; Akegarasu Takeo, a Buddhist priest from Hilo, who repatriated with family members Sumie, Wake and Tomei; Toyama Takinosuke, a sake brewer from Honolulu; Suetomi Koten, Buddhist priest from Honolulu, repatriated with family members Kinuyo and June; Tofukuji Koshiro, a physician from Wailuku, Maui; Matsuda Ishichi, a businessman from Honolulu; Tanaka Yaroku, general manager of the *Volcano Times* in Hilo; Asaeda Horyu, a Buddhist priest from Honolulu, who repatriated with family member Chisato; Hirama Teruzo, manager of Island Barber Supply in Honolulu, who repatriated with family members Mine, Evelyn Etsuko and Harry; Hori Minetaro, a Shinto priest from Honolulu; Yamane Goichi, a gas station owner from Honolulu, whose brother Mitsuo was also interned and later repatriated; and Tominaga Asahei, of Honolulu. – Trans.

Hirama Teruzo

Hori Minetaro

Yamane Goichi

Tominaga Asahei

Three men from Barrack 58 also are on the list:*

Kudo Isamu

Isobe Misao

Wada Takashi

At this point, I am sure they will be able to repatriate. Their dreams are coming true. I wish to congratulate these people with a round of applause.

Segregation of Loyal and Non-loyal Internees at Issue in the Centers[21]

At this time the segregation of loyal and disloyal internees† seems to be a hot topic at the various centers. Like the saying, "One barking dog sets all the street a-barking," rumors beget more rumors. The power of the spreading rumor is amazing, but something that can be dismissed simply.

Mr. X in Barrack 56 received an airmail letter from his family at the Gila River Center [in Arizona]. Since this letter was said to refer to the segregation issue, I visited him to learn the details of the letter. I would like to describe the atmosphere that surrounds this particular center.

This internee's family, at Gila River Center, consists of his wife and two sons. A son, who has reached the age of conscription, has rejected military service, so he is considered disloyal.

In a letter sent recently to Mr. X, his son said there was a rumor at the Gila River Camp that individuals identified as disloyal were to be segregated, keeping families from being able to live together. Thus the son asked Mr. X if he was going to repatriate, because

---

*Kudo Isamu, a carpenter from Hilo, who repatriated with family members Sumie and Takekazu. Isobe Misao, a Shinto priest from Honolulu, who was repatriated and returned to Japan aboard the second exchange ship. Misao's brother Isobe Shigemi also was a Shinto priest in Honolulu who repatriated aboard the second exchange ship. Wada Takashi, an insurance agent from Honolulu. – Trans.

†During World War II, the "loyalty" of all people of Japanese ancestry, incarcerated in internment camps, who were over the age of seventeen, was tested using the "loyalty questionnaire." Two of the questions formed the core of the loyalty test: #27 – Are you willing to serve in the armed forces of the United States on combat duty, wherever ordered?; and #28 – Will you swear unqualified allegiance to the United States of America and faithfully defend the United States from any and all attack by foreign or domestic forces, and forswear any form of allegiance to the Japanese Emperor or any other foreign government, power, or organization? It was widely believed among internees that a "no-no" response to the two questions would indicate disloyalty and that those who did so would be sent to a separate camp from those who responded "yes-yes." Indeed, many who answered "no-no" were moved to Tule Lake in California, designated a segregation center, which would separate "loyal" from "disloyal" internees. – Ed.

the family would then be able to live together, if all were identified as disloyal. The son also said that he would be separated from the rest of the family, if the father were not to repatriate. He requested a prompt reply, and Mr. X obliged, saying the decision to repatriate had already been made even before the letter had arrived.

Other stories have come out of the Gila River Camp. One tells of some *kibei* with backbone who, on the anniversary of the attack on Pearl Harbor, hoisted the flag of the Rising Sun on the mountain behind the camp. It seems that a rift exists in the relationship between the administration and the internees at this camp that is greater than that at any of the other nine relocation centers.

[In another story,] Mr. Y, an internee, wanted his son, who was confined at Gila River Camp, to come and visit him. He sent the young man a visitation permit approved by Mr. Johnson, the [camp] director. Confident that there would be no problems, the young man applied for a leave permit, but his request was rejected outright. No reason was given, but it was probably because he was in the disloyal group. He had been allowed to leave when he was at Livingston Internment Camp, but not while held at Gila River. I bear some ill feelings over the attitude of the authorities there because of this incident.

Reportedly No Announcement about Exchange Ship List at Kenedy Camp[22]

Japanese internees from Panama who had been with us at the Livingston Internment Camp moved to Kenedy Internment Camp in Texas.* This morning I received a letter from Mr. Hiroshi Kawahara, who had served for a year as their secretary while at Livingston. Apparently the [exchange ship] list has yet to be announced, and he says, everyone is impatiently waiting to see it. His letter is as follows:

Mr. Ozaki:

Please forgive me for the long silence. I presume that you are well and are again serving the Hawai'i group. What is your impression of the new camp? Since the management of the camp was transferred from the military to the Department of Justice, life here seems to have become more like that of the outside world. Still, those days when we suffered and laughed together at Fort Sill and Camp Livingston remain the most memorable for me. Even after the war ends, they will remain so.

---

*A Department of Justice internment camp located near San Antonio, Kenedy held internees from the United States and Latin America, as well as Japanese and German POWs. – Trans.

Construction of additional housing for cohabitation camps progresses quickly, and the day when you will be able to move in seems not too far away. Now, if there was no barbed wire, I think life here would return to normal, like shaba.

News about the exchange ship seems to be on everyone's lips. Do you have any good news? It is rumored that the repatriation list has already been announced at your camp. According to the news here, the M.S. Gripsholm *is expected to sail by August at the latest, and everyone is eagerly looking forward to seeing the list of names.*

Life at this camp is essentially the same as it was at the previous camp. Baseball, soccer, and tennis are very popular here. There are baseball games nearly every day, keeping both players and spectators busy. I go to the office every day, but there is not much to do. Since I have the time, I am studying English. There is a good teacher here, and we are now reading Gone with the Wind.

Outside the barbed wire, beautiful flowers are in bloom and the days of beguiling sights continue. I look forward to seeing you on the exchange ship. Many apologies for my bad handwriting. Please extend my best regards to the others.
July 20

The "beautiful flowers in bloom" and "days of beguiling sights" are probably references to the women who can be seen outside the barbed wire enclosure. The fact that the list for the exchange ship has not been announced at Kenedy seems to be frustrating the internees, for it could mean that those from Latin America have higher priority or that a similar thing could happen as in the case of the *Gripsholm*, the first exchange ship, in which some women and children were sent back to Japan, while their patriarch was left behind.

FAMILY TIES IN HAWAI'I, 1942 – 1944

There is no greater happiness for a family than to be together, regardless of the difficulties we may face. It would be a tragedy for us to live apart. I feel sorry for the children.

—Hideko Ozaki, in a letter to her husband

ONE OF THE richest contributions of the Ozaki Collection to the literature on World War II internment is the letters from friends and family back in Hawai'i written to Ozaki while he was in camp. They provide a fascinating glimpse into what life was like in Hawai'i during wartime. The letters are filled with vivid details of the day-to-day concerns of those left behind, including making a living, surviving illness, selling property, and sending gifts and money to the internees. They contain snippets of announcements of births, marriages, and deaths of people in Ozaki's community. Equally important, letters from Ozaki's wife and father reveal the effect of internment on the lives of the families left behind.

Most remarkable about life in wartime Hawai'i revealed through these letters is the strong network of help and support offered one another among Ozaki's family and his community back in 'Amauulu. Through the letters we witness the lives of five families intertwined through their generous gifts to each other of in-kind, financial, and emotional support. These five families are:

1. Ozaki's immediate family, his wife Hideko and four children, Earl Tomoyuki, Carl Yukio, Alice Sachi, and Lily Yuri;
2. Ozaki's parents, his father Tomoya and his mother Shobu;
3. The Kosaki family of Ozaki's older sister, Kayo: husband Kazuki, wife Kayo, and six children, Nobuko, Frank Mineyuki, Richard Hiromichi, Kazuo, Mabel Yoshiko, and Albert Hidemichi;
4. The Uejio family of Ozaki's younger sister, Haruko: husband Fumiwo, wife Haruko, and five children, Grace, Roy, Katherine, Hope, Clifford;
5. The Kobara family of Ozaki's wife, Hideko: husband Takeji, wife

Haru, and Haru's son George Terada, and Hideko's half-brother Thomas Yoji.

Ozaki's father writes to him often while he is in camp; he updates Ozaki regularly on the lives of the other three families. In fact, when Hideko Ozaki and her four children leave 'Amauulu for a Mainland camp, Ozaki's parents move to Honolulu, and live with the Kosaki family in Honolulu. The Kosaki family is the most active of letter writers to Ozaki while Ozaki is in camp. Kazuki Kosaki works at a hotel where most of the guests are soldiers, while his wife, Kayo, runs a laundry business. Their daughter, Nobuko, at this time is in college to become a teacher. Upon graduation, she takes a position on the island of Moloka'i, and later marries Robert Fukuda from Hilo. Richard Hiromichi is in college, after graduating from McKinley High School, where he was student body president.* He later volunteers for the U.S. Army and leaves for Camp Savage, Minnesota.†

The Uejio family is wealthy; husband Fumiwo Uejio is "quite a businessman," having started the Royal Trading Co. that carried the well-known Peace brand of packaged food products. He also had the Aji-no-moto franchise for a while.[1] The Kobara family, Mrs. Ozaki's family, is also very wealthy. They own a successful restaurant called the Blue Ocean Inn that Takeji Kobara started right before the war. During the war the restaurant teems with workers at breakfast, lunch and dinner.

The Kobara family hires Ozaki's father when he moves to Honolulu. He writes to Ozaki often about how well the restaurant is doing and how he works hard many straight days without a break. He mentions that the restaurant serves 1,700 to 1,800 customers on Sundays and that Mr. Kobara has purchased three fee simple houses to the right of his present house

---

*Richard Hiromichi Kosaki, son of Ozaki's older sister Kayo, served in the Military Intelligence Service during World War II and as an interpreter during the American occupation of Japan. He would go on to hold a number of university chancellorships in his home state and found the University of Hawai'i's community college system. McKinley, the first public high school established on the island of O'ahu, developed a reputation for providing a progressive education and employing democratic ideals in the mentoring of students whose parents had been immigrants. It was nicknamed "Tokyo High," and many prominent Nisei graduated from McKinley, including U.S. Sen. Daniel Inouye and Hawai'i Gov. George Ariyoshi. See, Dorothy Ochiai Hazama and Jane Okamoto Komeiji, *Okagesama de: The Japanese in Hawaii, 1885-1985* (Honolulu: The Bess Press, Inc., 1986), 104-08. – Trans.

†Site of the Military Intelligence Service Language School (MISLS) outside of Minneapolis, it was established to train Nisei and *kibei* soldiers in the Japanese language and in military intelligence. The school opened in June 1942 with 200 students and graduated some 1,600 Nisei linguists by August 1944, when it was moved to nearby Fort Snelling. Graduates were sent to the Pacific theater, where they interrogated Japanese POWs, translated captured documents, and monitored Japanese radio broadcasts. See *The Pacific War and Peace: Americans of Japanese Ancestry in Military Intelligence Service 1941 to 1952* (San Francisco: Military Intelligence Service Association of Northern California, 1991). – Trans.

for $14,000, a tremendous sum of money at the time. Because Ozaki's father lives with the Kosakis and is employed by the Kobaras, he often expresses his troubled feelings about having to depend so heavily on these families.

In the letters we read that the Kosaki family and Ozaki elders send many goods to Ozaki's family while they are in camp. They send Japanese canned goods to ease their lives with a taste of home, as well as bolts of fabric. Because only American citizens are allowed to remit money during the war, funds are sent to Ozaki and his wife and family through Mr. Kazuma Kataoka in Hakalau. Ozaki's father often frets having to trouble "Kazuma-sama" all the time. He clearly is not comfortable feeling indebted to others through their kindnesses.

The letters, in their everyday detail, are richly textured and are an enormous contribution to the literature on internment and wartime in Hawai'i.

English original
Date: February 25, 1942[2]
From: Richard Hiromichi for Kayo Kosaki, Honolulu, Hawai'i
To: Otokichi Ozaki, c/o Immigration Station, Honolulu

Dear Uncle,
    We hope that you are well.
    We have received your letter and [are] sending you the suitcase.
In the suitcase are:

1 leather jacket
1 woolen bathrobe
1 knitted sweater (mama knitted it)
1 pr. of slippers
8 prs. of socks
1 pr. of long underwear
4 handkerchiefs
Some letter writing paper and envelopes
1 pr. of pajamas

    We hope that you will find the above things useful. If there are any other things you want, please write to us.
    We are sending a letter to Mrs. Ozaki.
    In closing, we sincerely wish that you will take good care of yourself, and may you always have pleasant thoughts and always be in the best of health.

Very sympathetically yours,
Kayo Kosaki
(Hiromichi Kosaki)

P.S. Grandfather is now safely back in Amauulu so please do not
worry. If you need more money, please do not hesitate to ask for it.

Translated into English for Hideko Ozaki
by Shiho Shinoda Nunes[*]
Date: May 6, 1942[3]
From: Hideko Ozaki, Hilo Hawai'i
To: Otokichi Ozaki, Fort Sill Internment Camp, Oklahoma

Dear Husband,

Your two letters, one written March 30th, the other April 16th,
reached me at long last. The letter arrived yesterday. I was glad to
hear that you had reached your destination safely. I worried thinking of the long journey across the sea, the change again in food
and climate and living conditions. I hope and pray that this letter
finds you well and in good spirits.

Do not worry about us for we are all fine. The children have
been surprisingly well. Yuri, especially, you will hardly recognize.
Since you left, we have not had to have a doctor called, not even
once! Grandfather and Grandmother, too, are well, working harder
than ever now that you are away. Grandfather goes up to his
garden to work everyday, while Grandmother looks after the house
and children. You would be pleased and happy if you could see
them. I know, for they are all so healthy.

I am well, too, so you must not worry about me. Recently I
have started working at the Kobai Kaisha at the Amauulu Camp.
Our friends have been exceedingly kind to our family. They got
me this job, not to mention the financial help they have been
giving us monthly since you went. They really have been kind and
generous.

The work is easy, the hours short, from 4:00 to 6:30 p.m.
Grandmother looks after the children while I am gone. I come
home to a late supper by myself.

Recently I heard from Mrs. Koide that she had been told to be
ready to leave. She was also told to consult me. Apparently Mr.
Koide[†] thinks I, too, would like to accompany you to Japan, since

---

[*]Hideko Ozaki had to have her letter translated because correspondence to and from internees
had to be in English early in the war. Shiho Shinoda Nunes is the daughter of Yoshio Shinoda, principal of Dokuritsu Gakkō. – Ed.

[†]Shoichi Koide, a staff member of the *Volcano Times* in Hilo. – Trans.

we are being given a chance to express our wishes in this matter. I shall make very clear my stand.

Grandfather and Grandmother wish to remain here. Nothing will persuade them to go. I have only one feeling on the matter—I want to do what you wish me to do. If you want to go to Japan and have me join you, I will. If you wish to remain and have us wait for you, that will be my wish. Your wish will be my wish. Please let me know soon.

The school has been taken over by the Army. Sensei and his family were moved out, too, in March. They went to Piopio where Dr. Sugamura used to live. Sensei has been detained. It is now over a month since he was taken. Ryo-chan is in the Army, Minoru is working as an interpreter at the Honolulu Police Station, Shi-chan is married. Yes, many changes have taken place.*

I am sending for you to sign an application blank for withdrawal of funds from the American Savings and Loan Association. Mrs. Yamakawa and Mrs. Saito have been insisting that their share be returned. The withdrawal cannot be made without your signature. The lines on which you are to sign have been indicated with an x. When the check is issued later, it will have to be sent to you again for signature. I would prefer to wait, but they are insistent, so I am attending to it now. Please attend to this and mail back the blanks by clipper. (Fill in the other necessary blanks of information on these cards.)

Please write as often as you can. We are anxious to hear from you.

Take good care of yourself. We think of you and pray for your quick return everyday and every night.

---

*This paragraph refers to the Shinoda family of Hilo Dokuritsu Gakkō, where Ozaki taught before the war. All Japanese language schools were shut down following the attack on Pearl Harbor; at Dokuritsu, the Army occupied the school, turning the campus into the headquarters for the Hilo military police, the kindergarten building into a jail, and the Shinoda family's residence into a temporary detention facility for enemy aliens. The Shinodas were forced to move into a unit of a private hospital on Pi'opi'o Street. Principal Yoshio Shinoda was arrested in April 1942 and incarcerated for a time in his former home at Dokuritsu, before being transferred to Kīlauea Military Camp and then Sand Island, from where he was later released. Ryo-chan is the endearment for second son, Ryo Shinoda, who served in the 442nd; Minoru is elder brother Minoru Shinoda, a member of the MIS during the war, and later a renown scholar of Japanese history; Shi-chan is Shiho, who has translated this letter for Hideko. See Shiho S. Nunes and Sara Nunes-Atabaki, *The Shishu Ladies of Hilo: Japanese Embroidery in Hawai'i* (Honolulu: University of Hawai'i Press, 1999), 41. – Trans.

English original, translator unknown
Date: May 20, 1942[4]
From: Hideko Ozaki, Hilo, Hawai'i
To: Otokichi Ozaki, Fort Sill Internment Camp, Oklahoma

Dear Mr. Ozaki,

How are you getting along? We are getting along fine.

Earl and Carl are going to school everyday. Alice and Lily are very strong but she (Lily) drinks milk from me. Sometimes the girls go to somebody's house and forget to eat and I have to call them.

Grandfather came home from Honolulu and everyday he goes to Pali. Grandmother is very well. She said till you come home you cannot be sick.

We worried because you did not send any letter to us. May 8th we got a letter that you reached safely so we are very glad.

Miss Shiho was married to Mr. Nunes, so Mrs. Shinoda and Takashi* are very lonely.

Please do not worry about us. The camp people treat us very good.

Will you send letter with airmail always?

Translated for Hideko Ozaki by Shiho Shinoda Nunes
Date: June 3, 1942[5]
From: Hideko Ozaki, Hilo, Hawai'i
To: Otokichi Ozaki, Livingston Internment Camp, Louisiana

Dear Husband,

I received on Monday your letter of May 5th asking us to be ready to leave. I wrote you not long ago on the matter. You must have received that letter by this time.

I am still of the same mind. I would like to go where you go, and I would like the children to come with me, for I believe that a family belongs together. Grandfather and Grandmother say they will remain in Hawaii; they have no desire to go back to Japan.

It is true that I prefer to live here and have the children grow up here where they were born. If there is any possibility that you will be allowed to return, I would wait for you here. However, from what has been told me, there is slim chance of that, so I have quite decided to go with you.

Our friends, when I discussed the matter with them, strongly urged me to remain. They feel the best thing for the children and us is to wait until this awful war ends. I have been thinking of

*Takashi is the youngest of the four Shinoda children. – Trans.

their many arguments and I am unhappy about it. However, I am still of this mind: I shall do whatever you wish me to do.

The family is well and happy. Life goes on as usual, with Grandfather going out to work. Grandmother [is] taking care of the children, and the children [are] quarreling happily among themselves as ever. Sachi has learned to sleep alone without her father, and Yuri-chan has not once been ill these many months. I am working now, as I told you.

Please write as often as you can. There is so little news of the kind we want to hear.

Your friends send their good wishes, and we all send you our love and prayers.

Date: July 6 [1942][6]
From: Hideko Ozaki, Hilo, Hawai'i
To: Otokichi Ozaki, Livingston Internment Camp, Louisiana

I was worried when I did not hear from you for a spell, but three letters suddenly arrived on one day. It made me so happy to see that they were written in Japanese. I immediately wrote back in Japanese, too.

There has been no change among the people in this ['Amauulu] camp. They are worried about you.

The children have been fine, but they have caught a cold that is making the rounds now. It is not serious; they are running around during the day, but cough at night. It is nothing to worry about. Grandfather is fine, too. He works everyday in the cane field and is always boasting about how nice his section is. Grandmother is also well; she has not caught a cold at all. The camp people are really surprised at how well we are doing. We owe it all to the gods.

You mentioned an exchange program for those who wish to return to Japan. I discussed the matter with Father and Mother,* but they do not wish to return to Japan. I suppose they have become accustomed to the life here and prefer to remain in Hawai'i. We purchased land here with the intention of staying forever, so I have regrets about leaving it behind. After all these years, I too would like to stay here, but it is only proper that I go with you, if you are returning to Japan. No matter how poor we may be or how difficult things may be, there is no greater happiness for a family than to be together. It would be a tragedy to be separated and to live apart. I feel sorry for the children. We will do whatever you say. What worries me is leaving behind the seventy-plus-year-old

---

*Otokichi's father and mother, i.e. Tomoya and Shobu, whom Hideko also refers to as "Grandfather" and "Grandmother." - Trans.

elders.

I understand the exchange ship route will take us through the Indian Ocean, skirting the eastern coast of Africa, but it is such a long trip. Just thinking about it makes this seasick-prone woman shudder. I am worried about the four children, who will be with us. If they become ill, it may be difficult for me to care for them. Mrs. Koide often comes to visit us. She and her husband plan to return [to Japan], but they have just one child, so it will be easier for them. Would it not be better for us to return after the war is over? If it can be easily arranged, I will go back. What about travel expenses? The tickets alone will be costly.

The teachers would like to withdraw their collective savings, so I sent you the [request] form and the [savings] book. I received the form back with your signature, but not the book. Did you receive it? Your signature is also needed for the book. I, too, withdrew my savings and have already used up the money, so I will need to rely on government aid and have turned in my request.

There is still more to say, but I shall save it for the next time. We are all fine, so you must not worry. Be in good health. We eagerly look forward to the day when we can see you again.

English original
Date: July 7, 1942[7]
From: Shiho Shinoda Nunes, Hilo, Hawai'i
To: Otokichi Ozaki, Livingston Internment Camp, Louisiana

Dear Mr. Ozaki,

I hope that this letter finds you in good health and cheerful spirits, and hopeful that some good and happiness may come out of this terrible conflict. Mrs. Ozaki, in her loneliness, is a frequent visitor at our house, and on her last visit asked me to write to you. She has written one letter in the past week in Japanese, but is afraid that censorship may delay it, so she has asked me to write you.

Your letters sent from Louisiana, one in English, one in Japanese, reached her a few days ago. She was overjoyed to get them, for she had almost given up hope, and had almost concluded that you had been among the nationals recently sent away. She brought them to our present place at Piopio for me to translate, but I was out then, just two days ago. I met her in town. We had a dish of ice cream at Machida, while I translated the letter for her.

The first thing she would like me to tell you is that the family is well. Grandfather works without rest in his field. Even Sundays [we] see him going off to work. Grandmother looks after the children uncomplainingly. Lily is well, just now getting over a slight cold. Sa-chan* is as fat as usual. This being summer, the children are at home, and Earl and Yuki-chan† play all day long.

Yuki-chan was with his mother the other day when she came to Piopio. While she and my mother talked, Yuki and I went downstairs to fish for shrimps and mosquito fish. He was quite excited and kept chatting away in English, something which is rare to me because he has always been so shy with me. He is as dark as ever. One big front tooth is coming out a bit crookedly for he still has his front baby teeth. I think he should have the baby ones pulled. When he opens his little mouth to talk, there is the one big tooth shining white, eclipsing all the other small ones. He took home that day a jar full of shrimps and one mosquito fish to show the family.

Mrs. Ozaki says that she and the children will join you if you wish them to, but that it would be better to wait until the war is over. Nothing further has been said about families being allowed to join detainees, and she is not sure whether it would be possible at all. Besides, the dangers involved in a long sea voyage at such times are too great. For herself she does not mind, but there are the children to think about. Even if it were possible for families to join the fathers, she feels perhaps it is better to wait until peace time.

Your letters are a bit confusing about the request for money. The Japanese letter, which was written earlier, asks for some money. The other, written later, says that it isn't necessary. She takes the word of the second letter and will not send any until such a time when you should ask for it. Don't hesitate to ask, she says, and she will wire you whatever you need. If possible and if necessary, she suggests that you wire collect (she pays for the wire here) and she will immediately wire the sum.

Right now she is not particularly hard up for money. The Amauulu people have been more than kind, helping out financially. She has the job at the store that helps out a little. In August she may go on relief, since the Public Welfare people have O.K.'d her application. Many other families of detainees are being helped by the agency. You are not to feel sorry about the family finances. They will manage somehow.

Yes, many changes have taken place. Hilo will never again be the Hilo you knew, and many old faces will be gone, many new faces will be here. My father has been away 80 days, but we are hoping he will be returned to us. Mother is well. She sends you

---

*Alice Sachi
†Carl Yukio

best wishes.

Mrs. Ozaki asks that you write oftener, since the gaps between letters are so long, and she worries so much. Please write her more often. She sent with her other letter in Japanese, some 20¢ air mail stamps. Did you get them?

Take good care of your health. May a kind and loving God protect you from harm.

English original
Date: July 16, 1942[8]
From: Earl Tomoyuki Ozaki [eldest son], Hilo, Hawai'i
To: Otokichi Ozaki, Livingston Internment Camp, Louisiana

Dear Father,

Thank you for the letter. I am glad to know that you are very well. We are very well in our health. Now it's summer vacation so we can play as we want. We also read book from the public library. Some times we help Grandmother and, mother and others. Lily very big now so when you see her you will be surprised. Some times when a ship come she says that you came home. When Lily go downtown she walks everywhere I go. Alice is very fat now because she eat plenty. She always play with Lily. Carl is fresh and always play with Alice and Lily. He doesn't want to read book so mother had to scold him. Mother works at Amauulu store in the afternoon that's why she is very busy. She has to work hard to let us eat and live. We heard from your sister that she sent one hundred dollars. Did you get it? Are you going to Japan? If you go we will [be] sad because we cannot get letter from you. If you go to Japan please do not worry about us. My eye glass broked so we bought another glass. It is the same as the [one] I had. Mother said she wanted to know how to take care of the orchid. Please write how to take care. You know the biggest orchid has eight buds now. When you go to Japan do not [get] sick. Please come home soon as you can. We're waiting for you. When ever we have good things to eat we put it where you was sitting and we eat. The camp people and friend is very good to us. Please write a thank you letter to Mr. Sato or to us. We are always waiting for your letter to come. Good-by.

English original
Date: July 28, 1942[9]
From: Tom T. Okino, Attorney at Law, Hilo Hawai'i
To: Otokichi Ozaki, Livingston Internment Camp, Louisiana

Dear Sir:

Upon the request of your wife, Mrs. Hideko Ozaki, I have prepared the enclosed instrument, to-wit, Power of Attorney, to be executed by you before a notary public in the State of Louisiana, so that your wife shall thereby be authorized to lawfully manage your property in Hilo, Hawaii.

The enclosed Power of Attorney must be notarized by a notary public and the certificate of a clerk of a court in which the notary public is residing should be executed by the clerk of the court knowing that the person taking the acknowledgment is a duly commissioned notary public. A copy of said certificate is attached to the said instrument.

The execution of this Power of Attorney before a notary public is necessary because the power includes interest in and to real property situate in Hilo, Hawaii.

After the same is duly completed, you may return the same directly to your wife.

Date: August 3 [1942][10]
From: Hideko Ozaki, Hilo, Hawai'i
To: Otokichi Ozaki, Livingston Internment Camp, Louisiana

It is quite hot. Are you doing all right? We are fine, so please be reassured. Yukio and Tomoyuki are staying at the Kataokas' house.* I understand they go to the stream everyday to catch shrimp and return darkly tanned. It has been so lonely without them that I sent a letter asking that they come home. They will probably be back today. Yuri and Sachi are doing very well and are getting into mischief constantly. Lately they have become naughty and do not readily obey Grandmother. Grandfather works in the cane fields from early morning until sunset. He returns home so late that it is worrisome. Now that Yuri needs less supervision, Grandmother spends her time doing personal things.

Thanks to the kindness of the camp people, I am allowed to work at the 'Amauulu store in place of Goto-san. I stock the shelves once or twice a week and learn dressmaking once a week.

---

*The family of Kakuma Kataoka, who lived in Hakalau, about fifteen miles north of Hilo. The Kataokas, including wife, Momoe, and sons Kazuma and Yoshikata, appear frequently in the letters of the Ozaki family. – Trans.

The work keeps me quite busy. Thank goodness for my strong body. Now and then I get to enjoy lunch with Madam at her house.

What is happening with the Japanese and American exchange plan? A few days ago, there was an article in the newspaper, which stated that those [internees] with families in Hawai'i will not be returned [to Japan]. We are happy. It may be an inconvenience, but we hope you will bear with it. If there is some urgent need to return, there is no other choice. Just the fact that we can communicate with you is reassuring. Please give careful thought to this matter.

At my request, a Power of Attorney document was drawn up by Mr. Okino and sent to you a few days ago. Please sign and return it quickly. Even if you return to Japan, there is absolutely no need to worry about us. No matter how difficult it may be, I will look after the elders and the children. Besides, the camp people and our friends are very supportive, so rest assured. We will be waiting eagerly for your earliest return. The day will come when we will be together again and enjoy a happy life. I look forward to just that.

The largest of your carefully tended orchid plants now has eight shoots with twenty-seven buds. They are so pretty. I wish you could see them. I plan to take them over to Kogawa very soon. I could go on, but I shall stop here.

P.S. If you need anything, I can send it at any time. Please let me know.

Date: August 7 [1942][11]
From: Earl Tomoyuki Ozaki, Hilo, Hawai'i
To: Otokichi Ozaki, Livingston Internment Camp, Louisiana

Last year at about this time we were in Honolulu having fun at Waikīkī Beach. We all laughed at the baggy pants I used for swimming. Those were happy days. There is no place to go now, so Yukio and I spent two weeks in Hakalau with the Kataoka family. We had fun fishing, catching shrimp, and picking 'opihi.* We went home looking so dark that everyone laughed.

You may not be home, but we remember to make offerings of special food at the altar before eating them. We also bow before your picture before going to bed. Whenever I feel lonely, I go to look at your picture in the bedroom. We are anxious to have you come home as soon as possible.

---

*Hawaiian: limpets

The biggest orchid plant is in bloom. Mother says she wishes you could see the thirty-one flowers. They are so pretty. Your letter of July 26, which came today, said you are going back to Japan soon. We will miss you. If it could be done without problems, we want to go with you. As of now, we cannot, but I hope the day will come when we will see you again.

English original
Date: August 12, 1942[12]
From: Nobuko Kosaki, Honolulu, Hawai'i
To: Otokichi Ozaki, Livingston Internment Camp, Louisiana

Dear Uncle,

I am writing this letter on behalf of mother and she is sitting across from me telling me what she would like to have included in this letter to you.

Today we received your letter which you wrote on the [censored]. So you see despite the air mail stamp the letter took more than [censored] to arrive here. On [censored] we received your radiogram asking for money so immediately we sent you a hundred dollars which we hope you have already received.

We receive letters from Hilo once in a while which tell us that the family is doing fine. We here in Honolulu are also in the best of health. Every morning mother makes four lunches, for Mineyuki, Hiromichi, Kazuo, and I are working. Mineyuki is still doing very well at Fair Dept. Store. Hiromichi is trying to make enough money to pay for his tuition for he is going to the University in September. Kazuo is working at a doctor's office and I am working at a school office. We will all go back to school soon. Yoshiko is helping with the laundry at home and Hidemichi is very busy making model airplanes for the Navy. So you see life in Hawaii is still the same and this is the same in Hilo. So do not worry about us back in Hawaii.

In your letter you speak of having applied for repatriation. We have talked it over and we feel that it would be much wiser to remain in the United States than to be sent to Japan. It would be entirely too difficult for the rest of the family to be reunited with you in Japan. All things being considered we definitely feel that it would be very much wiser for you to remain in the United States. Of course, there may be other problems to be considered, of which we know nothing. The decision rests on you but the above is our opinion.

Sincerely yours,
Nobuko Kosaki and Mother

P.S. We will write again. Mr. Kawazoe is not at home now so Mrs. Kawazoe and the children come over quite often. Mrs. Kawazoe will have a baby in October.

Date: not dated[13]
From: Earl Tomoyuki Ozaki, Hilo, Hawai'i
To: Otokichi Ozaki, Livingston Internment Camp, Louisiana

For a change I got up at five this morning. Mom was sure it would rain. I followed Grandpa to the vegetable garden. At lunch time, I had five bowls of rice, because it tasted so good. I like books, so I still spend a lot of time reading.

We want to return to Japan with you. Mom is getting a few things ready for the trip, but she is worried about how we will manage on the high seas.

Date: August 25, 1942[14]
From: Kayo Kosaki, Honolulu, Hawai'i
To: Otokichi Ozaki, Livingston Internment Camp, Louisiana

I was so relieved when I received two letters from you. At about this time last year we were all having such a good time in Waikīkī. Who would've thought we would be at war a few months later?

The anthurium and orchid plants are doing very nicely. I enjoy looking at the flowers throughout the day. It helps me to forget everything for a while.

Your decision to return to Japan is fine, but you shouldn't take your family with you. Wait until the end of the war. In the meantime, I'll look after your family, so don't worry. It's too much of a burden for Hideko to care for an elderly couple and four little ones. Why not have them come to Honolulu? Maybe Hideko can learn dressmaking here. Please let me know.

Date: August 30 [1942][15]
From: Hideko Ozaki, Hilo, Hawai'i
To: Otokichi Ozaki, Livingston Internment Camp, Louisiana

Are you doing all right? We are fine. These days the children play without undershirts, but they are doing well and do not catch colds.

What is the latest information on the exchange ship? Can our family accompany you? I am worried. The elders will not return to Japan. I don't know what I should do. You know, the elderly can be quite difficult. Once they say something, they do not listen to others. When I mention taking the children with me, they imply that we are running away after all the years they spent on the children's upbringing. I am really at a loss as to what to do. In the next breath, they say it would be a relief to have everyone gone. All I hear on this matter are complaints. I am praying for the day when we are at peace again and can be happy. Brother [Kazuki] and his wife [Kayo] have said that they are willing to look after the elders, but I feel it would be an imposition. The elders prefer to remain here, because they have nowhere to go, even if they return to Japan. At any rate, please give the matter careful thought and make a decision. If you decide to return to Japan, please ask the camp superiors to send a telegram. Please don't forget to let me know. P.S. I am enclosing five postage stamps.

Date: September 4 [1942][16]
From: Hideko Ozaki, Hilo, Hawai'i
To: Otokichi Ozaki, Livingston Internment Camp, Louisiana

I received three letters at the same time – the ones dated August 23 and July 13, and the one addressed to Father. You seem to be fine, so I am relieved. Here at home the elders and the children are in very good health, so please rest assured.

I understand that you have no information on when you will be boarding the exchange ship. I shall take some snapshots and send them right away. Since you have not seen the children for some time, you will be surprised to see how much they have grown. Please look forward to receiving them.

We have submitted our application to the Swedish Consul declaring our wish to return to Japan if an exchange ship is available. I do not know, however, what will come of this. Father in Honolulu* and my brothers and sisters are suggesting that we not return to Japan but move to Honolulu instead. They want us to join them. They say they will look after all of us, and with everyone in one place, there would be less to worry about. The elders are insisting on staying. Grandfather has additional land to look after and works very hard in the cane fields every day. He says that as long as he can work he will stay here, and when he is no longer able to, he will depend on those in Honolulu. We cannot leave them behind and go to Honolulu. I am wondering what I should do. If we are not returning to Japan, I think it would be better to remain here. The camp people have been very helpful, so please send thank-you

---

*Hideko's father, Takeji Kobara. – Trans.

letters to Yahata-san, Sato-san, Watanabe-san and Tango-san.*

We will do as you say, so please think carefully and let us know what you decide. I am sewing some children's clothes with the intention of going to Japan. Mrs. Koide is also returning to Japan. With four little ones, I am worried about being aboard a ship. Oh, well, there is nothing I can do except to wait until the time comes.

If you need anything, please let us know, and we will send it to you. There is nothing to be concerned about, because we will manage somehow. As long as we keep ourselves in good health, we will be able to see you. With this in mind, I am being careful. Please keep well. We will have peace some day, and happy days will come.

Until the next time.

English original
Date: October 15, 1942[17]
From: Hideko Ozaki, Hilo, Hawai'i
To: Otokichi Ozaki, Livingston Internment Camp, Louisiana

Mr. Ozaki:

The Power of Attorney which you executed to me was not properly completed by the notary public, Mr. Arnold L. Price because Mr. Price did not complete the Certificate which was attached to it. The Certificate must be signed by a clerk of the Court of Record or the Secretary of the State of Louisiana, confirming that Mr. Price is a duly commissioned notary public in and for the State of Louisiana of the county in which he resides.

You will find enclosed herewith a new Power of Attorney to be executed by you. Please without fail instruct a notary public to complete the Certificate attached to the Power of Attorney.

The new Power of Attorney designates Kazuma Kataoka as Attorney in Fact. Please mail the Power of Attorney to Kazuma Kataoka at Hakalau, Hawaii. I am doing this because I may leave the Territory of Hawaii to join you in the future.

Very truly yours,
Hideko Ozaki

English original
Date: October 29, 1942[18]
From: Nobuko Kosaki, Honolulu, Hawai'i

---

*Likely Bunnosuke Sato and Rokutaro Tango. See their letters, pp. 233 - 234. – Trans.

To: Otokichi Ozaki, Livingston Internment Camp, Louisiana

Dear Uncle,

Auntie wrote to us just the other day and asked me to write to you. I am sorry that I have neglected to do this so far. Mother suggested that I send you a Christmas card but I believe she really does not understand. To me this is no time for saying "Peace on Earth, Good will to men." One would be contradicting oneself in this present day war-torn world to say so. I only hope that the day will come when I and all of us will be able to celebrate the real spirit of Christmas without any backward feeling.

But Christmas is Christmas and the New Year will follow. So in a limited holiday spirit may I hope for the best for you and pray that each one of us through this new suffering that we are going through will find a larger horizon of thought and philosophy and emerge a larger individual spiritually and mentally.

At present, I am doing my practice teaching at Teachers College Intermediate School. I am teaching the 8th grade class which happens to be the highest grade at the school. There are 15 students in the class and it is amazing how different each personality is. We spend the whole day from 8:00 a.m. to 2:30 p.m., teaching the class. Then from 2:45 p.m. to about 4:30 everyday we have conferences without our supervisors on the different problems we have met in the classroom. It is all very interesting and challenging to know that we are molding individual personalities and characters. Now, I can see why some teachers enjoy their work so much. But on the other hand it is hard work. There are all the planning, studying and thinking to do.

As I do my practice work I can think back to the days when you and I talked about the different theories of teaching—of developing the whole individual—of teaching a concept, etc. Right now, my main interest is to show these boys and girls the use of arithmetic. As you know my main interest has been in mathematics and in relation to all the defense activities going on now no one can over rate the importance of mathematical training. So if I can get my boys and girls to understand the arithmetic system and really see why it is so important, I would have done a large part of my duty to my country.

It is amazing when one stops to think of it how much the children are learning now. The things that the children of today know are entirely different from what we as children thought were fun. Now, they know all about airplanes, guns, tanks and all the firefighting and civilian defense activities. Even my brother Albert who is only in the 5th grade in school makes model airplanes to scale and talks about wanting to become an aeronautical engineer.

He has a certificate from the Navy giving him the rank of honorary cadet aircrafts man. He has this framed and hung up on the wall.

Auntie has been writing to us quite often about her plans. She said that there is nothing to worry about. Mother would like for you to write to Grandmother and Grandfather and tell them to come to Honolulu and stay with us if they are lonely in Hilo. In case anything should happen it would be very difficult for us to go to Hilo to look after them so if they are left alone please tell them to go to Honolulu and live with us.

Date: November 20 [1942][19]
From: Hideko Ozaki, Hilo, Hawai'i
To: Otokichi Ozaki, Livingston Internment Camp, Louisiana

I received your telegram just after two o'clock in the afternoon on November 20. My letter must have reached you.

We are fine, so please rest assured. We too have packed our things and are waiting, although we do not know when we will leave.

In your telegram, you asked to have your passport sent, but it could get lost along the way, so I shall carry it with me when we leave here. I had been planning to do that anyway. Please do not worry. If, however, you need it as soon as possible, please let me know, and I will send it. I do not have my birth certificate, so I have asked for help from my father in Honolulu. I think he only needs to write a request to the Immigration Office, but I am not sure. I am asking him to do so at the same time that I send this letter to you. I plan to carry both documents and the children's birth certificates with me. I will take your used coat, your trousers, and other clothing and buy raincoats.

The children are in school. Yukio has a new teacher at this critical time, so he is having problems in reading. It seems that he cannot pronounce the words. I am having him study at night. On Sunday, the fifteenth, Mrs. Goo came to visit, so I mentioned the problem. She kindly offered to help Yukio for fifteen minutes after school. I am so happy. She wanted to buy some of our [potted] flowers, but I will not sell a single one. She was very happy when I gave her two or three red anthuriums instead. There have been some outside requests for our flowers, but Grandfather and Grandmother are here [to care for them], so I will not sell anything. I don't want to sell them at a bargain price, after all your hard work. There are no offers for our property right now, so I will leave it as it is. When the war ends, let us return here.

I suppose it is cold on the Mainland, so I will take blankets and two *futon*˙ with us. I am worried that it will be too cold for the children.

They are happy that they are going to [their] father's place. I worry about the little ones on board the ship. We have everything ready, so I think we could be leaving soon, but I don't know. I will send a telegram when we do. The children are too busy playing to have the time to write to you. I think it would be nice if you could possibly write to the ['Amauulu] camp people. They have been very good to us, so please thank them.

It will be getting cold, so please be careful not to catch a cold. Until the next time.

Date: November 24, 1942[20]
From: Kazuki Kosaki [Ozaki's brother-in-law, husband of Kayo], Honolulu, Hawai'i
To: Otokichi Ozaki, Livingston Internment Camp, Louisiana

On November 22, I received your letter dated October 15 addressed to Kayo.

Please forgive me that I have not visited you nor written to you. I am glad to note in your letters that you are in good health and keeping yourselves busy. We are all in good health. In Hilo, Grandpa, Grandma, Hideko-san and her children are quite in good spirits, I am pleased to tell you. They seem not to feel insecure in their lives at all, although mental hardship is another matter.

This emergency happens only once in a lifetime. In the past year, when the blackout came, I saw the full moon through the coconut trees from the veranda of my house, which reminded me of the old days. Since it is getting severely cold on the continent, please take care of yourself.

I still work at the hotel, and most of the guests are soldiers. They are all good people. The master is kind to us. Kayo is busy at laundry, but since Yoshiko helps the master and his income is very good and he eats well everyday, he seems to be happy.

Nobuko is a senior at a college and soon graduating. She will become a teacher this February. Hiromichi is a freshman (400 students) at a college, and was elected president.[†]

---

*comforters
†Richard Hiromichi was elected freshman class president at the University of Hawai'i before he left for the Army. He was elected president of the student government, The Associated Students of the University of Hawai'i at Mānoa, when he returned to campus after three years in the Army. – Ed.

Kazuo and Yoshiko are students at McKinley High, and Hi-demichi is in the fifth grade at a primary school. Mineyuki works at Fair Department Store.

We worry about your future, but cannot say anything definite. You have to follow the destiny of the trends.

I hear that you plan to go back to Japan on an exchange ship. It is natural that you want to go back. It will be most fortunate if you can go back safely with the family. Since, it is a long journey, I worry about your wife and children.

Since Hideko-san is firmly determined to go to the Mainland and get on board the exchange ship, we try to assist her for the preparation as much as possible. However, a ship bound for the Mainland does not seem to be leaving any time soon. The grand-parents say, "Journey not in the cold winter, but in the spring-time," and it seems that they do not wish to go back to Japan. However, do not worry about them. We will take full responsibility of taking care of them, but they have to come out to Honolulu.

They say they would like to stay in 'Amauulu, even if it means living alone. It seems that they do not want to come out to Hono-lulu. If they stay in 'Amauulu and are cared for by the camp people for a long time, we in Honolulu will not be able to save face, I'm afraid.

Will you please write to them and half-force them to come out to Honolulu and live with us? There are plenty of easy jobs for them in Honolulu. They need not worry about anything.

We have gradually repaired and expanded the house we had bought, and now we are painting it. We grow many kinds of vegetables in our yard. We also built a hothouse that is ten-by-eighteen [feet]. The anthuriums bloom beautifully everyday. The orchids also have begun to bloom.

When I see people in the park or cheerful children playing at the seashore, I sometimes wonder if we really are waging a war. I pray sincerely that peace will come soon.

Mrs. Kawazoe gave birth to a baby girl in the beginning of October. Both mother and baby are in good health. Now the baby is very cute.

It seems that their family intends to go to the Mainland. They say they might live with the family from Hilo. Now Mrs. Tanaka of Hilo is in Honolulu and taking care of the baby.

Mr. Kobara is in good health, and his restaurant is prospering. He sends money to Hideko quite often. All members of the Uejio family are also in good health. Mr. Uejio works at the farm, as usual.

Kayo plans to send some clothes to you, since the continent is very cold now. These days it is getting difficult to buy enough clothes.

When this letter reaches you, you may be greeting the New Year.

We do not know what will be the outcome of this war, but take care of yourself so that you may ride out this emergency and wait for the arrival of a bright future.

Date: December 1, 1942[21]
From: Kumataro Yoshioka, Hilo, Hawai'i
To: Otokichi Ozaki, Livingston Internment Camp, Louisiana

How have you been? The other day I asked your wife for your address. She was kind enough to reply immediately. Thus, I am writing this letter of greetings and to let you know about my life of late. We live without too much inconvenience, and in peace, despite the present war situation.

I heard that Mrs. Ozaki was arranging to come to you soon. I hope your reunion will be a happy one.

I have been in a hospital here since July of this year, and my health has greatly improved (weight increased by ten pounds). I will be discharged from the hospital by the time this letter reaches you.

While in the hospital, I composed some short poems. Some of them are as follows:

White-tipped waves break	何時となく
Along the beach,	今日も暮らしぬ
Another day	白波の
In a convalescent home.	濱邉にそうる*
	療養所にて

As I read God's words	聖書よめば
My daily blessings grow	日毎の恵
Helping me forget	くはわりぬ †
Theses afflictions	病める身をさへ
Of body and soul.	忘れらりける

---

*沿う
†加わりぬ

A world in chaos   世は乱れ
Nation pitted against nation   國と國との
Where city and country   争闘ひの
Will be fields of combat.   ちまた*となりぬ

ひな†も都も

Please laugh at my ignorance. Just jotting down my congratulations and the recent news of my life.

Wishing you all the best.

Date: January 13, 1943[22]
From: Kazuki Kosaki, Honolulu, Hawai'i
To: Otokichi Ozaki, Livingston Internment Camp, Louisiana

Please rest assured that your parents, Tomoya and Shobu, live in good health with us in Honolulu.

Hideko and her children, Tomoyuki, Yukio, Sachi, and Yuri, left Honolulu on December 27 of last year. I feel relieved to have read a newspaper report that they arrived safely in San Francisco with people from the Hawai'i camps.

Let me explain the situation whereby our whole family, including our parents [Tomoya and Shobu], moved from Hilo to Honolulu.

Our parents were determined not to go to the Mainland. Father, especially, did not want to go even to Honolulu; he wanted to stay in Hilo to lead a comfortable life. However, we received in the middle of December a stern order from the military government to move to the Mainland. Since this order was undreamed of and unexpected, our parents were more than shocked. They were not prepared for the journey, and time was limited. Thus, they were quite confused, as they discarded and packed their household goods. Friends pleaded in vain with the authorities to not move them to the Mainland. Finally, our parents made up their minds and calmly picked up their belongings.

All the people at 'Amauulu Camp and the parents and children of the Kataoka family and Mr. Okazaki at Hakalau helped them clean up. Our parents distributed the leftover goods to the people at 'Amauulu Camp in order to save face for you. They received a sizable amount of farewell money. All the family, that is, seven people, arrived in Honolulu on December 25.

We felt it was too much for our old parents to take a long journey on the sea and on the land in the cold winter. As soon

---

*巷
†鄙

as we received a letter from Hideko that they had left Hilo, with Nobuko representing us, we applied to the Red Cross, the Swedish Consulate, and the military government. After the officers concerned met at the INS office, they approved the wish of our parents not to go to the Mainland on the condition that we take care of them, and they were generously allowed to remain in Honolulu. They were happy, but at the same time, it was hard for them to part with the grandchildren. I can understand that.

Through the gentlemanly and generous treatment of the military government, we were able to meet with Hideko and her children at the INS office. We were able to talk freely in the yard from morning until five o'clock. Hideko was in good spirits and looked somewhat fatter. We were surprised to hear that Yuri, whom we had worried about, was also in good health; she did not get seasick at all and had *kaukau.*ˑ Tomoyuki and Yukio were OK. Sachi was *momona,*† as usual. The children will not be too much of a bother to Hideko. Rather, they could be of help to her.

Father hates to be out of work and at present works at Kobara Restaurant. Mr. Kobara is quite satisfied with him. His restaurant is doing very well. At any rate, please do not worry about our parents, since the families of Uejio and Kobara and we will take good care of them. Please take care of yourself and live with the hope that we will meet again when peace returns.

Your postcard to Tomoyuki and your package to the children were forwarded to us from Hilo. Unfortunately, however, the postcard and the package arrived after they had left. Hiromichi keeps the rare pine tree leaves and pebbles of the river.

I gave your children lots of candies and crackers in Honolulu. Since they are prepared well, you need not worry about them during the journey. Mr. Kobara sent not only money, but a lot of clothes.

Mother asked me to tell you this. Mother used to take sleeping pills when she went to bed in Hilo. However, since she came to Honolulu, she does not need the pills. She can sleep well. She is very helpful to us.

We asked Mr. Kazuma Kataoka to take care of the revenue from sugar cane on the island of Hawai'i. Hereafter he will send the proceeds to Honolulu.

I spent many days writing this letter. I hope you will understand it, if you read it repeatedly.

Please take good care of yourself. Please write to me as soon as you receive this letter.

---

*Pidgin: food; to eat
†Hawaiian: plump

P.S. Nobuko graduated from the university and will work at a high school on Lāna'i as a teacher on January 28 (until June).

_____

English original
Date: January 20, 1943[23]
From: Edward J. Ennis, Director, Department of Justice, Alien Enemy Control Unit, Washington, D.C.
To: Otokichi Ozaki, Camp Livingston, Louisiana

Dear Sir:
    Reference is made to your letter of January 5, 1943 wherein you request that your family be allowed to reside with you at a family camp upon their arrival from Hawaii.
    Since your request comes under the jurisdiction of the War Department I am this date forwarding same to General B. M. Bryan, Jr., Chief, Aliens division, Provost Marshall General's Office, War Department, Washington, D. C., for proper consideration.

Very truly yours,
Edward J. Ennis
Director

_____

Date: February 17 [1943][24]
From: Kazuki and Kayo Kosaki, Honolulu, Hawai'i
To: Otokichi Ozaki, Livingston Internment Camp, Louisiana

    On February 10, we received your letter of December 30 of last year. We understand you are in good health and accumulating invaluable experiences everyday. I hope you will be patient.
    Here, our father and mother are also in good health. Father works at Kobara Restaurant everyday. Mother either works at the vegetable farm or helps out with Kayo's and others' laundry. The flower seeds you had sent us sprouted and grew everyday. I think they will bloom within a few days. Mother takes good care of them.
    We feel relieved to know that Hideko-san and her four children have arrived safely at Jerome Relocation Center, Denson, Arkansas. [Kayo]* carefully made *shio konbu*† with the thought to send it to you, but we gave it to Hideko-san since she was to sail soon. We will make it again and send it to you. These days we cannot find

_____

*"Kaneo" in the original. – Trans.
†Salted kelp

Japanese foods like *konbu** and *narazuke*† any more, and we are inconvenienced. Getting pickles is also difficult. Even in Honolulu, it is very difficult to get fresh fish and vegetables, so we grow vegetables in our yards.

We cannot get fish at all. The lifestyle has completely changed. Meat is abundant in supply. When ships do not come in, however, we can get nothing. We bought and stocked up on quite a bit of rice and canned foods (American-made). These days butter is getting scarce.

This time we sent to you: tempura, *hokkigai,*‡ *narazuke*, green tea, *tai no shio-ni,*§ *kinugai Yamato-ni,*¶ one roll of *wakame,*** two bottles of *shio konbu*, and a bottle of *daikonzuke.*†† We also sent you a set of black and white stones for the game of *go*. Please look forward to their arrival. When you receive them, please let us know. We are keeping our fingers crossed that they reach you soon. We feel sorry that we cannot help you as much as we wish. Please understand our situation.

We work everyday without holidays. [Kayo]‡‡ is too busy everyday to take on any more. Nobuko is on Lāna'i to practice teaching. She will come back in June and go back to the university. She will get a diploma in September and go to other islands to teach. Hiromichi is a freshman at the university. Mineyuki signed up at Volunteer Combat Units. He received an A-1 card. If he passes the physical examination, he will go to the Mainland to begin military life. It seems he will go to Camp Shelby in Mississippi.§§

Both Mrs. Kawazoe and her baby are quite well. They visit us once in a while. We mailed out the package today. It is insured. It weighs about thirteen pounds. We believe that the U.S. government treats you well. Since we are at war, let's be patient. Take care of yourself.

English original
Date: not dated[25]
From: E. B. Whitaker, Project Director, War Relocation Authority

---

*Kelp
†Squash pickles seasoned in *sake* lees.
‡A type of surf clam; likely canned. – Trans.
§Sea bream simmered with salt in a seasoned broth.
¶A type of long-necked clam, simmered Yamato-style in a sauce of *shoyu*, sugar and ginger; a common preparation for canned foods. This is a popular military ration even today. – Trans.
**Seaweed
††Pickled radish
‡‡"Kaneo" in the original. – Trans.
§§In early 1943, the Army put out a call for volunteers to fill the ranks of its newly created all-Japanese American 442nd Regimental Combat Team. Some 10,000 men from Hawaii signed up; and from among them more than 2,600 inductees left in March for Camp Shelby, Mississippi to begin basic training. – Trans.

To: Hideko Ozaki, Jerome Relocation Center, Arkansas

You are hereby notified that your application for leave clearance
dated March 8, 1943 has been considered by the Director. Your
application for leave clearance has been denied because: There is
reasonable ground to believe that the issuance of leave would inter-
fere with the war program or otherwise endanger the public peace
and security.

This notice does not authorize departure from the relocation
center. A suitable application must be made separately at any time
you wish to apply for leave.

Date: March 1 [1943][26]
From: Tomoya Ozaki, Honolulu, Hawai'i
To: [Hideko Ozaki, Jerome Relocation Center, Arkansas]

I am well, as always, but Bāsan* has had some trouble. Her
lungs are not good. When she was given a tuberculin test by a
government doctor,† she and Kayo‡ were found to be positive, and
they were asked to come to the public health center for an x-ray
check-up. On their way back, they dropped in at the Kosaki family
doctor to review the x-ray results. According to the doctor, Kayo
had tuberculosis years ago, but now it has been cured completely.
On the other hand, Bāsan has a slight shadow in her right lung.
Thus, the doctor recommends that she begin treatment as soon
as possible. He says that she does not need to be hospitalized and
that she can recuperate at home.

He says that this disease does not infect old folks, but it does
younger people. He advises us that since Kosaki's house is small,
we had better rent a house and let her recuperate at leisure for a
quicker recovery. Now I am looking for a house to rent, but it is
very difficult to find a suitable house these days. If she stays in
a hospital, the children may suffer, and they say the food situation in the hospital is not good. But if she stays with them, the
disease may infect the children. I am quite at a loss. I have not yet
disclosed this news to the Kosaki, Kobara, and Uejio families. I'm
sorry to be giving you bad news.

As requested, I bought three aloha shirts and other things for

---

*When writing to Otokichi, Tomoya often uses the expression *jiji-baba* 爺婆, lit., "old man and
old woman," in reference to himself and Shobu. He also often refers to his wife as *bāsan* 婆さん,
"old woman." Thus, the translations will retain the use of "Jiji and Baba" and "Bāsan," as Tomoya
uses them. – Trans.

†I.e., a public health official. – Trans.

‡"Kaneo" in the original. – Trans.

Otokichi for $20.20. I will mail them shortly.

Today I asked Kazuma in Hakalau to send $100 to Otokichi in care of you. It will reach you soon, so please keep it for him. I cannot sell the land in Hilo yet. As soon as it is sold, I will let you know.

Around February 20, Toshio Okazaki of Hakalau had surgery to remove kidney stones, and he is now recuperating. They say he is getting better day-by-day. I sent him a get-well letter and *omimai.*ˑ When you write to the Kataoka family, please enclose an *omimai* letter.† Since I am not writing to Otokichi separately, please tell him about this.

I will write again.

I have a most unhappy life, too.

Please send a thank you letter to the Kosakis.

Take care of the children. Take care of yourself.

Bāsan will get well in six or seven months, I'm sure.

I often have problems sleeping, because I feel so badly about the Kosakis having to take care of us.

Afterall, I do have one happiness, and that is that this old man has not gotten sick, and so from here on out I shall work hard.

Date: March 22, 1943[27]
From: Tomoya Ozaki [Otokichi's father], Honolulu, Hawai'i
To: Otokichi Ozaki, Livingston Internment Camp, Louisiana

I received your letter on March 18. I was relieved to note that you are doing well. The Kosaki, Kobara, and Uejio families are all fine. I am in good health and work everyday.

Bāsan's lungs are bad, and everybody worries about her. She went to Mr. Kosaki's family doctor on March 15 to have an x-ray taken. The doctor found two small spots in her left lung and a small cloud in her right lung. The doctor said he would take an x-ray again in three months. Another doctor says that at her age these are not rare, and she does not need to worry about them. She takes medicine. He says that being careful about her diet is most important.

Since Mr. Kosaki worries about her, we are trying to find a house to let her stay in, but I have not found it yet. She used to get cold and stay in bed once in a while, when we were at 'Amauulu. Since moving Honolulu, she has not been in bed for even a day because of illness. She eats well and is fine. I cannot see anything wrong with her. I do not think you need to worry about her.

---

*A gift, often monetary, to express concern about one who is sick.
†For Toshio Okazaki, which the Kataokas would presumably pass on. – Trans.

The land in Hilo that you mentioned will be very difficult to sell. Recently we applied to Honolulu for a permit through the kind offices of Mr. Mukai. If the permit is issued, we can sell [the land]. I have to pay a tax of more than $60 beginning this year, and I am at a loss as to how to pay it. Thus, if the land is sold, it will be a big help to me.

We receive letters from Hideko once in a while. We are relieved to know that all four children go to school and are in good health.

By the way, I bought three aloha shirts, a sweater, and towels for $20.20. I will send them to you soon.

Last year, the profit from selling sugar cane from our 'Amauulu field was $237 and $100 from the uncultivated part of Shishido's field. I will have to give up these three fields this year, because [the price of] sugar cane has come down and the cost of labor has risen. I now work for a salary.

I give all of my salary, except for [what I need for] personal expenses, to Mr. Kosaki. I put [money for the] *tanomoshi** in the bank. Last year we spent a fair amount of money on clothing, since we did not have any. We thought it would be better this year, but we have to spend on medicine now.

The daughter of Mr. Mukai is now in Honolulu for medical treatment. Mrs. Mukai came here to see her at the beginning of February, and she cannot leave and is still here. I gave three dollars as *omimai* and treated them to a meal together with Mr. Kosaki.

I do not know when we will be able to live together. The only thing we can do now is wait patiently. I pray that peace will come as soon as possible, and I look forward to seeing you. I will work hard again this year.

If peace comes soon, do you want to come back to O'ahu? I cannot work for or depend on Mr. Kosaki forever. It would be nice if all of the family could live together where you are living. However, it may take a long, long time for this to happen. In the meantime, we are at quite a loss as to what to do. I am sorry for the burden we have put on everyone.

I will write you more news next time.

Please take care of yourself.

---

*A mutual financing group, described by Dorothy Hazama and Jane Komeiji: "(*Tanomoshi*) were organized among friends. Each of these groups was made up of ten or twenty persons or families who put a specified amount of money into the pot each month. The first month's pot automatically went to the 'house' or person in charge. Beginning with the second month, the members bid for the pot. The highest bidder took the pot and paid each remaining member a portion of his bid. Once a person took a pot, he was not eligible to receive ensuing dividends. The members, therefore, tried very hard to be one of the last to take the pot." See Dorothy Ochiai Hazama and Jane Okamoto Komeiji, *Okagesama de: The Japanese in Hawai'i, 1885-1985* (Honolulu: The Bess Press, Inc., 1986) 74, 76. – Trans.

Date: April 28 [1943]²⁸
From: Tomoya Ozaki, Honolulu, Hawai'i
To: Otokichi Ozaki, Livingston Internment Camp, Louisiana

I have not written to you for a long time. I am glad to know from your occasional letters that all of you are in good health. All of the Kosakis, and Jiji and Baba, are in good health.

Bāsan and I came to live in Honolulu from December 25 of last year, and thanks to the help of Nobuko-san, we are able to stay here [with the Kosakis]. Healthy as always, I began working at Kobara's restaurant from January of this year. My job is to peel potatoes and to help wash dishes. They use one bag of potatoes a day. On Sundays about 1,700 to 1,800 customers visit the restaurant, and we are busy. The restaurant is doing very well.

Since I work everyday without taking even a day off and eat two times a day at Kobara's place, I need not worry about food. Since coming here, I've become nine pounds more *momona*, and everybody smiles at me and says, "You've gotten younger." I am very healthy now.

Last February, I took out [a life] insurance [policy] for $3,000. This year after we came to Honolulu, I asked Mr. Kosaki to go to the insurance company to extend the policy. Since [the premium on] $1,000 of the insurance will be due by next year, I will pay the premium in May, and in June I will pay the real property tax on the land [in Hilo].

I will cut cane at 'Amauulu this year. Since I cleared grass at Shishido's farm last year, I can cut cane at three places. So, I do not need to worry about money.

Our only inconvenience is our clothing. It went to the Mainland with our children's clothing and has not come back yet.* This is a big problem for me. My two pairs of pants and three shirts are gone.

We are greatly indebted to the Kosaki family.

No matter what we say, there is nothing we can do under the circumstances. I can only pray that peace will come soon.

I pray for your good health.

P.S. Kazuma sent $200 to Hideko on April 24. Bāsan has been in better health since she left 'Amauulu.

Date: May 7 [1943]²⁹
From: Kazuki Kosaki, Honolulu, Hawai'i
To: Hideko Ozaki, Jerome Relocation Center, Arkansas

---

*What Tomoya probably means is that his and his wife's clothes were packed up, along with those of Hideko and the children, during preparations for the family's move to Jerome. – Trans.

Excuse my long silence. Thank you very much for your letters. Thank you for the beautiful postcard yesterday. I feel relieved to note that you are all in good health and it is getting warmer and easier to live.

As for us, both our father and mother are quite healthy. Our father works at the restaurant without taking days off. The restaurant is closed every Wednesday. He is gifted with his hands and he makes all kinds of things for other people. He is happily loved by neighbors and at the restaurant for this ability.

Our mother is a wonderful woman. She practices *katakana*[*] characters. She can read the newspaper. After lunch, we let her rest. She is in good health. She looks forward to the day when peace will come and she can see everyone again.

Recently, I bought sticking plasters to put on the chest to bring down fever. I will mail them soon. I checked at the post office and found out to my regret that we cannot send foodstuffs, like candies and the like, to the continent. Please understand our situation.

I heard a story that someone sent out candies and other goods from Hakalau. This may be possible because handling is more generous in the countryside, or they do not know the regulations.

We, foreigners, are not allowed to send money. I feel sorry for you, but please understand. I received a correspondence from Hakalau that they sent about $100 to you. I hope you have received it by now.

The package for the old folks has not yet arrived. Upon checking at the Consulate office, I found that the ship had not arrived but would be arriving shortly. As soon as the ship comes in, the package should arrive, I hope.

I received a letter dated April 16 from Otokichi-san. He says he is in good health and is keeping himself busy, which is good. He also says that you and Yuri paid a visit to him. He must have been very pleased.

A few days ago, a newspaper in Honolulu reported that the Japanese in Arkansas had collected $1,000 to purchase warm clothing, which was donated to the evacuees from Hawai'i. I am quite impressed by the news.

About ten days ago, I sent you a letter from our father and mother. I hope you have already received it. All members of the Kobara family are in good health and work hard. Since I will not write to Otokichi-san, will you please forward this letter to him?

Praying for the day of peace to come soon.

---

[*]The noncursive Japanese syllabic writing system, usually used for loanwords or for emphasis.

English original
Date: July 13, 1943[30]
From: Edward J. Ennis, Director, Department of Justice, Alien
Enemy Control Unit, Washington, D.C.
To: Otokichi Ozaki, Santa Fe Internment Camp, New Mexico

Dear Sir:

I am in receipt of the petition dated June 21, 1943, which you
signed and in which you request reunion with your family in a
family internment center.

I wish to advise you that the Department of Justice and the
War Department have recently collaborated in reviewing your case
and it has been decided that you may be paroled to a War Relocation Center provided this arrangement is satisfactory to the War
Relocation Authority.

Negotiations are now under way between the War Department
and the War Relocation Authority to effect your parole as soon as
possible. However, in this connection I wish to point out that a
delay may be encountered since many such cases are being handled
in the same manner. You will be notified by the War Relocation Authority if and when arrangements for your transfer are
completed.

Very truly yours,
Edward J. Ennis
Director

Date: November 14, 1943[31]
From: Tadasuke Koryu Nakabayashi, Hilo, Hawai'i*
To: Otokichi Ozaki, Santa Fe Internment Camp, New Mexico

Thank you very much for your letter. I am very sorry for not
having written even one letter to you. I am pleased to hear that all
of your family is well. Please take care of yourself. I pray for your
health.

I learn a lot from the righteous men who display strength,
greatness, manliness, and nobleness while fighting against all of the
hardships.

I am quite all right, but feel miserable for not having even written a letter to you, despite my peaceful life. I scold myself for this.

As you say in your letter, I am quite impressed with the heroic

---

*Tadasuke Koryu Nakabayashi, appears in subsequent letters, sometimes referred to by just his
poetry name, Koryu, the characters for which mean "red flow," i.e. "lava flow." He was an employee
of Amfac, also known as American Factors, one of the Big Five corporations that wielded incompa-
rable economic and political clout in the territory. – Trans.

fighting of the Nisei combat teams under the Stars and Stripes. I offer my deep appreciation and respect to them. At the same time, I offer my everlasting appreciation and respect to you, teachers and managers of the Japanese schools, who worked long and hard to educate these great Nisei citizens. Yours efforts have been rewarded. You have made invaluable sacrifices.

When will wars ever disappear from our world? But as long as there are wars, enlisting and sacrificing oneself for one's country is invaluable to the United States, which values democracy and freedom. Those Nisei and Sansei are doing their duty, leaving behind their elderly parents, young wives, many beloved children, and high monthly salaries, for some. They are willingly risking their lives in the face of severe bombing by the enemy. Moreover, their families sent them out happily and cheerfully. I cannot help but pay my utmost respect and express my appreciation to every one of them, who has made such a great sacrifice.

Some of them may have already died on the battlefield, and still others may have lost legs or hands. I feel we have a huge responsibility not to waste their great sacrifices. I must take this fact very seriously and, for the sake of these Nisei, Sansei, and Yonsei,* try to shoulder even one millionth of their responsibilities.

The flowers of the pink shower trees already lie scattered on the ground, and golden shower petals are now falling. The ripe fruit of yellow guava trees lie on the roadside near the gulch homes. Autumn is deepening, and the cold autumn moon is rising. The same cold moonlight may be shining on dead bodies on the battlefields. The explosions of bombs may be heard as well.

Please give my best regards and those of my wife to Mrs. Ozaki. Japanese schools have been closed and our country is at war. It is difficult to educate our children. Educators and priests are having a hard time. Everything has to be sacrificed to win the war. I pray that the war will end as soon as possible.

Mr. Fujita of "Kokusui" died of pneumonia at four o'clock this morning.†

Date: December 3, 1943[32]
From: Kazuki Kosaki, Honolulu, Hawai'i
To: Otokichi Ozaki, Santa Fe Internment Camp, New Mexico

I am sorry for my long silence. I hope you are not angry with me. Forgive me, please.

---

*A fourth generation Japanese American.
†This is probably Shigeru Fujita, an employee of the Nichi-Bei Sake Brewery in Hilo. "Kokusui" is the name of a brand of *sake*. – Trans.

From your letter to Grandfather, I am pleased to note that you are doing fine, as usual. However, I am sorry to hear that you have not been able to live together with your family.

I receive letters once in a while from Hideko-san. I sympathize with your children, because they have to live in an unfamiliar land. The influence of the war is spreading quite widely.

Our lives are now under martial law, and the new laws are quite different from the old days. However, in Hawai'i, the treatment is fairly generous, and we are thankful for that.

The only trouble is that we cannot help you as much as we wish. We cannot remit money. There is the restriction on what we can send and the list of prohibited items that we cannot send out.

Hideko-san often asks us to send money. Since we cannot do anything, we have to ask Kazuma for help.

They are pleased to read letters from the Mainland, but at the same time, the old people worry about you, and they say that they sometimes cannot sleep at night. So please be careful about what you write.

Your parents always think about you. Parental love is always beautiful. However, if they cannot do things that they wish to do, it is better to let the future take care of itself.

Your father is in good health and does not easily yield to younger folks. However, he is very stubborn and difficult to deal with. Kayo cannot stand him once in a while and talks back to him with harsh words. Since he was raised in the countryside, even I feel he is somewhat awkward.

Your mother is a quiet woman. She does not know much about cooking nor house cleaning. However, she is very good at heating a bath and cooking rice. These days she is very busy at making straw sandals. Caucasians buy them for one dollar a pair. Since there is not even a pair of wooden clogs or sandals in the market, they are very valuable.

On holidays, your father makes wooden clogs and brooms from coconuts and dustpans from oil cans. He also makes soy sauce and *takuan.*[*] Everybody is grateful to him.

When he has a drink at dinnertime,[†] he repeats the same story many times. Hearing him, we share the opinion that everyone does the same thing when he gets old.

Since the outbreak of the war, we do not go downtown unless we have business. We have a one-day holiday once in twelve days. At that time, we go there to pay bills for the phone, electricity, gas, water, mortgage, etc.

---

*Pickled turnip
†The making of *sake* was prohibited with the outbreak of the war. However, citizens with the proper permit were allowed to purchase one bottle of whiskey or wine a week. – Trans.

In the morning and at the lunch break, we clean the house, weed the yard, and take care of the vegetables and watering in the hothouse. These are pleasures. Since nine people live in a small house, there are lots of things to do.

I get up at six o'clock in the morning and come home at around eight-thirty at night. On my way home, I buy foodstuffs. Everyday I have to think about what we should eat. This is hard. Most difficult is that we cannot get vegetables and fish. Since there are no Japanese fishermen anymore, we can seldom buy fish. When we can, it costs one dollar per pound.

At the hotel, we work mostly for soldiers. American soldiers are very good people. They treat us well.

Hiromichi applied for an interpreter position. If he passes the physical test, he will go to Camp Savage, Minnesota, at the beginning of January. Mineyuki also applied last year, but he could not pass the eye test. Now he works at a pineapple company.

Nobuko graduated from the Teachers College of the university[*] after five years' hard work. She is now a full-fledged teacher and teaches at a high school on Moloka'i. Because of her good performance, she received an award.

Hiromichi is now a sophomore. He is always ranked number one or number two on tests and is a scholarship student. If he goes to the Mainland and lives the military life, he will gain more valuable social knowledge than living as a student. I hope he will cross the life and death line successfully.

I cannot get away from the god of poverty, and I still have several thousand dollars of mortgage on my house. This year, I painted the roof and the whole outside of the house and renovated the inside and painted it all white. Now my home feels good. I have waited for my children to grow and help me. I feel sorry that we cannot do anything for you. However, please rest assured that we take responsibility to care for the grandparents.

Mr. Tango, Mr. Sato, Mr. Watanabe, and others at 'Amauulu are always kind to us. The parents and sons of the Kataoka family really take care of us from the bottom of their hearts.

Mr. Kataoka informed us that, through the kind offices of somebody, the land in Hilo could be sold at $1,500 net. Grandfather says that after due consideration, it is better to sell it.

I agree with him. We do not know how long your present situation will continue, and you need money. Thus, it is better to sell the land and keep $1,500 in a deposit in your name at a bank. This way, when you need it, we can withdraw it and send it

---

[*]The Teachers College was formed in 1931, when the Territorial Normal School was merged with the University of Hawai'i's School of Education, requiring graduates to earn a bachelor's degree. – Trans.

through Kazuma.

However long I write, I cannot finish writing, but let me stop here. My writing is in disorder, but I hope you can understand it. P.S. The second son of Mr. Kataoka in Hakalau goes to a business school in Honolulu, but he applied for an interpreter and translator position. Since he applied without consulting his parents, his mother was surprised.

Date: December 3, 1943[33]
From: Kazuki Kosaki, Honolulu, Hawai'i
To: Hideko Ozaki, Jerome Relocation Center, Arkansas

Hideko-san, it is very nice of you to write often to your father-in-law, but it is better not to write anything that will cause a headache for them. I feel sorry to note that you cannot yet live with your husband, but it is very cowardly for you to say, "I should not have come to the Mainland," or "I would like to go back to Hawai'i."

First of all, I am afraid that you did not go to the Mainland with a firm determination. You expected that you could go back to Japan as soon as you went to the Mainland. You did not bring household goods and kitchen utensils with you and left them in Hawai'i. You left Hawai'i as if you were going on a short pleasure trip, didn't you? That is why you say you want this and that now.

Even in Hawai'i, we cannot buy pots and pans and other kitchen utensils, electric appliances, and alarm clocks anymore. There is none of them in stores. We are surprised to note that we cannot find even a yard of window cloth. We hardly see cotton fabric.

On the other hand, an abundant supply of foodstuff, canned goods, and meat comes from the Mainland, for which we are grateful. The food situation is even better than in the old days. However, we can hardly get fresh fish. We eat fish only several times a year.

Since a large amount of clothes, dress fabric, flannel, and other goods come by ship, we do not feel inconvenienced. We may be able to send you these fabrics once in a while.

A headache in your letter is your request to send money to you. As explained to you before, the present law prohibits the Japanese from remitting money. Neither Grandpa, nor Father Kobara, nor I can do it. The only way is to ask Kazuma in Hakalau. When you need money, please contact him in Hakalau. I know you need money for your children.

Since a family of nine lives in a small house, we are quite busy.

These days, stores do not contact us for our daily orders, so I do the shopping for food everyday. Meat is abundant, but vegetables are scarce. Thus, I have to go to three or four shops.

Kayo is busy doing laundry work, as usual. On top of that, she takes care of the vegetables, anthuriums, and orchids. Grandpa is in good health and works hard. On the other hand, he is stubborn and annoys us once in a while. Grandma is busy making straw sandals everyday. She does not know much about cooking and cleaning house. Her job is to cook rice and heat the bath. Since she was born and raised in the countryside, I feel sorry for her. Maybe you should have taught her a little bit more. I pray that peace will return as soon as possible, so that both of us can live comfortably.

When we get old, will we be like the grandparents? It is good to beware due to other men's harm.

Kayo will not let Grandpa do anything. She makes others laugh by saying, "He cannot do anything sensible." She is especially strict. However, please rest assured that we will not do anything that would cause headaches to the old folks. Since both of them came to Honolulu, they have never been sick. They are looking better than we do. I believe that they are happier here than they would have been on the Mainland.

Sometimes, reading your letters, they worry about you people so much that they cannot sleep at night. It is natural that parents love their children and grandchildren. Nonetheless, I feel sorry for them.

Please write letters to them as before, but it is better not to write wishes that cannot be fulfilled. We cannot understand how hard the position is that you have been placed in. In the same way, you may not understand our living conditions as enemy aliens under martial law. We have to endure the present hardship.

I have not written to you for a long time, since I did not want to write these things. Now I have decided to write. As a matter of fact, we do not have much to write. Both the old folks and we are in good health. On top of that, I have become lazy with a pen. Please forgive my long silence.

I do not know how Otokichi-san will feel about this letter, but please let him read this. I will definitely write to him after the turn of the year.

On reading what I wrote, I find that I wrote my one-sided view only. If you find any mistakes, please feel free to let me know. I feel sorry that I cannot do anything much for you, since I am still poor. The business of Father Kobara's is prospering and he is rich. However, since you married into the other family, you cannot depend on him too much. I hear that he bought and sent you various goods. I am thankful to him.

However long I write, I cannot finish. Now let me finish here. Take care.

English original
December 11, 1943[34]
From: J. Lloyd Webb, Counselor, Community Welfare, Jerome Relocation Center, Arkansas
To: Hideko Ozaki, Jerome Relocation Center, Arkansas
Dear <u>Mrs. Hideko Ozaki</u>:

You have been receiving a monthly grant of assistance from the War Relocation Authority in the amount of <u>$10.25</u> because you have no one in your family who is able to work for wages to meet your need for cash income.

Beginning in December, you will receive a monthly clothing allowance of <u>$13.50 </u>instead of the public assistance grant. Such clothing allowances will be provided to families in which there is no person able to work and thus provide cash for clothing and incidentals. If it should become possible for you to work and you refuse to accept a job, you will no longer be eligible for clothing allowance.

If, for some reason, your income including this clothing allowance is not enough to supply you with the necessities, you are welcome to call at the office of the Welfare Section and explain your problems to Miss Saliba. Before additional assistance can be allowed, it will be necessary that you discuss frankly your financial situation.

Sincerely,
J. Lloyd Webb

Date: January 5, 1944[35]
From: Tomoya Ozaki, Honolulu, Hawai'i
To: Otokichi Ozaki, Santa Fe Internment Camp, New Mexico

I have not written for a long time. Your letter dated October 29 arrived at the beginning of December. I was relieved to hear that all of you have been spending your days in good health. Jiji and Baba and the Kobara, Kosaki, and Uejio families are all doing well.

I like to work, so from January of last year, I began working at Kobara's restaurant for $80 a month. I worked continuously through the year, without taking even an hour's rest. I am the *yokozuna** among the twenty or so workers. The wage was raised three

---

*A *sumo* grand champion; but here Tomoya is referring to the likelihood that he is senior among the workers. – Trans.

times to $110 a month with three meals a day. Everyone says, "The old man works hard for his age." Hoping that the wages will be raised again, I have once more begun to work with energy in the New Year.

During the two months of August and September of last year, Kosaki's house underwent extensive renovation work, and we – totaling ten people, including eight from the Kosaki family and the two of us – stayed at the Uejio house during those two months. Jiji and Baba felt so sorry for the Uejio family that we behaved as quietly as borrowed cats.

I am sure that you also are feeling a lack of freedom these days. However, under the present circumstances, this cannot be avoided. Likewise, our life during those months was nothing short of a living hell. Let's pray that peace will come as soon as possible and that we will be able to see each other again.

On the morning of December 15, a baby boy was born to the Uejios.* Both the mother and the baby are fine. Bāsan went to help them from December 13. [The Uejios] are very happy.

Hiromichi Kosaki enlisted in the army as a language specialist at eight o'clock in the morning on January 2. I think he will go to the Mainland.

Yasuo Kawano was killed in battle.

I have been paying thirty-two dollars and some-odd cents in tax annually on the land in Hilo. Since this is too much, I have decided to sell it. If sold, I can send money to you. We cannot spend even a nickel now.

I just now sent $120 to Hideko. Since Hideko left, I have sent $550 to her in total. I do not know how many years this situation will last. I still have some savings, but I have to plan in advance. If the land is sold, I will send the money.

During the last year, I have received a total of $250 from Hideko's father. He is very kind. He gave me $150 in secret from under the [cooking] oil [cans] today. Please do not disclose this to others, including the Kosaki family. This is just between the Kobara father and you and me. Please write a thank you letter to the [Kobara] father for his generosity to me, address the letter, "To our parents," and put it in an envelope and send it to me.

First, I received eight yards of cloth for Hideko from the Kobara family, and I bought another twenty yards, all of which I sent. Then, I paid $6.25 to Mr. Uejio for five yards of fabric, bought an additional fourteen yards, and sent it all. Separately, I received from the Kobara family twenty-eight yards of fabric, a wallet, two pairs of pants, a sweater, and five shirts. I paid some forty dollars

---

*Clifford Kiyoshi

in cash for all of it and sent it to you. Since the Kosakis also have sent [Hideko] a lot of fabric, I hope clothing will not be a problem for them anymore.

The [Kataoka] family in Hakalau is very kind to us. Kazuma-sama takes good care of us.

Thirty-five dollars and several dimes of the *tanomoshi* came back [to me] from Oshima-sama. As to the smaller one, I received $23.65 thanks to the help of Aunt Fujimoto, and I left it with Kazuma-sama.

I sent twenty-five dollars to Kazuma-sama as a Christmas gift, ten dollars to Yoshitaka-kun as a farewell gift, and a piece of high-quality fabric for a dress for Mrs. Kataoka.*

If you need money, I can send some. There are so many things to tell you, but I will write them in the next letter.

Date: January 6 [1944][36]
From: Kazuki Kosaki, Honolulu, Hawai'i
To: Otokichi Ozaki, Santa Fe Internment Camp

Please don't worry about your parents. We'll take good care of them. It's the responsibility of those remaining behind on the home front. Live your life as you see fit and with confidence. Actually, it's Hideko and the children that I feel sorry for. Psychologically this will probably turn out to be one of the most difficult experiences in their lives. I pray you'll be together as a family soon.

Grandfather's such a good worker that he's indispensable to Grandpa Kobara. He earns $120 now, and he was especially happy to receive a $100 bonus for New Year's. On busy days like Sunday, he gets an extra two to three dollars. Wages are going up here as elsewhere, but so is the cost of living. In other words, the value of the dollar is going down.

The government is showing more leniency now. Curfew's been extended to ten o'clock at night, but I don't go out unless I need to. Lights, too, are allowed until ten at night. After that, it's pitch black until five-thirty in the morning. Life's become easier.

It's the first week in January, but the New Year celebration here really leaves something to be desired. People go to work as usual, and we see nothing but men in uniform. Thanks to these soldiers, business is booming. It doesn't feel like New Year's at all.

P.S. Since it's so cold there, I bought long wool socks for you.

---

*Although the Kataokas' son Kazuma is a much younger man, Tomoya refers to him here with the respectful "-*sama*" in order to show his appreciation for the care Kazuma has given to Otokichi's family. Brother Yoshitaka is called by the more informal "-*kun*," implying familiarity and youth. The farewell gift is for Yoshitaka, who has enlisted in the Army. See the letter from Hideko to Ozaki, dated January 7, 1944, p. 149 - Trans.

I'll send them together with some old but unused bowls and tea cups. We can't find Japanese things anymore. The lack of chopsticks is a problem.

Date: January 16 [1944][37]
From: Kazuki Kosaki, Honolulu, Hawai'i
To: Otokichi Ozaki, Santa Fe Internment Camp, New Mexico

The parcel I mailed today contains rice bowls I had bought before 1941 and tea cups I managed to get from a certain store. You'll also find two pairs of wool socks and a pair of slippers that Grandmother made. I wish I could send more things, but perhaps you can look forward to the next parcel. Chopsticks, unfortunately, are not available. Kayo says you can probably make them there, so we should ask you to send us some.

Date: March 8, 1944[38]
From: Tomoya Ozaki, Honolulu, Hawai'i
To: Hideko Ozaki, Jerome Relocation Center, Arkansas; to be forwarded to Otokichi

How have you been? The Kosakis, Kobaras, Uejios, and Jiji and Baba are all doing well. As for the disease in Bāsan's lungs, she had another x-ray yesterday thanks to the kindness of Mr. Uejio. As a result, the doctor says that this is quite common among older people, that it is nothing to worry about, and that it will not infect other people. We all felt quite relieved. Mr. Uejio was kind enough to drive her in his car to and from the hospital. She is taking medications that the doctor previously prescribed. Since she is old, I think it is better for her to eat a lot of nutritious foods and take it easy.

Your father told me that he had dreamed of you a few days ago, and he asked me to convey his best wishes to you. As soon as you see this letter, send this to Otokichi, please. Our faces were pale with worry [about Bāsan], but now we are relieved.

Take care of the children and yourself.

FATHER AND MOTHER IN SEPARATE CAMPS, 1943-1944

> Adversity makes us stronger, so I shall practice forbearance and wait patiently.
>> --Hideko Ozaki, in a letter to Otokichi Ozaki

THIS CHAPTER FOCUSES on the correspondence from Hideko Ozaki to Otokichi Ozaki before the family was reunited—when Mrs. Ozaki and the children were interned at the Jerome Relocation Center in Arkansas, and Ozaki was in Camp Livingston, Louisiana and Santa Fe, New Mexico. These letters document daily life in camp, especially that of the children—their activities, minor illnesses, and concerns. Unfortunately, only a few letters from Mr. Ozaki to his wife are in the collection.

Foremost on the minds of the couple is, of course, the children. Mrs. Ozaki recounts the children's lives in detail, from their school grades to their illnesses and minor injuries. According to Florence Sugimoto, translator of Mrs. Ozaki's letters, her worry and concern over raising four young children on her own in an unfamiliar environment are clearly and emotionally expressed. For example, in one letter Mrs. Ozaki complains to her husband that she is getting fat. While in our twenty-first century society, mentioning getting fat would be viewed as a complaint due to one's vanity, in Japanese culture, gaining weight is considered a good sign, one of prosperity and robust health. What this may be disguising, however, is that Mrs. Ozaki is gaining weight due to inactivity and lethargy. She also comments on her aging appearance, which may be another way of signaling that the strain of camp life is wearing on her.

The other major concern of Mrs. Ozaki is getting the family back together again. In nearly every letter, she mentions her desire to reunite the family, whether it be in another camp or on a ship headed toward Japan. Her children often express missing their father, and Mrs. Ozaki would have no doubt wanted her husband with her to share in the child-raising duties. When Yukio brings home a less than satisfactory report card, or when Yuri comes down with swollen lymph nodes that the doctor's medication does not help, the burden of childcare would have no doubt been alleviated if both parents had been present. Also striking is the effort to maintain the semblance of home and normality, as a turkey dinner is served for Thanksgiving, there is a Christmas play starring the children in camp, and *mochi* is made for the New Year.

The letters in this chapter shed further light on the network of support among the Hawai'i families documented in the previous chapter. Many families back in Hawai'i have sons who enlist in the army and who are sent to Mainland posts. These sons visit Mrs. Ozaki in camp, and she treats them to home-cooked dishes just like their mothers would have made. So just as the families back in Hawai'i support the Ozakis by writing to them and sending them gifts, the Ozakis reciprocate by taking care of their sons who are far from home.

Date: March 10 [1943][1]
From: Hideko Ozaki, Jerome Relocation Center, Arkansas
To: Otokichi Ozaki, Livingston Internment Camp, Louisiana

I received your postcard to Tomoyuki and your letter dated March 1. I feel better now that Mrs. Tagawa,* the Kokuzo family, and the others went there [to Livingston] and learned about the situation at your camp. Tomoyuki and Yukio are going to school, as usual. Sachi is fine, too.

It was a relief when Yuri got over her cold, but then the area around her chin became swollen, so I had the doctor examine her right away. He said the problem was her lymph nodes. I have been applying ointment and giving her medicine orally, but the swelling persists. She had the same problem five or six months ago, and I had her drink some medicine I got from Dr. Yoshina. She got well after two-to-three days. This new swelling is in the same place as the last time. Her body is probably weak. I guess she feels no pain, because she is eating and playing [as usual]. She has no fever, so I think the problem is not serious.

I am waiting for the visitation pass. I think I shall take only Yuri with me. I understand the train gets filled to capacity, and we are discouraged from taking children. I plan to go with Mrs. Ochiai.†She is waiting for my pass to arrive. If we will be together soon, I intend to cancel my visit. After all, as one who speaks no English, the trip would be problematic. Yuri is too young and will

---

* Mrs. Tagawa is Kazu Tagawa, whose husband, Shizuma, was the general manager of American Trading Co. in Hilo. The Kokuzos, Zenkai, a Buddhist priest from Hilo, his wife, Yoshino, and their son, Yoshinao, were all interned. – Trans.

† Katsuko Ochiai, wife of Keikichi Ochiai, a member of the Japanese Chamber of Commerce in Hilo. – Trans.

probably not wait patiently, so I intend to take her and leave the other three children with others. You probably want to see all of them, but please be patient. I hope to make the trip as soon as the pass arrives and Yuri is well again.

I received a letter on March 3 from Brother [Kazuki Kosaki] in Waikīkī. He said that money is not easy to come by, so I should not be extravagant, but I did not mean to be extravagant. I only bought something warm in preparation for the winter, since we have nothing. I wanted one set of clothes for each of the five of us, but there were problems. When I sent my requests all at once, it may have been too much of a shock for my family, but asking for a few things at a time is such a nuisance. I do hope my requests are filled, however, if even a little at a time. I understand it was Hiromichi who sent the last parcel.

I asked for a number of other things I cannot get here, but I suppose they cannot be sent. Oh, well, I guess I shall bear with the inconvenience. The children have been saying that Grandfather will send them candy. They have been looking forward to it day after day and are disappointed [when it does not arrive].

Mrs. Ochiai has been very good to us. She trims our hair. There has been a stage show every week, but I have not seen any of them. Somehow I am not in the mood. I prefer to spend my time with the children. Some of the ladies here will go anywhere to see the shows, but I cannot get into the spirit. I look forward to reading the newspaper. Doing nothing only makes me forget how to write.

Until the next time.

Date: April 13, 1943[2]
From: Hideko Ozaki, Jerome Relocation Center, Arkansas
To: Otokichi Ozaki, Livingston Internment Camp, Louisiana

I feel relieved now that I have seen you. Our group returned safely at 8:30 in the evening, so please be reassured. Apparently we were not expected that night, so the children and our neighbors had gone to see a movie and were not at home. Children do manage without their parents. I was told that Tomoyuki and Yukio worked well together, doing the household cleaning and mopping, while I was away. Sachi behaved well, too, sleeping in the other room. She decided to do the laundry for me, putting all the clothes in the washtub and using her little hands to scrub them. The woman next door saw that and took it upon herself to do the work. I feel badly about it. [According to her] the children were very good, and there was no fighting whatsoever. I had not brought home any gifts for them, because there was no time, but none of them complained.

It was wonderful to see you after a year and two or three months. I was shocked to see so much gray in your hair. You must have had a difficult time this past year, but thank goodness, your health has been good. I was not able to buy those carpenter tools on the way back [from Jerome]. I have been told I cannot order them at this time either, which presents a problem. If we cannot be reunited as a family for quite a while, I hope to visit you again. Mrs. Koide may be going again, too, [to visit her husband].*

I must write to our parents in Honolulu right away to reassure them [about my visit]. I should have told them sooner about my safe return, but I have been busy and I am still in a daze [from the trip]. I am sorry for the delay in writing to you.

Until the next time.

Date: April 27, 1943[3]
From: Hideko Ozaki, Jerome Relocation Center, Arkansas
To: Otokichi Ozaki, Livingston Internment Camp, Louisiana

How are you? We are fine, so please be reassured. If there is no possibility that we will be living together anytime soon, I hope to take the children to see you in May. Please send visitation passes right away for ten-year-old Tomoyuki, seven-year-old Yukio, five-year-old Sachi, three-year-old Yuri, and me. It will be costly, but I think you would like to see the children too, so I have decided to do it. I also have a little more experience now. Of course, there is no need for all the expense, if we will be together soon, so please keep that in mind and send a reply.

Tomoyuki and Yukio are to have their tonsils removed on the twenty-eighth. Sachi goes eagerly to kindergarten every day. I wish our family back home would send money quickly. Other families here are receiving some, but I suppose not everyone knows how to make the necessary arrangements.

I bought some dried shrimp and will send it to you. I also ordered some *miso* for you and was surprised by how much it costs. The shrimp is so expensive – seventy-five cents a pound! I also ordered *shōyu*,† so I shall take it with me [when I visit you].

Once in a while, please write to the Nakauchi boy. Mrs. Koide has received her pass but does not plan to use it for now. If this separation continues, she suggests we go together to visit our husbands. Mrs. Takeda has received her pass today and says she

---

* Masakatsu Koide, the wife of Shoichi Koide, an employee of the *Volcano Times* in Hilo. While she was in Jerome, her husband was with Ozaki in Livingston. – Trans.
† Soy sauce

will join us.

Until the next time.

Date: May 11, 1943[4]
From: Hideko Ozaki, Jerome Relocation Center, Arkansas
To: Otokichi Ozaki, Livingston Internment Camp, Louisiana

I read your two letters dated May 2 and May 4. It must be quite hot there, too. The heat here is wearing me down. I dread to think what it will be like in the coming days. The children are all fine. Yuri is completely well and running around again. School has been in session for only a half-day since yesterday, probably because of the heat, but it begins early and the children have trouble getting up. I cannot help but worry that they have too much extra time for play.

There was something like a classroom visitation for parents on the night of the seventh, so I attended with the children. There were report cards and drawings displayed on the walls. Tomoyuki and Yukio are not doing too badly. I think Yukio is poor in reading. His spelling is good. At lunchtime I had seen Tomoyuki working on a picture of a palm tree with the sun behind it. He drew it quite well. There was a student performance, too. Children, dressed as all kinds of flowers, danced at a wedding ceremony for two very young children dressed as the bride and groom. I understand the wedding costumes were special-made.

The very first high school graduation ceremony at this camp was held on the eighth. The students in their blue caps and gowns looked like college graduates. It was an impressive ceremony with a large crowd in attendance. It reminded me of our school a year ago. It was so hectic then.

It rained a little in the morning, and the loud thunder was frightening. I understand lightning fell twice not far from us. Here one can see it even in the daytime. At night it is a very pretty sight. This area seems to be famous for its loud thunder. For three days, beginning on the seventh, there was an arts-and-crafts exhibit sponsored by the Denson Women's Club.* Embroidery work, knitted articles, hand-made flowers and the like were on display. My contributions were a scarf and a bedspread.

For Mother's Day, on the ninth, the young people did all the work in the mess hall, latrines, bathing area, etc. We mothers had a pleasant day of rest. Sachi said she would do the mopping and worked with her little hands. Yuri said she would walk without being carried and played nicely. Their thoughtful gestures brought

---

* The Jerome camp was located in the city of Denson, Arkansas. – Trans.

tears to my eyes. Yes, you're really out of luck, if you don't have girls.

On this Mother's Day, about ten of the older women gathered to play volleyball. Feeling ten years younger, I played to my heart's content, but I probably will not get over the pain in my legs for a while. No more volleyball for me.

A few days ago I received a letter from Matsuko Sakai. It seems that eight young men enlisted and are on the Mainland now: Yahata-san, Mitsuo-san, Goto-san, Kubota-san, Sato Takeo-san, Toyama-san, Watanabe Sanji-san, and Nakamura Saburo-san.* I may be able to see them one of these days. I wrote back [to Matsuko] right away. I understand Toru-san is here [on the Mainland], too. How unfortunate for Basuya-san.† He was very good to us.

This letter has gotten quite long. I shall be waiting for the pass. It may be the end of May or the beginning of June, when I can make the trip.

Who knows when we will be able to live together? I can only bide my time and wait.

Date: May 31 [1943][5]
From: Hideko Ozaki, Jerome Relocation Center, Arkansas
To: Otokichi Ozaki, Livingston Internment Camp, Louisiana

I received two letters, one sent on the nineteenth, the other on the twenty-first. I am happy to hear you are well. Now that your address will be changing, you must be preparing for the move. What a shame it is that I cannot take the children to see you. All I can do now is wait for the day when we can be settled in the Family Center quarters. ‡

Tomoyuki and Yukio had their tonsils removed on the twenty-eighth. Yukio was released from the hospital on the twenty-ninth, but Tomoyuki stayed an extra day because of continued bleeding, and he returned on the thirtieth. They are fine, but swallowing is difficult, so I am giving them fruit juice, *okayu*,§ *miso* soup, and the like. They should be back to normal in two-to-three days. I think I shall keep them out of school for about a week. I had

* All are residents of 'Amauulu. – Trans.

† Lit., "Mr. Bus Man." This is most likely the nickname for Ichiro Kasai, who was an employee of a bus service in Hilo. By late 1943, he was with Ozaki in Santa Fe, where he remained until the end of the war. See his June 1945 letter to Ozaki, p. 210. – Trans.

‡ Crystal City Internment Camp, located in south Texas. Crystal City housed internees of Japanese, German, and Italian descent, along with Latin American Japanese, initially intended to be exchanged for American POWs. Also known as the "Family Camp," because it held Issei and their families, Crystal City was one of the largest camps, with a peak population of some 4,000. – Trans.

§ Rice porridge

been worried, but the good doctors here gave me no cause to be concerned.

Sachi goes to kindergarten every day. When she brings home art work, she asks if it can be sent to you. Now she can even write her name, Alice, in English. Going to school is important, after all. Yuri is healthy and plays nicely every day. No longer does she cry at night, and she has been sleeping well, since having been weaned from the bottle. I guess she has gotten stronger physically. Once she says something she will not easily change her mind. She is exactly like her mother (giggle).

The *tsukemono* I asked Mrs. Takeda to take to you probably was not very tasty. It was just that I thought you might enjoy something different.

I often write to the families in Honolulu and Hakalau. About four days ago I received a letter from Hakalau, which said that everyone is fine. If the grandfathers [in Honolulu] approve, the family [in Hakalau] will send the money [I requested]. I understand [Grandfather] earns ninety dollars as a dishwasher. The expenses for the two of them [Grandfather and Grandmother] probably are less than half that amount. The word is that Grandfather has gained eight pounds and looks ten years younger. He claims that his work is more like play compared to working in the cane field. The thirty-first marks the ninth year since Younger Brother passed away, which brings back all sorts of memories. As I thought about him, I felt so sorry. I think I shall buy some fruits and place them on the [Buddhist] altar.

A letter from Older Brother [Kazuki Kosaki] gave details regarding the insurance. The insurance company says it will not pay out the policy even though it has matured, because this is wartime. If we return to Japan on the exchange ship, payment will not be made either.

The children don't like to write letters, and it is a problem. Since [the boys] are at home now, I shall have them do it. This letter is getting too long, so I shall write again. You need not worry about Tomoyuki and Yukio. They should be fine in a week.

Date: June 3 [1943][6]
From: Earl Tomoyuki Ozaki, Jerome Relocation Center, Arkansas
To: Otokichi Ozaki, Livingston Internment Camp, Louisiana

I'm sorry I didn't write for a long time. Mother is always scolding me about this. I'm staying home from school now, so I decided to write.

On the twenty-eighth of last month, Yukio and I had our

tonsils taken out. Yukio went home the day after the operation, but I still had bleeding so I had to stay in the hospital for three days. For a while I couldn't eat any kind of food, even though I wanted to, but I'm all right now. I'm going back to school next week.

I was happy when Mother said she was going to take us to see you, so I was disappointed when it didn't happen. I guess we'll just have to wait.

It's been five months since we got here. It was cold at first, and we even had snow, which I saw for the first time. Now it's hot. We are playing hard and getting tanned.

There are lots of fireflies now. I was going out with my friends every night to catch them, but then Mother said, "I don't want you to get eaten by the snakes, so don't go out anymore." So that put an end to it.

A few days ago, Hidemi sent from Honolulu some model airplanes he made, but they were broken when I got them. I bought glue to fix them, but the pieces won't stick together. I have no other toys, so I'm playing with them anyway.

I heard that you're working with *oshibana*.* Please show me some the next time.

Date: June 10, 1943[7]
From: Hideko Ozaki, Jerome Relocation Center, Arkansas
To: Otokichi Ozaki, Santa Fe Internment Camp, New Mexico

I read your letters dated May 25 and May 31.

I am happy to hear you are all right. By now your address probably has changed. The change in surroundings may be good for you. Living in the same place can become depressing. We are fine, so please be reassured. Yuri, too, is fine. Two or three days ago she began saying she was going to school, which created a problem. She may be too young, so I had thought of postponing it for a while, telling her that a child who must be carried piggyback cannot expect to go to school. This morning she got up early, said she was going to walk to school, then went to the mess hall [for breakfast], singing in a loud voice a song Sachi had learned. Since she wants to go so badly, I am considering taking her. What do you think?

If this kind of life must go on much longer, I am afraid I must find work. By coincidence there are jobs now for waiters and waitresses. What do you think? Since I would need to leave for work at about five-thirty in the morning, it may be a hardship

---

* Pressed flowers

for the children, but I do want to work. I don't know what to do. Spending thirty to forty dollars every month without working makes me feel helpless. I am considering other options. Please give me your opinion. Three days ago I received one hundred dollars from Hakalau. I am very thankful. If you need something I shall order it, so please let me know.

According to Kazuma's letter, Mr. Tango has asked several times that we write to 'Amauulu. I have sent a letter to Mr. Tango and no one else, because I do not want to create problems. I correspond with only our families and brothers and sisters.

When Mrs. Koide left on her trip [to see her husband], I could have gone too, if the bus had still been here. What a shame. She brought back candies and other things I had asked for, and the children were very happy.

Sachi, too, needs to have her tonsils taken out. Should we wait until she is a little older? It would be a problem if she has continued bleeding after surgery. The two boys are fine, and they are back in school. Children heal quickly. Exchange ships seem to be available, according to the newspaper, but my prayers are more about being together as soon as possible.

Until the next time.

Date: July 2 [1943][8]
From: Hideko Ozaki, Jerome Relocation Center, Arkansas
To: Otokichi Ozaki, Santa Fe Internment Camp, New Mexico

There was nothing following the letter that said you had reached Santa Fe safely, so I had been worrying every day. I feel better now that I have read today's letter. Some residents here receive letters about every other day. I begin to worry if I don't receive one once a week.

After reading about the huge fire, I worried all the more, wondering if anyone had been injured. Fortunately everything turned out well. We here are doing well, too. The children go to school everyday. The weather has turned cooler these past few days, which is very good. It was so cool this morning that I had to take out a sweater. Of course, when it gets too hot it is unbearable, even though I may not be doing anything. Still, when I think of the soldiers [in battle] I cannot complain. Adversity makes us stronger, so I shall practice forbearance and wait patiently.

I sent you twenty-five dollars the other day by telegram, but I suppose it has not reached you yet. I understand you are allowed to carry cash, so I sent a small amount. If you need clothing, please let me know. I have some money with me, so you need not request any from Hakalau.

This coming Saturday, I understand about thirty people from Hawai'i, who are in Mississippi and play baseball, will be here. I am waiting to see if there will be someone I know in the group. I am learning to sew in my free time, but I have no sewing machine, so I am using someone else's. It is so sad. I should have brought everything from home with me.

Camp residents from the Mainland are growing vegetables for their meals. Cucumbers, tomatoes, beans, cantaloupe, green onions and other vegetables grow very well. Those of us who are expecting to go to the Family Center regret not growing anything; after all, we still could have enjoyed the food. Some of us feel there is still time and have begun planting seeds. We cannot even be sure when we will get to live together. I shall just think of it happening this year.

Sachi can be irritable. Sometimes she gets up in the morning and announces she will not go to school, which creates a problem. Then Yuri speaks up, saying she will go to school in her sister's place, so I should dress her right away. Placed in an awkward position, Sachi changes her mind and goes to school.

Tomoyuki kept begging me to get him a baseball glove and ball, so I have given in and decided to order them. The poor boy has nothing to read or play with. The cost will be only about two dollars, so I have decided to do it. The two boys have promised to share the set and play nicely.

You must have enjoyed meeting new people from Hawai'i [who are in Santa Fe]. It must have been rejuvenating.

Until the next time.

Date: July 10 [1943][9]
From: Hideko Ozaki, Jerome Relocation Center, Arkansas
To: Otokichi Ozaki, Santa Fe Internment Camp, New Mexico

I am sure you are fine. We are all doing well every day in this hot weather.

I understand that the Spanish consul went there on the seventh and answered questions about the sixteen items.* It seems to be taking forever to get the Family Center built. I guess I shall just wait patiently. It seems that there may be an exchange [ship] soon, but here again no details have been given, so we cannot count on it.

---

* See the minutes to a similar meeting held at the Fort Missoula Internment Camp in December 1943, Ch. 3, p. 56

Yesterday, I chatted with the temple minister's wife,* whom I had not seen in a while, and we spent about two hours together. No matter whom I talk to, the main topic is family reunion. Her two children are fine. The elder daughter, quite grown up, is very bright. Her father would surely be happy, if he could see her. Last night there was a variety show at Block 11. Sachi and Yukio danced, and they did well. It was the first time I had seen them perform. On the way home Yuri fell asleep, so I *oppa*-ed† her. I was so tired, and my shoulders and back ached.

Watermelons are in season now, and we can get some delicious ones. When I think how much better they would taste chilled, I wish I were back in 'Amauulu. When the children see others with watermelons, they pester me to buy a watermelon for them, too. I do buy the fruit often, but it is expensive, so I struggle to avoid overspending.

Mumps is going around now. The lady next door has it. One of her children has already recovered, but the other two have it now. I have my fingers crossed that it will not get passed on to me, but it probably will, since we are next door and the children play together. I understand the quarantine period is three weeks. How inconvenient. Yukiko, who goes with Sachi to kindergarten, also has the mumps, so Sachi will have to go to school alone beginning Monday. She says she will not go, making things difficult. I shall have to take her for the time being. There has been no word from Hawai'i. Are you receiving any letters?

Until the next time.

Date: July 21 [1943][10]
From: Hideko Ozaki, Jerome Relocation Center, Arkansas
To: Otokichi Ozaki, Santa Fe Internment Camp, New Mexico

I had been happy to see your letters arriving so quickly, but now it takes about a week before I receive one. I read your letter of the fourteenth, and I am happy to hear that the weather is good and you are well.

For about three days it was so uncomfortably hot here that we dripped with perspiration. It was really unbearable. At night the bed felt so hot that it was difficult to fall asleep until after midnight. I feared those of us who are not accustomed to the heat would become ill if this continued. Fortunately it is a little cooler today, and I feel better.

We are doing well. The family next door and the one in front

---

* This is most likely Yoshino Kokuzo; see Hideko's letter to Ozaki, March 10 [1943], p. 126 – Trans.
† Pidgin: to carry piggyback style

have the mumps, but they are [otherwise] fine. If possible, I would just as soon not come down with it. Yuri and Sachi seem to be unfazed by the heat and continue to play hard. Their clothes are so full of dirt that cleaning them is somewhat of a problem, but I am happy because what is important is that they are well.

Tomoyuki's grades are mostly "A's," while Yukio's are much lower. I think Yukio is a little slower. We need not worry too much about Tomoyuki. Mrs. Aoki, who says too much play leads to delinquency, has had the boys make *geta* and has let them play with all kinds of toys at her barrack. Mrs. Aoki's husband has them do *sumō* and play ball games. [Tomoyuki and Yukio] get along well with the two [Aoki] boys, and they go everywhere together. They do not play with others. Sachi goes to school every day. I understand she will be able to go to the first grade in September. I think she is receiving extra help at school to prepare for the transition. She can write her name nicely, but arithmetic seems to be quite difficult for her. She spends her free time practicing [her writing]. Many of the letters she writes are reversed, but time will probably take care of that. Yuri is like Tomoyuki and loves books. When her brother has one [in his hands], she looks on quietly. It is a shame that there is a shortage of books. I practice sewing in my spare time.

On the seventeenth and the eighteenth Obon dances* were held. About 3,000 people attended, and about 500 of them were dressed in beautiful multi-colored kimono. It was the first time I had seen an Obon dance like that. It was a spectacular sight.

You mentioned meeting many old friends [there]. What a small world this is. One can never tell who one will meet. The accident sometime ago must have caused many problems. I feel for you. It seems unlikely that families will be reunited before October, and everyone seems resigned to it. The rumor is that the exchange ship will be leaving next month. I heard that some people have already been notified [that they will be on the ship]. I have no idea when it will be our turn. I continue to pray that we will be living together before long.

Until the next time.

_____

Date: July 29 [1943][11]
From: Hideko Ozaki, Jerome Relocation Center, Arkansas
To: Otokichi Ozaki, Santa Fe Internment Camp, New Mexico

_____

* Dances that are part of the annual Buddhist Bon Festival (Obon), occurring in July or August, to welcome visiting ancestor spirits. Participants in summer cotton kimono (*yukata*) dance in unison around a raised platform (*yagura*), upon which accompanying musicians and singers perform. – Trans.

I kept waiting and waiting for your letter to arrive, and before I knew it a whole week had gone by. I do not understand it, but letters for others at this camp are dated the same day as yours, yet they arrive one week sooner than the letters for me. Today I received your letter dated the eighteenth.

It is a relief to know that you seem to be fine. We are well, too, but exactly one week ago Sachi finally came down with the mumps. An infectious disease warning sign printed in red letters was posted on the door, and no one could go out. Sachi had a high fever for about two days, but with the rest and quiet, the swelling is gone, and she is full of high energy again. For about two days she really looked like Okame.* Besides being chubby, she had that puffiness—on both sides, now—so you can imagine how she looked. Now I worry that our other children may get the mumps, too. All of the children next door have gotten over it. It seems that communicable diseases are unavoidable.

The wife of the temple minister† came twice to give us the latest information. Her family is fine. It seems that disloyals and internees requesting repatriation are to be sent to Tule Lake. We will probably be going there, too. The authorities in Washington have probably notified those of you in Santa Fe who are to be sent to relocation centers to join their families. Where we go makes no difference to me, as long as we can live together. The sooner it happens, the better. The ladies here gather and talk about the prospects, so our children are happily talking about the day they will join you. The children next door have said their father has written that their family will be together soon, and even the youngest one is excited about it. I guess the desire to be together is the same for everyone.

I understand the new mess hall has been completed, which is good. For the children, I bought just one toy. A slightly larger blackboard would come in handy, but if we are to move soon, it would be better to have less luggage to carry, so I am reconsidering that idea. What do you think? Whenever Tomoyuki is free, he works on the so-called puzzle that I bought for him. I also spent two dollars on dolls for the two girls, but they break things, so it is discouraging.

We are being served all kinds of fresh vegetables lately, which is unusual for this time of year. I am glad that we can often eat tomato, cucumber, cantaloupe, and eggplant. Light and refreshing, they whet the appetite in burning hot weather. I often order *miso*

---

* A comic mask of a laughing woman with fat cheeks, it is a symbol of prosperity and is also known as Otafuku. Okame is usually paired with the male mask Hyottoko, and they are often worn during comic dances and plays that are a part of rural agricultural festivals. – Trans.
† This is likely Yoshino Kokuzo. – Trans.

and make soup for the children. I hope to do some knitting for winter wear, so I ordered about ten dollars' worth of yarn today. In his letter, Grandfather said I should send a letter to Hilo, but I shall not write to anyone.

This is getting too long, so I shall end here.

Until the next time.

Date: August 5 [1943][12]
From: Hideko Ozaki, Jerome Relocation Center, Arkansas
To: Otokichi Ozaki, Santa Fe Internment Camp, New Mexico

Today I received the letter you postmarked [July] thirtieth. It was an unexpected and pleasant surprise to receive two letters this week. Everyone waits eagerly for the mail. We may not write any letters, but we look forward to receiving them. Human beings are so self-serving.

I am happy to hear you are busy and well. We are fine. Sachi has gotten over the mumps and has received permission to return to school next Monday. The rest of the children are mumps-free, but I am not sure for how long. In other families, no one has been spared. It seems that only bad things spread. I worry most when the children become ill. As of now, they are healthy, so I have gotten as plump as a pig. When I see my friends, they invariably tell me I have gained weight. What a problem. Since two or three of my dresses have become too small, I must have put on pounds. I am still taking sewing lessons in my spare time, but the hot weather makes it difficult to sew. I feel like doing nothing in the afternoon. The sweltering heat is giving the children heat rash.

I understand that the "disloyals" will soon be segregated from the "loyals" at each relocation center. We will probably be sent to Tule Lake. We should know by the end of the month. I hope we go to the Family Center—the sooner, the better. Since I have persevered up to now, I shall be patient for a while longer. Please make many pairs of *geta* and have them ready, because we can use them all. The roads are bad, so the *geta* will wear out quickly. Yuri's *sashi-geta** was not wearable, because the support came off. You need not send another pair, however. Instead, please take good care of it until we join you. I have bought a ball and glove set, so that should be enough.

The children next door are well now. Every day they have been excitedly waiting for their father to come home. Whenever they

---

* The exact term is *sashiba-geta*; the *sashiba* being the support, or "teeth," of the *geta*. Hideko uses the term *sashi-geta* to describe *geta* in which the "teeth" were inserted into the platform, as opposed to *geta* that are carved from one solid piece of wood. – Trans.

see a train go by, they eagerly say, "Daddy's come home!" How pitiful. They probably miss him.

I think it will not be long before we are together again. Let us be in good spirits and be in good health when we meet.

Until the next time.

_____

English original
Date: August 7, 1943[13]
From: Paul A. Taylor, Project Director, Jerome Relocation Center, Arkansas*
To: Hideko Ozaki, Jerome Relocation Center, Arkansas

In accordance with a recent announcement of the Director of the War Relocation Authority, it is now the policy of the Authority to locate in a separate relocation center those persons of Japanese ancestry presently residing in various relocation centers who prefer to live in Japan, or whose declarations have indicated that their loyalties lie with Japan during the present hostilities, or that their loyalties do not lie with the United States.

This position has been taken in order to promote the general welfare and to provide a place of protection for those evacuees who are known to favor the cause of Japan.

You have by your acts or declarations indicated your desire to live in Japan, or that you are sympathetic to the war aims of that country, or that you are not loyal to the United States.

It will be necessary that you transfer to the Tule Lake Center. You should discuss this situation with your family group. The representatives of the Welfare Section will be at Block 38 messhall at 10:30 AM, Sunday, August 8, 1943 to interview all of the repatriate or expatriate families of your block.

At the interview with the Welfare representative, each member of your family should be present. Each and every member of your family who has not requested repatriation or expatriation should be prepared to indicate what he or she has elected to do – whether to accompany you to the Tule Lake Center, or whether to live elsewhere. Plan for family welfare should be discussed.

After the decision has been made in regard to the plans of your family, you will be notified of the date the transportation has been arranged for you and certain other important items and information regarding the preparation for travel and transfer.
Very truly yours,
Paul A. Taylor

_____

* Taylor was the administrative head of the camp. – Trans.

Date: August 10 [1943][14]
From: Hideko Ozaki, Jerome Relocation Center, Arkansas
To: Otokichi Ozaki, Santa Fe Internment Camp, New Mexico

On the ninth, I received your letter dated August 2. I am glad to hear that you are well and very busy. We are fine, too. Yuri came down with the mumps yesterday. Apparently it cannot be avoided. Everyone else will probably get it, but it is not a frightening disease, so please do not worry. There is swelling on both sides, but Yuri is fine, and the four children are noisily chasing each other now. As I write this letter, I am scolding them for the loud commotion. What is most distressing is that they cannot go outside. Yuri does not go to school, so there is no problem, but the two boys will miss three weeks of instruction if they get the mumps. Sachi has been back in school since yesterday. She is preparing for the first grade and is studying hard. On each page, she practiced writing her name and basic numerals and took both papers to school today. Her writing has gotten much better.

I received the notice about going to Tule Lake, and I was questioned about it on Sunday. It was nothing out of the ordinary. Since I do not know if you will be paroled, it is not possible to know where we will go. Those paroled will probably go to Tule Lake, but those who are not paroled will probably go to the Family Center. In either case, we must leave this camp. My reply was that I would like to decide after you make your decision. More information should be coming from Washington. People are saying that families will probably be together by about October. In any case, it may be best not to count on it.

After sending you some *nori-no-tsukudani** I found at the [camp] store, I learned from Mrs. Koide that you have it there, too. She said her husband had sent her some, in which case it will not be very special [for you]. On the other hand, our *tsukudani* may be tastier, so please try it with that in mind.

I understand the weather is good there, and I am very envious. It is so hot here that I cannot fall asleep until past midnight. Just as I feel comfortable and begin to doze off, I must get up. You can imagine how I look as I rub my sleepy eyes and go off to wash my face. I feel most sorry for the children. I guess Hawai'i is the best place to live. Everyone here is suffering from heat rash and scratching away at their itching bodies. It is unbearable.

Please make as many *geta* as possible and have them ready for us.

Until the next time.

---

* Soy sauce-seasoned seaweed.

Date: August 20 [1943][15]
From: Hideko Ozaki, Jerome Relocation Center, Arkansas
To: Otokichi Ozaki, Santa Fe Internment Camp, New Mexico

I see that interviews were conducted at your camp, too; however, we will probably not be among those boarding the exchange ship leaving soon. I understand that only single men and those with very young children qualify for this trip, so we cannot expect to be considered this year. Now that the matter has been settled, I can concentrate on my knitting. No longer will I believe those rumors about family reunification. The word was that it would take place in August, but nothing has come of it. The transfer to Tule Lake seems to have been dropped, and we are to be sent directly to the Family Camp. This, too, may change. Oh, well, I shall wait patiently for the day we are allowed to be together again.

Date: not dated [sometime between August 14 - 27, 1943][16]
From: Hideko Ozaki, Jerome Relocation Center, Arkansas
To: Otokichi Ozaki, Santa Fe Internment Camp, New Mexico

I received your letter of August 14. I guess the *tsukudani* was nothing unusual, after all. All of us here are fine. Tomoyuki is still not able to go to school, but I think he will be permitted to do so soon. For now it seems that we are not scheduled to go to Tule Lake. I understand the Family Camp will be our destination, but I doubt we can count on it.

Those who are returning to Japan on the exchange ship are working furiously to prepare for the trip. I went to help the Higashi Hongwanji Temple minister's family with their packing.* When we were in Hilo, we imposed on them a number of times, so I left a token farewell gift of ten dollars. I am thinking of making a similar token gift to Sumie and to the person from Honolulu. The rumor is that the group will be leaving this coming Saturday, so everyone is busy. I am praying that we will be able to live together as soon as possible.

I presume Koryu-san† and the others are fine.

Every Saturday, a number of enlisted men from Hawai'i, who are here on the Mainland, take turns and pay us a visit. Yesterday it brought back memories, when I met Luna-san.‡ He laughingly

---

* Rev. Takeo Akegarasu of Hilo, his wife, and their two children. – Trans.

† Tadasuke Koryu Nakabayashi – Trans.

‡ The name appears as ルナさん. Thus, it is unclear whether this is a personal name, or possibly a nickname based on the Hawaiian word *luna*, which means foreman or boss, and was widely used to refer to supervisors on the sugar and pineapple plantations. – Trans.

said he had been naughty in school, but that he is now a "good boy." This weekend I understand that about seventy soldiers will be coming to see us. Someone I know may be among them, so I am looking forward to the visit. It will be like old times to see friends from Hilo.

This morning I went to see Mrs. Arakawa.* It was a social call, and we talked about her family. She was shocked [to hear that the Ozaki children had contracted mumps]. Sensei,† too, had come down with the mumps, and after resting for about three weeks, returned to work yesterday. Since my arrival [at this camp], I have made only about three social visits. Although the distance is not great, going out is not a simple task. I am focused on knitting right now. I have no cooking to do, so I can do a great deal of knitting, but it makes my shoulders ache. At this point there is no one to scold, and the children get along nicely, which is good. I received a registered mail notice, so I am going to the post office. The money has probably arrived.

Until the next time.

Date: October 23 [1943][17]
From: Hideko Ozaki, Jerome Relocation Center, Arkansas
To: Otokichi Ozaki, Santa Fe Internment Camp, New Mexico

Thank you for the letter. I am glad to hear you are doing well. We, too, are passing the days in good health, so please be reassured.

Mornings and nights here are very cold, but during the day sweaters are not needed, so the weather is not really cold. I am very sorry about Mr. Odachi's death.‡ I immediately went to see his wife to express my condolences. I feel for her and the four children. If the family had been together, Mr. Odachi could have been cared for by his wife and children. He could have died a happier man. With the great distance separating them, there was nothing they could do, which makes it all the more unfortunate. Let us resolve to take care of ourselves.

I received your parcel the other day. There was so much candy that I wondered if some of it was meant for someone else. I worried about it as we helped ourselves, but I did give some of the candy to five or six of our friends. In our present circumstances,

---

* Possibly Haru Arakawa, the wife of a civil engineer from Hilo, Frank Futoshi. The family, including six children, was interned at Jerome. – Trans.

† I.e., the camp doctor. – Trans.

‡ Kinzaemon Odachi of Hilo, a priest of the Tenrikyō sect, died on October 21, 1943 in Santa Fe. His wife, Kameki, and children Michiko, Masako, Mitsuko, and Michio were interned at Jerome at the time of his death. – Trans.

we all try to share whatever we have. It's delicious!

Yukio has been waiting every day and wondering what you will send him. I have told him he cannot expect to get a reply so soon after having written to you.

Did you receive the photograph of your parents? They seem to be fine, so you need not worry. The Higashi Hongwanji minister and his family probably reached the exchange point and safely boarded the exchange ship.* It is a long trip, so they are probably exhausted.

About twenty Nisei soldiers have come for a visit, but there seems to be no one I know. It would make me so happy to see our [former] students. There are some soldiers who are embarrassed about being recognized and hide their faces. My guess is that they were like that, too, when they were in school.

Yuri goes to school regularly. I suppose it is still a new experience for her. In the middle of the night, she cries for no particular reason, which concerns me. She must feel frustrated. As time passes and she gets better adjusted, she will probably get over it. Among the four children, I think she requires the least attention. She seems to understand English well, learns songs and sings them, too. Her older brothers and sister are there to teach her, so she probably learns quickly. We are all happy that our letters reach you so quickly.

Your birthday is coming soon. How old will you be? I no longer look forward to my birthdays and the added years.

Until the next time.

Date: November 22 [1943][18]
From: Hideko Ozaki, Jerome Relocation Center, Arkansas
To: Otokichi Ozaki, Santa Fe Internment Camp, New Mexico

We had warm and comfortable weather the last two-to-three days, but it is a little cooler today.

The elderly gentleman [internee], who left yesterday, stopped by earlier, accompanied by his daughter-in-law. The news they provided about the situation at your camp gave me a sense of relief. Their Tosa dialect† made me feel as though Grandfather and my sister were speaking to me. I was teary-eyed after hearing the woman's story about the assistance you provided until her father-in-law was paroled. I can understand how anyone in a

---

* The Akegarasu family travelled aboard the second exchange ship when they repatriated to Japan. The point at which those of Japanese ethnicity were exchanged for those of U.S. nationality was Goa, India. – Trans.

† Tosa is the traditional name for today's Kōchi prefecture, from where the Tomoya Ozaki family immigrated. – Trans.

similar situation would want to do everything possible to bring a family together. It was Friday night when the gentleman left, but I understand the family had shared stories throughout Thursday night until the next morning. I can imagine how happy his wife must be. The daughter-in-law knows your brother well. Some people do not like to deal with the elderly, but you were very helpful, and both father and daughter-in-law were grateful. They asked that we consider them as relatives and treat them as such. I thought it was so nice of them to say that. Apparently, the gentleman had been given something from you to deliver to me, but his luggage had still not arrived. I will probably receive it sometime soon. I was also able to meet the other person. The most welcome news is that you are well.

On Saturday night there was a thirtieth-day memorial service for deceased members of the Tenrikyō religious group. Internee families in attendance made token condolence gifts, which were collected and presented as a group offering. I felt so sorry for the mourning families, and tears welled up in my eyes. I extend my deepest sympathies to them.

The scarf is almost finished, but I am a little short of yarn. I have already ordered some, so please wait.

Date: November 25 [1943][19]
From: Hideko Ozaki, Jerome Relocation Center, Arkansas
To: Otokichi Ozaki, Santa Fe Internment Camp, New Mexico

Yesterday morning after my sewing lesson, it was firewood chopping all afternoon until five o'clock. I was so exhausted that I went straight to bed, after making sure the children had their bath. Yukio made one mistake in his spelling test yesterday, although I had helped him with the ten words to be studied. I scolded him for misspelling the word for tomorrow's dinner – turkey.

It is very cold this morning, so we promptly used the heating pad you sent through a third party. I told the children to stay in bed and left to help with the chopping of firewood again. As we worked, Mrs. Koide and I reminisced about our Thanksgiving celebrations in Hilo.

As I write this letter, the laundry and ironing are all done. I can hear the Japanese music—primarily pop songs—from the radio next door. It must be coming from within this camp. Sigh . . . those were the days.

Today we received a large fruitcake from Sears. We could not tell whom it was from, but we guessed it was you.

This evening we had our Thanksgiving dinner and a special

program of songs and dances by children and grown-ups.

Date: November 26 [1943][20]
From: Hideko Ozaki, Jerome Relocation Center, Arkansas
To: Otokichi Ozaki, Santa Fe Internment Camp, New Mexico

It was quite cold this morning, and the children would not get up, so I went to the mess hall alone. I had nothing special to do, so after finishing the laundry I worked on my knitting. It was a few minutes after eleven o'clock, when I heard the mail carrier's footsteps. When I went outside, I was told I had four letters and a parcel. I was very happy to receive so many letters. They were from [the Kataokas of] Hakalau, Grandfather [Tomoya], the mother of Mitsuo in 'Amauulu,* and Nishioka-san.

I guess the elders are fine. My father and older brother and sister are also well. A news article about Tule Lake came with their letter. The strong message from Grandfather was that since the government is looking after us, we must do nothing disloyal. I have been asked to relay this message to you as well. I received three *zabuton*† that I had requested. Aunty‡ also sent some dress fabric for the children and me. Her frequent acts of kindness are appreciated. I understand that Mrs. Kubota of 'Amauulu and Mrs. Fujimoto asked her about us and that they became teary-eyed after hearing about us.

Someone seems to be interested in buying our property. He is a poetry friend of yours and runs a restaurant now, but he used to be the druggist at the Matayoshi Clinic.§ What shall we do? I am in favor of selling. We need to send a response, so please let me know right away. The yearly tax is thirty dollars, as you know, which presents a problem. You may want to send a letter directly to Hakalau.

I learned that the Missus was seen recently.¶ She said that she would feel lonely if the Ozakis were to sell the land, for she would lose her connection to 'Amauulu. She also said that everyone is waiting for our return.

Mrs. Tachibana sent a thank-you card for the hospitality we extended to her son, Mitsuo, when he paid a visit during his furlough. We gave him our recent photograph, which he sent to

---

* Mitsuo Tachibana was a member of the 442nd Regimental Combat Team. His father, Shingo, was a farmer in 'Amauulu. – Trans.
† Floor cushions
‡ This is probably Momoe Kataoka of Hakalau. – Trans.
§ A clinic run by the physician Zenko Matayoshi of Hilo. – Trans.
¶ This paragraph in its original Japanese form is very ambiguous. Hideko has omitted many of the subjects and objects in the sentences. – Trans.

his mother. She says that when she saw how much the children had grown and how well they looked, she felt as though she had seen us in person. She had also seen your photograph when she was in Hilo, and she was very happy to see you looking well. Her letter brought tears to my eyes. I wonder if everyone else is eagerly looking forward to our return. We must have peace soon, I thought to myself. The people in 'Amauulu are fine, according to Mrs. Tachibana. The young men have enlisted and are gone, so the older women are working. Mrs. Tachibana is keeping her area clean and spending her days counting her blessings.

We were unable to get the Oshima *tanomoshi*. Oh, well.

Today was a very happy day for me. Letters are what I look forward to most. Receiving one is such a joy, but writing one is so difficult. In his letters Grandfather always says I should write to various people, but the words do not come easily.

Until the next time.

Date: December 6 [1943][21]
From: Hideko Ozaki, Jerome Relocation Center, Arkansas
To: Otokichi Ozaki, Santa Fe Internment Camp, New Mexico

It was unusual, but we had heavy rain last night, which made conditions very warm. This kind of weather is fine with me. How are you doing? We are all well, so please rest assured.

Many people are coming down with colds. Thank goodness, we are all right. Yuri has a slight cough, but it is not serious and she goes to school regularly. The children have been practicing for their Christmas program everyday after coming home from school. Last Friday and Saturday I carried firewood* for two consecutive days. I was exhausted, and my back and shoulders ached. It will be a real problem if we cannot be together soon. There are rumors about possible transfers to Tule Lake, but I am simply waiting to join you. I understand someone from Hawai'i is going home, and we are waiting to see him. His children are very excited, as they wait for his arrival. After a two-year separation, they may not be able to recognize one another. The husband of the woman next door has requested a parole, but I suppose he does not know when he will return home.

I am guessing that you are the one who sent us that cake the other day. I really have no idea who it was from.

Christmas is coming, but we probably need not send Christmas presents to those in Hawai'i. There is nothing special we can

---

* Hideko uses the phrase *maki-happai* 薪はっぱい; *maki* from the Japanese word for firewood and *happai* from the Hawaiian word *hāpai*, which means to carry. – Trans.

send, and under the circumstances our families will probably understand. For about two months now, no money has come from home, and I am waiting for it. The expenses are shocking. With the government providing the meals, you may be wondering why the money is needed. With four children, when they see other friends with something, they want to have the same thing. Managing their spending money is no easy task. Are the Basuya-san and Uncle well? Please give them my regards.

The other day I sent you the scarf and socks I knitted, as well as the slippers Grandmother made. Did you receive them? The pair that Mrs. Kitajima sent her husband is the same color as yours, so I suggest you put your name on yours to avoid confusion. Knitting socks has become a great fad since I began doing it, and now many ladies busily knit away. After all, the socks keep us nice and warm.

Until the next time.

Date: December 27 [1943][22]
From: Hideko Ozaki, Jerome Relocation Center, Arkansas
To: Otokichi Ozaki, Santa Fe Internment Camp, New Mexico

It was a careless mistake, and I apologize, but is everything all right there? I presume you had a pleasant Christmas. We were able to spend this Christmas in good health, too. The Christmas program scheduled for the twenty-fourth had to be postponed for a day, because the electricity went out, leaving us in darkness. To make matters worse, heavy rain soaked the ground, making walking difficult.

On the twenty-fifth, the program began at 1:30 in the afternoon, and lively songs and dances were featured. Yuri, dressed as an angel in a pure-white costume, joined other young children and danced. The little ones looked so sweet, and they performed well in spite of their size. Yukio and Sachi were also in the program. Tomoyuki, the shy one, did not participate. Last year we celebrated Christmas at the Immigration Station, but this year's event was very festive. There were many toys. The children are very happy and are playing with them everyday.

On the evening of the twenty-fourth, your father sent a parcel containing fabric, *lauhala** wallets, sweaters and shirts of good quality, and other items. I was so happy. In an earlier letter Grandfather had said there were many other things that were sent. These were probably packed in another box, which has not arrived yet. I understand the cost was in the tens of dollars. I am so grateful.

* Hawaiian: pandanus leaf

The cold is spreading and as a precautionary measure, six ladies have been designated as volunteer nurses for our block. I am one of them. All six of us were selected because we are not employed. I intend to do whatever I can, but with four children to look after, I am not sure I can take care of others. I may be the very one requiring care. At any rate, I shall do my best for the sake of the block and for my fellow residents. Fortunately there are only two or three in our block who have colds at this time.

I did not get to meet the two internees from Hawai'i, who are said to have returned home.

Until the next time.

Date: December 30 [1943][23]
From: Hideko Ozaki, Jerome Relocation Center, Arkansas
To: Otokichi Ozaki, Santa Fe Internment Camp, New Mexico

I received your letter addressed to Tomoyuki and the postcard for me. I also received the beautiful sewing box, and I really like the design on it. Thank you very much. Since we had luggage restrictions [when we left Hawai'i], I had not bothered to bring such things with me. It was so inconvenient until now. The rest of the articles, which my father in Honolulu had sent, arrived today. The parcel contained two apron pants,* three sweatshirts, a pair of high-quality scissors, and toys. I feel badly about having imposed [on the family].

You had snow there. It is relatively warm here. Yukio has early signs of a cold and is sleeping, but it is not serious. I am taking precautions, however. The rest of the children are fine. It is cold [outside], so I am keeping everyone indoors. They play and also get into arguments. After today we have one more day before the year ends. As I look back, I can say that we were fortunate, since none of us had serious health problems. Being well is paramount. I understand that today another bag of *mochigome*† was delivered, so we should be able to have *zōni.*‡ It seems that *sashimi*§ has also been brought in. I am looking forward to enjoying this once-a-year treat.

I see you received your fingerprint identification card.¶ By now

---

* Hideko uses the term *heppuru pansu* ヘップルパンス, meaning *epuron* or *apuron pansu*, a type of plantation work garment that was a combination of long apron and pants. The term *epuron* or *apuron pansu* was also sometimes used to mean overalls. See Barbara F. Kawakami, *Japanese Immigrant Clothing in Hawaii, 1885 – 1941* (Honolulu: University of Hawaii Press, 1993). -- Trans.
† Glutinous rice, used for making rice cakes
‡ The customary New Year's Day soup made of rice cakes and vegetables.
§ Sliced raw fish
¶ Hideko uses the phrase *shimon pēpa* 指紋ペーパ; literally, "fingerprint paper." – Trans.

the sweater is probably in your hands, too. I thought we would be together by New Year's Day, but I guess it is not to be. Surely, it will happen next year.

The children thoroughly enjoyed the peanuts from the package [that you sent]. Besides the letter to you, Older Brother [Kazuki Kosaki] sent me a long, long letter.

Please welcome the New Year in good health.

Date: January 7, 1944[24]
From: Hideko Ozaki, Jerome Relocation Center, Arkansas
To: Otokichi Ozaki, Santa Fe Internment Camp, New Mexico

I received a letter dated December 30 from Grandfather [Tomoya]. He writes that since February he has been working without taking even a one-hour break. Grandmother [Shobu] is doing very well, too, and is able to go without naps. I am really happy to hear this.

A baby boy was born to the Uejio family on the morning of December 13. Everyone is very pleased, says Grandfather.

Hiromichi volunteered for the Army, passed his test, entered the service on the third and will be leaving for the Mainland soon. Yoshitaka of Hakalau has also enlisted. Mr. Chikazawa took a bride in January and welcomed a baby boy in October. Shiho gave birth to a baby girl, naming her Miho. What a series of auspicious events so early in the new year.

It was Mrs. Kawazoe who sent us the cake the other day. We are grateful.

At Christmastime, Kazuma was given twenty-five dollars for gasoline expenses; after all, Grandfather does impose on [the young man] a great deal. Grandfather has a number of social obligations and has given quite a few congratulatory gifts.

There are many children in the Kosaki family and [Grandfather] feels sorry for them because of the crowded conditions. Sometimes he feels like a borrowed cat.*

Nobuko is home [for the winter break], so Grandfather is staying at my father's place. Grandmother has gone to the Uejio's to help the family.

[Grandfather's letter] also mentions Yasuo Kawano's death on the battlefront.

It seems that many [internees] are being paroled and are returning [to their families]. I understand that [the internee] whose family lives next door is expected to return, possibly

---

* One who keeps a low profile and tries to be unobtrusive. – Trans.

tonight, but it is not certain.* I have high hopes that in time things will work out for us as well.

I am hopeful that we will see Hiromichi and Yoshitaka one of these days. Since about fifty volunteer soldiers are coming to the camp tomorrow morning, I may see someone I know. I look forward to seeing former students and listening to their stories.

I am glad everyone in Honolulu seems to be in good health. I will write again.

Date: January 17 [1944]²⁵
From: Hideko Ozaki, Jerome Relocation Center, Arkansas
To: Otokichi Ozaki, Santa Fe Internment Camp, New Mexico

I received your letter dated the twelfth. I am deeply sorry to hear that you have been worrying because my letters have not reached you. The new year began with all four children coming down with a cold, one after the other. The fever at night was a problem, but they are well now and have returned to school. On the fifteenth we had a heavy snow, which piled up about three inches. The children were thrilled, throwing snowballs and making snowmen. The cold does not bother them at all. It is just a matter of adjustment. Compared to last year, even Yuri needs much less attention. When we first arrived she refused to leave my side, which was a problem. This year she has become more confident about going to school. Lately she does not want to go, however, so I am keeping her home on very cold days.

[The other day] as Tomoyuki and I were carrying in the firewood, he accidently dropped some on the first toe of my left foot. For two days the toe throbbed and kept me awake. I could not walk, so Tomoyuki brought my meals to me. Thank goodness, it was not the children who were hurt. They would surely have cried all night and kept me awake. I have been applying medication on the toe. The pain is gone now, and I am able to walk, but I probably cannot wear shoes for a while. The toenail is sure to fall out. I am reminded of that time twelve years ago when my finger was crushed. How awkward it is when one has pain in certain spots.

Tsutomu [Nakauchi] paid us a visit before six this morning. We were very happy to see him. He seems fine. He looked a little thinner than before, possibly because he has so much on his mind. He brought gifts of dolls and woodcraft for the children. For me, he had a beautiful sweater that must have cost at least five dollars.

---

* Hideko uses the word *kaeru*, "to return," with the meaning that male internees are *returning to their families*, reunited in another camp. – Trans.

I fear we have greatly imposed on him. He said he has a three-day leave and plans to see his younger brother and go on to New York. Mrs. Ideno was happy to see him, too. Tonight we had chicken *hekka** for dinner at Mrs. Ideno's place. Tomorrow night we will be the dinner hosts.

Having struggled through two years, accompanied by four children, there is no doubt in my mind. I wish for the same things as you do. You may have heard all kinds of rumors, but you need not be concerned about me. I am your wife, so please have faith in me. Everything will be clear when we meet. I am anxiously waiting for the day when we will be able to live together.

Until the next time.

Date: January 21[1944][26]
From: Hideko Ozaki, Jerome Relocation Center, Arkansas
To: Otokichi Ozaki, Santa Fe Internment Camp, New Mexico

I received your letter dated the fifteenth. I am happy to hear that you are fine. We are doing well, so rest assured.

Lately it has been very warm, perhaps because I have become accustomed to the weather. Yuri goes to school everyday [now].

Tsutomu was here for two days, then visited his brother, Hideo, and continued on his trip to New York. He looked fine, which was reassuring. He felt sorry for the children when he saw they had no play equipment, so he spent eight dollars and bought a softball set for the boys. He also spent four dollars on each of the girls, buying them both a doll. I feel very badly about having imposed on him. He must have done it because Grandfather and the others have been good to him. He is such a nice young man. The children are thrilled with the gifts. Another young man from Hilo, who had visited Mrs. Arakawa, brought me a message from Minoru. I wish Minoru himself would come to see us, but I realize how far he would need to travel.

One person's misconduct does not necessarily apply to everyone. Please trust us.

A letter from my brother arrived today. Everyone there is fine. My brother writes that it was a busy New Year's Day without rest, which left the family with an empty feeling. The business is doing so well that the bonuses given out [to the employees] amounted to $2,000. Grandfather is said to have received $100 – how nice.

It seems that our property can be sold for $1,500. The money would be deposited in the bank, and we would receive monthly

---

* Chicken cooked with vegetables in soy sauce. Similar to sukiyaki, it is a dish that originated on Hawai'i's plantations. – Trans.

checks. It is shocking, but true, that we need spending money.

I went to school for the children's report cards. Grades for Tomoyuki, Yuri, Sachi and Yukio are the same as the last time. Yukio somehow is not doing good work in the basics, such as reading, arithmetic and spelling. His grades in music and penmanship are good. His schoolwork is not good. Tomoyuki's grades are very good. There is no need to worry. I am glad he has such a good friend in Mrs. Yoshimasu's son, a very good student and a nice young man.* Yukio's friends are limited to those he plays with, which is a problem. The fact that he is strong is a good thing.

Until the next time.

***

Date: January 25 [1944][27]
From: Hideko Ozaki, Jerome Relocation Center, Arkansas
To: Otokichi Ozaki, Santa Fe Internment Camp, New Mexico

I received your letter of the nineteenth. I am glad to hear that you are fine. The weather has been as warm here as it is in Hawai'i, and all of us are happy for it. I hope it will continue, but I am quite sure that it will become colder once again.

We are relieved to hear that you have been notified that we will be sent to Tule Lake. I guess we [in Jerome] will be notified sometime soon. I do not know when that will be, but I will sit back and wait patiently.

The children are well and attending school. I was unaware of it, but an article that Tomoyuki had written was in the school newspaper the other day. He belongs to a newspaper club, and he collected the information by himself. He did not bring one home, because there were not enough copies, but I am happy to hear that someone else sent a copy [to Santa Fe].

I have no idea who spreads rumors about the lives of the internees' families. Everyone is very kind to us.

Noboru came to visit us the other day. I heard that his older brother had been injured but not very seriously. Your former students are visiting us one after another. Their visits have become our greatest pleasure.

I heard that you had received a gift from Fudeko's mother. I feel badly for her, but I am happy to hear that everyone is willing to help her. Please ask her to send a picture of Fudeko's baby. I don't have her address, and so I can't write to her.

Machiyo and Eiko Arakawa have left camp to work in Chicago.

---

* Masayuki Yoshimasu, a Japanese language school teacher from Hāmākua Poko, Maui, was interned at Jerome with his wife, Fumiko, also a teacher, and their three children. – Trans.

People are gradually leaving camp.*

Have you got a fountain pen? I can order one for you, if you want.

Please buy some laundry soap, if it is available, and keep it for us. I can only buy one [piece] of it at a time here.

Until the next time.

Date: January 29 [1944][28]
From: Hideko Ozaki, Jerome Relocation Center, Arkansas
To: Otokichi Ozaki, Santa Fe Internment Camp, New Mexico

How are you? It is warm here. We have not had to use our heater for the past week. We are hoping that it will not turn cold again. The children are well and attend school everyday. Yuri is also doing well and enjoys playing. I feel more at ease nowadays. Our life seems to have settled down now that we know where we will be moving to, although we still do not know when it will be. The children are very happy and look forward to seeing you again. Yuri asks me every day if she will be joining you at Tule Lake.

Tomoyuki sent a card to Toshiko in 'Amauulu, and she kindly replied. She has not married yet. Kazuma also wrote to us, asking to give you his best, as he was not able to write in Japanese. Enclosed is their family photo, most likely taken at Yoshitaka's departure.

My foot is better, and I can wear shoes now.

According to Kazuma's letter, he and Mr. Mukai are trying to sell our land.

Until the next time.

Date: February 23 [1944][29]
From: Hideko Ozaki, Jerome Relocation Center, Arkansas
To: Otokichi Ozaki, Santa Fe Internment Camp, New Mexico

How are you? We are fine, so please rest assured.

We received your parcel. Thank you for the soap, candy, honey and [chewing] gum. I guess the food was not packaged well, so there was soap powder on it, giving it a nice fragrance. Next time, you should pack it well. What a shame to waste such delicious candy. The bag was torn. It can still be eaten if we wash it.

Tsutomu Nakauchi's younger brother, Hideo, came to see us. He had gone to Chicago and, on the way back, stopped by here

---

* The children of Frank Arakawa, a civil engineer from Hilo, whose family was interned at Jerome. The government closed Jerome in June 1944 and converted it into a camp for German POWs. – Trans.

for a five-day visit. He left yesterday. He has four [former] high
school classmates [here in Jerome], so apparently they had a very
good time together. He said he liked it here. When I spoke to him,
he said he did not understand Japanese very much. He seemed
embarrassed, so I avoided speaking to him. He bought many
things for the children, which made them very happy.

According to the announcement yesterday, this center will close
by June 30. In due time, I suppose residents will be transferred
elsewhere, but we will probably be going to Tule Lake. I have
bought all kinds of things, so packing will be quite a job. I shall
have to do it a little at a time.

There was a hearing last Saturday to segregate the loyal from
the disloyal. There have been so many of these sessions since we
came here, each one the same as the one before.

No letters have come from Hawai'i, and I am worried. I am
wondering if anyone has gotten sick.

Until the next time.

Date: March 1 [1944][30]
From: Hideko Ozaki, Jerome Relocation Center, Arkansas
To: Otokichi Ozaki, Santa Fe Internment Camp, New Mexico

I received your postcard dated the twenty-fourth. I am happy
to hear you are fine. We are well, too. The children are going to
school everyday. I went to get their report cards today. The grades
are good. I had been worried about Yukio, who had ten "N's"
the last time, but his grades were all "S's." I praised him for his
achievement, and now he has begun to study a little every night.
I am happy about it. He seems to be able to do the work once he
puts his mind to it. He was probably spending too much time
playing. Sachi seems to be doing well, too. I was told that she is a
good girl and behaves well in class, so yesterday I brought home a
book of *katto dore** for her. She was very happy. I am so glad that
all four children are in good health and their grades are good.

Beginning today I have a dishwashing job. Since I have been
a lady of leisure for more than a year and we have no idea when
we will be transferred, it seems really odd to be taking a job.
The fact is there are no workers available, so after being asked so
often to help the block residents, I simply could not refuse. I feel
somewhat sorry for the children, but I have no choice. Yuri is able
to do things for herself now, so there is no problem. Conveniently
enough, both she and Sachi go to school from one in the
afternoon.

---

* Lit., "cut doll;" i.e., paper dolls.

The Ochiai family is going to Crystal City, and there is much hustle and bustle as they prepare for the departure. I went to give them a little help. A farewell party will be held tomorrow night, probably with all kinds of dishes to enjoy. Whenever a family is transferred, the men in the camp help with the packing. It is gratifying to know we can rely on them. I do not know when we will be transferred, but I can prepare for it. By June everyone will be gone, so we will probably leave in the coming months.

Hiromichi sent some special candies. There was no accompanying letter, but it probably will come later.

No letters have come from Hawai'i. I am worried.

Former students and soldiers have been sending us candy, so the children are eating quite a bit of chocolate candy. The gum [you sent] was tasty and special. Please buy more of it, if you can. If possible, please make some *geta* and have them ready for us. There is no need to send them. I hope the trunk you ordered is a good one.

I picked quite a few *kikurage** and have left them out to dry, so that I can make *namasu†* for you. I can tell you, it will be delicious.

Until the next time.

* * *

As suggested in the above letters, one of the bright spots of camp life was the visits by and gifts from Nisei soldiers, sons of friends from Hawai'i serving in the military on the mainland. These visits were filled with warmth and nostalgia of home for both the camp internees and the soldiers. The soldiers were often treated to good homestyle cooking and treats, while the internees caught up with news from home. The last letters in this chapter are written by Tsutomu and Hideo Nakauchi, sons of family friends in Hilo, as well as other Nisei soldiers who visited Mrs. Ozaki and the children in the Jerome Relocation Center. Inserted is a letter from Mrs. Nakauchi, expressing her gratitude to Mrs. Ozaki for her hospitality.

English original
Date: February 18, 1944[31]
From: Tsutomu Nakauchi, Camp Savage, Minnesota
To: Earl Tomoyuki Ozaki, Jerome Relocation Center, Arkansas

Hello Yuki and Everybody,

---

* Edible wood ear fungus.
† Salad of pickled vegetables.

How do you do. Attending school every day and helping mother? As for me I'm OK and well, studying harder than you, I think. Did you have any snowfall lately? We had our first snowfall of this year two weeks ago. Do you know what we did? We played around like kids all week, fighting with snowballs and making snowmen.

Are you playing with the football? Be very careful and at the same time don't get yourself dirty, eh! Don't forget this saying by Bejamin Franklin. Play while you play, work while you work, and also study while you study.

Brother will be visiting you soon so I hope you have some fun with him.

Take good care of your mother and also your brother and sister and most of all don't neglect your health.

Date: 1944[32]
From: Hideo Nakauchi, Camp Shelby, Mississippi
To: Hideko Ozaki, Jerome Relocation Center, Arkansas

Mrs. Ozaki,

I thank you for your hospitality the other day. Thank you for the pickles. Today, I was invited to a friend's house, and I brought the pickles. They served steamed rice and everybody enjoyed the pickles with it. The pickles were gone in a moment.

When I returned here, I found that five of my friends had visited other camps. I hope I will be granted leave soon. I feel lonely now and wish that I could come to your place as soon as possible.

However, I do not know when I can get out of this place. In one month or in one year?

Give my best regards to the Missus next door.

Please read this letter to her. I may make some mistakes since I write only in *kana* characters.* Nisei men who had come back from Japan had to work and could not teach me *kanji* characters.

I hope that all of your children are in good health, and that Tomoyuki has recovered from the flu by now.

Please let me know if there is anything you would like to have. Bye-bye.

English original
Date: March 20, 1944[33]
From: Hideo Nakauchi, Camp Shelby, Mississippi

---

* *Hiragana* and *katakana*, the two Japanese phonetic writing systems in modern usage.

To: Earl Tomoyuki Ozaki, Jerome Relocation Center, Arkansas

Dear Tomoyuki,

Thank your Mom for the "Tsukemonos" and the things she did for me. There were some "musubis"* left over in some compartment so we had a swell time with them. Don't forget to thank her for them.

You know, Tomo, when we left Jerome we headed for Meghee† where we dropped some fellas and then it was a long ride to camp. Backaches and stiff necks—really hard to sleep on the bus. Reached camp at 4 A. M. Monday morning slept for a few minutes then it was reveille.

We changed house again. Now to Co. B. Only the house not the company. Maybe it was too crowded at Co. K.

Boy! If this thing keeps on going it'll drive us crazy. Walking back and forth. Chow time, reveille and retreat we go down (way down) to Co. K. and eat there. Boy some walk. I promised you a lot and I'm sending it later on with the sweatshirt and all.

I'm sending an album of our combat team and I hope you enjoy it.

Tell mom I'll not forget about finding the Hara boy. Don't worry.

Date: March 17 [1944][34]
From: Mrs. Nakauchi, Hilo, Hawai'i
To: Hideko Ozaki, Jerome Relocation Center, Arkansas

I feel sorry that I have not written for such a long time. I hope that all of you are doing fine. Please rest assured that we are all in good health.

I heard that Tsutomu and Hideo, who are in the military service, had visited you and had been indebted to you. I am so thankful that I do not know how to express my gratitude to you. I am so inexperienced that I do not know how to express my gratitude to you. Thank you very, very much.

One year has quickly passed since the two boys left my home, and they have lived without the warm feeling of home, and have experienced various hardships. Hideo wrote to me as follows: "When we visited their place, they treated us so well that we felt it was like being at home. When we left, they gave us nice gifts."

---

* Rice balls

† The writer means McGehee, Arkansas, the site of the Rohwer Relocation Center that housed Japanese Americans from Los Angeles and central California. McGehee is twenty-seven miles north of the Jerome Relocation Center in Denson. – Trans.

Thank you very much. I heard that both Tsutomu and Hideo had stayed at your place for many days.

Tsutomu will be finishing school next month and his destination is already decided. Hideo got his second holiday and went to your place. That should be the last holiday for him. They must have been very happy to be treated as if by their parents. Hideo will be leaving the school soon. I pray that peace will come as soon as possible.

I heard that your children had grown big, for which I wish to congratulate you. I sincerely hope that the day will come soon when you can join Mr. Ozaki. I am afraid that it is still cold at your place.

Please take good care of yourself.

Just a few words of appreciation.

P.S. I remitted a small amount of money. Please accept it. I thought of buying something for your children. I will do so next time.

English original
Date: October 14, 1943[35]
From: Bob Toyama, Camp Shelby, Mississippi
To: Mrs. Hideko Ozaki, Jerome Relocation Center, Arkansas

Thanks so much for the wonderful foods and the room to sleep with a soft bed and blanket. I have really appreciated all you have done for me and my boy friend. Yes! We had such a wonderful time at "Jerome" that my heart is full of happiness and memories which will be in my heart forever. And oh! How glad I was to see you and your sweet sons and daughters so cute and grown up. I bet they [are] all aching to go back to the paradise islands so much fun, so much friends and lots of amusements and recreation. I hope that day will come soon so all can go home to our sweet home and friends.

By the way I am sorry to say that your electric cords and plugs haven't got down here any more but I'll try this Saturday to have a day pass to go to a nearby town called Hattiesburg. Will you also tell Kokuzo Mrs. too. Just be patient and wait I'll try my best to get it. Yes! I never forget yet those promises. While coming all from "Jerome" I stopped [at] many large towns and roamed all over the town, every stores to look for the electrical cords, etc. but to a sad sack every dry goods [store], hardware stores were closed. So that's that.

Before closing this very letter will you please give my utmost thanks to Mrs. Takahata, Mrs. Kokuzo and Mr. and Mrs. Aoki.

Thanks. Well! Good night and good luck.

P.S. Excuse me for not writing in Japanese for I just can't. I forget most of it so you understand huh!

―――――――――

English original
Date: April 4, 1944[36]
From: S. Kubota, Camp Shelby, Mississippi
To: Hideko Ozaki, Jerome Relocation Center, Arkansas

Dear Mrs. Ozaki,

I must ask you to forgive me for writing to you in English. But to me this is the speediest method to express my appreciation for the fine comforting words you have sent me. Yes, I'll do my best in anything I undertake and we'll all get together in good old Hawaii.

Here it is spring. A long way since I last saw you, and I was happy to hear that all of you are fine. And may I ask how did it go for your husband. Was he granted his parole.

I'm glad the meager candies I sent you were appreciated. Yesterday I sent you towels and a sweatshirt. These I won't be needing any more. Will you please use it for yourself and the sweatshirt to your son. It isn't well but I hope you like it.

Well, I had better close now. Taps is blowing and we'll be headed for more work tomorrow. Will you please extend my regards to everyone.

Otokichi at ten years old with mother, Shobu, in Japan, August 1913.
Courtesy of Lily Ozaki Arasato

Hilo Dokuritsu Nihonjin Gakkō (Hilo Independent Japanese School), from which Ozaki graduated in 1921.
Courtesy of Lily Ozaki Arasato

The Hawaii Mainichi Building, where Ozaki began his career in 1924.
Courtesy of Lily Ozaki Arasato

Ozaki in front of the Hawaii Mainichi (The Japanese Daily News) Building, where he began his career in 1924.
Courtesy of Lily Ozaki Arasato

Otokichi Ozaki, *rear left*, with members of Gin-u Shisha, a *tanka* poetry club in Hilo, 1925.
Otokichi Ozaki Collection, Japanese Cultural Center of Hawai'i

Otokichi and Hideko Ozaki on
their wedding day, 1932.
*Otokichi Ozaki Collection, Japanese
Cultural Center of Hawai'i*

Takeji Kobara, Hideko Ozaki's father, in Hilo, c. 1930s.
Courtesy of Lily Ozaki Arasato

Hideko Ozaki in Hilo, c. 1930s.
Courtesy of Lily Ozaki Arasato

Otokichi Ozaki with his class in 'Amauulu Camp, c. 1933.
Courtesy of Lily Ozaki Arasato

Hideko Ozaki, *rear left*, with her *odori* (Japanese dance) class, 1934.
Courtesy of Lily Ozaki Arasato

Otokichi Ozaki and eldest son, Earl Tomoyuki.
Otokichi Ozaki Collection, Japanese Cultural Center of Hawai'i

Otokichi Ozaki, around the time of his arrest, c. 1941.
Otokichi Ozaki Collection, Japanese Cultural Center of Hawai'i

Family photo taken in Honolulu to send to Ozaki in camp, 1942: Ozaki's parents, Tomoya and Shobu Ozaki, *second and fourth from left*; and Ozaki's wife, Hideko, with the four Ozaki children, *from left*: Earl Tomoyuki, Alice Sachi, Lily Yuri, and Carl Yukio.
Courtesy of Lily Ozaki Arasato

A sketch by Hilo internee George Hoshida of an internee broadcasting the news in a Mainland camp.
Courtesy of the Japanese American National Museum; gift of June Hoshida Honma, Sandra Hoshida and Carole Hoshida Kanada.

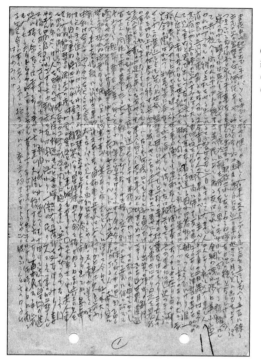

Ozaki's notes, written while he was in a Mainland camp.
Otokichi Ozaki Collection, Japanese Cultural Center of Hawaiʻi

A letter to Ozaki from his niece, Nobuko Kosaki, on behalf of her mother, Kayo Kosaki.
Otokichi Ozaki Collection, Japanese Cultural Center of Hawaiʻi

Kazuki Kosaki, Ozaki's brother-in-law, with
Ozaki's daughter, Lily Yuri.
Courtesy of Lily Ozaki Arasato

Haruko Ozaki Uejio, Ozaki's
younger sister.
Courtesy of Lily Ozaki Arasato

1943

Hideko Kobara Ozaki, *back left*, with a friend in the Jerome Relocation Center and the four Ozaki children: Earl Tomoyuki, Carl Yukio, Alice Sachi, and Lily Yuri.
Otokichi Ozaki Collection, Japanese Cultural Center of Hawai'i

Otokichi Ozaki, *second from right*, with internees in Santa Fe camp.
Otokichi Ozaki Collection, Japanese Cultural Center of Hawai'i

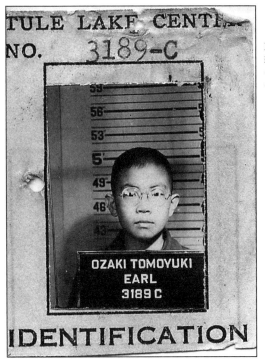

Earl Tomoyuki, Ozaki's eldest son, in his photo ID for camp.
Otokichi Ozaki Collection, Japanese Cultural Center of Hawai'i

Hideko and Otokichi Ozaki and their four children, reunited in the Tule Lake Relocation Center. *From left*: Lily Yuri, Earl Tomoyuki, Alice Sachi, and Carl Yukio.
Courtesy of Lily Ozaki Arasato

Tule Lake Relocation Center, c. 1944-45.
Courtesy of Lily Ozaki Arasato

The Kosaki family, 1945. *Back, left to right*: Albert Hidemichi, Mabel Yoshiko, Kazuo, Nobuko, Frank Mineyuki. *Front, left to right*: Richard Hiromichi, father Kazuki, mother Kayo.
Courtesy of Lily Ozaki Arasato

The Ozaki children, Carl Yukio, Alice Sachi, Lily Yuri, and Earl Tomoyuki, in Honolulu shortly after their return from camp, 1945.
Courtesy of Lily Ozaki Arasato

The Ozaki extended family on the occasion of Tomoya and Shobu Ozaki's sixtieth anniversary, March 1951.
Courtesy of Lily Ozaki Arasato

Otokichi Ozaki, upon his return to Hilo for the first time since his internment, December 1960. Posing with friends, *center front*, Otokichi and Hideko; *left front*, Lily Yuri.
Courtesy of Lily Ozaki Arasato

Otokichi Ozaki with the "Ozaki Red" anthurium he developed in 1935.
Courtesy of Lily Ozaki Arasato

Otokichi and Hideko Ozaki, after he was awarded the Sixth Class Order of the Sacred Treasure by the Japanese government, 1977.
Courtesy of Lily Ozaki Arasato

Honoring Ozaki for his imperial award, 1977. *From left*: Consul General of Japan Masao Tsukamoto; Hideko Ozaki; the Japanese film star Takamine Hideko, a friend of the Ozakis; Otokichi Ozaki; Tsuneko Tsukamoto, wife of the consul general; writer-director Matsuyama Zenzo, husband of Takamine Hideko.
Courtesy of Lily Ozaki Arasato

Receiving a commendation from the City and County of Honolulu, with city councilman Kekoa Kaapu. *Courtesy of Lily Ozaki Arasato*

Otokichi with his former Dokuritsu Gakkō student Herbert Matayoshi, then mayor of Hilo. *Courtesy of Lily Ozaki Arasato*

With grandson Nolan, beside his garden, at daughter Lily Yuri's home in Honolulu.
Courtesy of Lily Ozaki Arasato

Otokichi and Hideko with their grandchildren, c. 1970s. *First row*: Cynthia; *second row*: Kent, Trent, Nolan, Carlene, Gertrude (wife of Carl) holding Carolyn; *third row*: Kazue (wife of Earl), Otokichi, Hideko, Carl; *back row*: Earl, Lily, Bruce.
Courtesy of Lily Ozaki Arasato

Otokichi and Hideko Ozaki in their Waikīkī apartment, c. 1980s.
Courtesy of Lily Ozaki Arasato

Otokichi Ozaki, being greeted by Jean Ariyoshi, the wife of the governor of Hawai'i, at a reception for the publication of *Poets Behind Barbed Wire*, a collection of internment poetry, September 1983. This was Ozaki's last public appearance.
Courtesy of Lily Ozaki Arasato

FAMILY REUNITED, 1944 – 1945

> We are all very happy to have Daddy back with us.
> —Tomoyuki Ozaki, in a letter to his grandparents

IN THE SPRING of 1944, after years of application and rejection, Mrs. Ozaki and the children were finally reunited with Ozaki at Jerome, Arkansas and at Tule Lake, California. While life was still difficult in camp, some semblance of family life could resume. Ozaki continued to work as block manager and community leader, while Mrs. Ozaki worked on her sewing and tended to the children.

Ozaki was quite the correspondent, as a steady stream of letters from friends in Hilo as well as in other Mainland camps continued to pour into the Ozaki household. This is fortuitous for future historians, as these letters capture how the escalating Pacific War, in 1944 and 1945, affected the lives of those left behind. Sons of Hawaiʻi friends are killed in the European theatre, and awareness is heightened of these soldiers' acts of bravery and loyalty in spite of their parents being interned.

Life in Mainland camps, now going on three years, takes on a resigned atmosphere, as the earlier complaints of discomfort by internees are replaced by requests for items to enhance everyday life, such as fountain pens and sewing machines. Ozaki's land on the Big Island is finally sold, and the transaction completed, depositing $1,500 into his account. Ozaki and his family are still depending on those back in Hawaiʻi to take care of family business and send necessary items. Ozaki often expresses gratitude for all of the letters and care packages.

English original
Date: April 5, 1944[1]
From: Thomas B. Lyle, Agent Cashier, War Relocation Authority, Jerome Relocation Center, Arkansas
To: Otokichi Ozaki, Jerome Relocation Center, Arkansas

Dear Mr. Ozaki:
    We are holding funds, which was sent to our office from the U.S. Department of Justice, Santa Fe, New Mexico and same may be secured by calling at my desk in Administration Building No.

1, Saturday morning, April 8, 1944, between the hours of 8:00 a.m. to 11:30 a.m.

It will be necessary for the Block Manager to come to the office with you. You must come yourself, no one may secure these funds except the one to whom this letter is addressed.

Yours truly,
Thomas B. Lyle

Date: April 14, 1944[2]
From: Katsuko Ochiai, Tule Lake Relocation Center, California
To: Hideko Ozaki, Jerome Relocation Center, Arkansas

It must be a relief to have your husband back. I'm very happy for you.

Thank you very much for helping us as we prepared to leave the center and for the farewell monetary gift. Everyone had been very kind to us, so you can imagine our deep sadness at having to say goodbye. Being new here, we have no friends, and we miss all of you.

I'd been worried about the schools here, but everything's organized, and our children are attending both English and Japanese classes. There are some inconveniences with our housing, but I'm grateful that we can at least enjoy three meals a day as a family. Being new here, I could only find work at the sewing center. Together with the grocery shopping and cooking for the family, my daily schedule keeps me as busy as a bee. It's a far cry from my easygoing life there. Since I learned that your family moved into the quarters we had occupied, I feel the nostalgia even more.

If what I've heard is true, your family should be coming here in the near future. I'll be looking forward to seeing you.

Date: not dated[3]
From: Otokichi Ozaki, Jerome Relocation Center, Arkansas
To: Kazuki and Kayo Kosaki, Honolulu, Hawai'i

Your letter and package addressed to Santa Fe were forwarded here.* We are grateful beyond words for your kindness. Life is inconvenient in many ways, but thanks to the thoughtfulness of everyone in Hawai'i, we are quite settled now. I suppose I could have requested flatware and kitchen utensils, since our departure

---

* See Kazuki Kosaki's letter dated January 16, 1944, p. 124 – Trans.

for Japan is uncertain. Then the shipment might have reached me at some point. Well, it may be too late now.

I have no tools to work with, so I purchased a hammer, screwdriver, nails and screws, carpenter's square, and plane from Sears. I also ordered a saw, but it was not available. With pieces of wood and my tools, I managed to put together a cabinet for our footwear. Hideko's measuring stick for sewing took three days to take shape. Since we cannot get silverware, my next project is to make a wooden soup ladle and a serving spoon. They should be useful when we are moved to the next camp. I must admit that dealing with wartime inconveniences has been a challenge, but it is an interesting experience. Perhaps this is the penalty I must pay for the comfortable life in Hawai'i. Hideko regrets having given away her cookware and kitchen utensils in 'Amauulu, but we are in a war and there is nothing we can do.

We are forever grateful to the Kosaki family, Father-in-law Kobara and Mr. Kataoka for all their help. Many thanks, Brother, for the cups and bowls you took great pains to find. We handle them like precious stones whenever we have our *chazuke*.[*] Thank you for the aloha shirts, slippers, and other items. The tea set arrived without a scratch. For now, we have everything we need, so please do not worry. If you recall, there were two pairs of slippers in the care package you gave me when I left Honomū.[†] They were made by Grandmother [Shobu], so I cannot bring myself to wear them so casually. Instead, I have been repairing and wearing one pair over and over. Both pairs are now safely stored in my footlocker. Now that I have rejoined the family, Grandmother may be assured that I will make slippers for Hideko and the children.

And, how is Grandmother doing? Age is a problem, but her illness is probably not very serious. Right now she may feel that she is a burden to the family, but patience and endurance are important. Having experienced two years of confinement, I know something about persistence and perseverance.

A few days ago I received a letter from Mr. Tango in 'Amauulu in answer to the letter I sent from Santa Fe. I had avoided writing to friends for a long time on the advice of other internees. According to their correspondence, a guilt-by-association awareness is creating an awkward problem for everyone back home. My conscience is clear because I have never plotted against the government in my twenty-or-more years in Hawai'i. I have done my best to teach my Japanese American students to be good citizens. Even now, some of them are laying down their lives for

---

* Tea on rice.
† A town near 'Amauulu Camp.

the American flag. I am happy to hear that the internee parents of all these young men are gradually being released. This action reflects well on the United States.

Date: April 19 [1944][4]
From: Otokichi Ozaki, Jerome Relocation Center, Arkansas
To: Kazuki and Kayo Kosaki, Honolulu, Hawai'i

Your letter of April 6 arrived on the eighteenth. I am happy to hear that Grandmother [Shobu] is well. You and everyone there must be relieved, too. Please give my best regards to Grandfather [Tomoya]; I apologize for the great imposition and hope to write to him soon. I would like to write to Grandmother as well, but I hesitate to inconvenience her in any way. Please tell her I shall never forget what I owe her.

All of us are well. It seems to be the best season of the year, and the weather is pleasant. Yuri and Sachi go to kindergarten everyday in the afternoon. Sachi is *momona*, as usual. Yukio is often lectured about playing outside until dark, but at least he is well enough to stay out late. Tomoyuki had been complaining about his headaches, and we thought his eyeglasses could be the problem, so we had Dr. Kuwahara* examine him. Apparently, Tomoyuki's vision has worsened to the point where he probably cannot read what is on the chalkboard. A new pair of glasses will cost a shocking twenty-five dollars, but his eyesight cannot be compromised.

In these uncertain times, we try to limit our expenses as much as possible, but emergencies like this are a problem. When we are transferred next month, probably to Tule Lake, I hope to find work that is not labor intensive and will try to earn as much as I can. Right now, we must focus on packing preparations and the exhaustingly long four-day train ride ahead of us.

A boxful of fabric for children's clothing arrived from the Nakauchi family of Pāhoa. We also heard from Hideo Nakauchi, stationed at Camp Shelby, and Mr. Tango in 'Amauulu. Grandmother Tango hopes to send something special together with the large photo that was in my bedroom, which she had taken home with her. The kindness of relatives and friends is overwhelming. I cannot thank everyone enough.

As of now, we have no idea when we will return to Japan. After we are settled at Tule Lake, we may decide to return to Hawai'i first. The unreasonably harsh treatment we have been through has

---

* Ernest Mitsuo Kuwahara, an optometrist from Hilo, was interned with his family at Jerome. – Trans.

somewhat soured my positive feelings about the United States, but I myself have done nothing wrong, so my conscience is clear. This war is a battle for national survival; there is nothing that we can do.

Many of my former students in Hilo are at Camp Shelby. Some have already gone on to Europe and have died in battle. It is heartbreaking to think that these young men are giving up their lives for America. They are all serving with valor. There is some comfort in knowing that Americans are beginning to appreciate the greatness of the Japanese who will throw down their lives for justice, honor, and integrity, even if it means turning against their parents.

I shall write again. Please take care of yourselves.

Post-script*
Date: April 26 [1944]⁵

I received your letter of April 12 on the twenty-fourth. Selling the property in Hilo must have been difficult. Right now money is not a problem, but a government order could suspend all overseas cash transactions, so please have Kazuma send me $200 a month for the next three months. In case there is a last-minute departure for Japan, I would have the cash on hand. I can only take $700 with me.

Father, you cannot expect to work forever. With age, one tends to become stubborn and to complain more. When we are settled in Tule Lake, I shall consider my options for the future very carefully. Today, those of us who will be leaving had our pictures taken and were fingerprinted. This will be my sixth or seventh transfer. The thought sickens me.

I am relieved that you received the photos. I am fine except for more gray hair and forgetfulness -- a problem, indeed.

Date: April 22 [1944]⁶
From: Earl Tomoyuki Ozaki, Jerome Relocation Center, Arkansas
To: Tomoya and Shobu Ozaki, Honolulu, Hawai'i

Grandpa and Grandma, how are you? Yukio, Sachi, Yuri, and I are fine. We go to school everyday.

We are all very happy to have Daddy back with us. Mommy goes to work as a dishwasher every day. Hideo Nakauchi came to

---

* While this postscript comes at the end of the previous letter addressed to the Kosakis, it is clear from its content that it is intended for Ozaki's father, Tomoya. – Trans.

visit us recently. We will move to Tule Lake in May. I am eager to
see you. I hardly write in Japanese, so I've forgotten how. But I
shall write more often from now on.

Please take care of yourselves.

Bye bye.

Date: May 12 [1944][7]
From: Kazuma Kataoka, Hakalau, Hawai'i
To: Tomoya Ozaki, Honolulu, Hawai'i [forwarded to Otokichi
Ozaki]

Thank you very much for your letters. I wish to congratulate
you on the good health of your entire family. We are also fine. I
am glad to hear that the Ozaki family living on the Mainland is
also in good health. I am relieved that Otokichi's family has finally
joined him and that they are now living together.

As for the land in Hilo, I understand that you already know
the situation, since Momoe has told you about it. I went to a bank
in Hilo to remit the money, but was told that I could not remit it
with the paper I had. So, I went to a lawyer with the help of Mr.
Mukai. He said that the paper I had was the certificate of the land
sale and that I would need to get a remittance permit separately. I
have applied for the permit.

Since it may take some time for me to get the permit, I thought
that this would inconvenience Otokichi, and so I remitted, on
May 12, the $100 that you kindly sent to me from Honolulu.

Last but not least, please give my best regards to the Kosaki
family.

Note to Otokichi [from Tomoya]: On May 16, I received this
letter from Mr. Kataoka and am sending this to you for you to
read.

English original
Date: June 6, 1944[8]
From: J. Lloyd Webb, Counselor, Community Welfare Section,
Department of the Interior, Jerome Relocation Center, Arkansas
To: Hideko Ozaki, Tule Lake Relocation Center, California

Dear Mrs. Ozaki:

We received your letter of May 26 with the check for $3.50
enclosed and the question about whether your family could receive
an allowance for April and May.

The reason you received only $3.50 was because we expected
Mr. Ozaki to go to work and to count the children as his

dependents. He evidently failed to start to work, and because he was listed as the head wage earner for your family neither he nor the children got the benefit of the clothing allowance.

We understand that for some reason he did not go to work. It would have been more convenient if we had known what this reason was, but we assumed that there was some good reason for his failure to work. At any rate, he cannot benefit with a clothing allowance for your work, but we are able to issue an order for a supplementary cash allowance for your children.

We are ordering an additional allowance of $10.00 for the benefit of your children for which you can be considered eligible by your work. We are also returning the check you enclosed.

English original
Date: June 29, 1944[9]
From: H. C. Walters, Assistant Vice President, Bank of Hawaii, Hilo Branch
To: Otokichi Ozaki, Tule Lake Relocation Center, California

Dear Sir:

As requested we have charged your Savings Account No. 47198 $200.00 and we enclose our draft payable to your order for that amount less exchange and postage.

We have obtained from your Attorney-in-fact, Kazuma Kataoka, License no. 14227 which expires on July 29th. Inasmuch as this license does not authorize us to remit to you more than once in thirty days, we can only send you one more remittance of $200.00 under this license and will do so some time during the month of July. After the expiration of this license it will be necessary for it to either be renewed or for you to make an application to the Foreign Funds Control, care of the Governor's Office, Honolulu, T. H., for transfer of this account to some bank on the Mainland.

As the license requires that monthly reports be made of all deposits and withdrawals to the account under this license, we have advised Mr. Kataoka to that effect and he is making the reports.

Date: July 20 [1944][10]
From: Tomoya Ozaki, Honolulu, Hawai'i
To: Otokichi and Hideko Ozaki, Tule Lake Relocation Center, California

I had been waiting for your letter for a long time, when in the afternoon of July 17, I received your letter dated July 6. I am relieved to hear that everyone is in good health. The Kobaras, Kosakis, Uejios, and Jiji and Baba are all in good health, we haven't caught even a slight cold.

I received a letter dated July 5 from Hakalau. According to the letter, the Kataokas received a phone call from the bank in Hilo saying that they could now send a money [transfer], so they will send Kazuma to the bank. On the ninth, I received a notice that they [the Kataokas] sent $200 [to Otokichi]. I assume you have already received the money. Kazuma says that you, Otokichi, can now withdraw the money yourself. If possible, make arrangements yourself with the bank for the money [transfer], in order to save Kazuma the trouble of having to go to the bank [for you].

The Kataokas take very good care of us. I will never forget their kindness.

A memorial service for Yoshitaka was held at the Honolulu Hongwanji Temple.[*] I gave ten dollars as *kōden*.[†] Twenty-seven friends of Yoshitaka gathered.[‡]

I am in good health, as usual, and work everyday. Bāsan is also in good health and never catches cold. We are now at the Uejios'. Last spring, Hiroko Uejio got married and I gave her ten dollars as a wedding gift. On the coming thirtieth, Kiyoko is getting married. I will give her ten dollars as a wedding gift, and since we are at the Uejios', I will help them for a day [with the wedding].

Koki, the eldest son of Mr. Abe, recently enlisted. We had a farewell party for him, and I gave him five dollars as a congratulatory gift.

According to a letter from Mr. Chikazawa of Pāhoa, his second son, Toyoichi, will enlist shortly. I will write back to him soon. I will ask Toyoichi to drop in, if he has a chance to come to Honolulu. I am looking forward to meeting him, since I can get fourteen or fifteen dollars if he comes.

---

* Also known as the Honpa Hongwanji Hawai'i Betsuin, the headquarters of the largest Buddhist sect in Hawai'i. – Trans.

† Lit., "incense money." A gift, usually monetary, given to a deceased person's family to help defray funeral costs.

‡ Yoshitaka Kataoka, while serving in the U.S. Army at Camp Savage, Minnesota, died in a swimming accident in Lake Minnetonka. He was a family friend, and Richard Hiromichi Kosaki carried his ashes at the Camp Savage services. Email correspondence with Richard Hiromichi Kosaki, December 5, 2009. – Ed.

Bāsan takes care of [Clifford] Kiyoshi of the Uejio family, and
from the nineteenth, he began to eat baby food. Mr. Uejio sold
his sushi shop and bought the site of Migihata Shoten. He began
operating a wholesale business. Now he employs several staff
members and sells tens of thousands of dollars [of goods]. Mr.
Kobara's [restaurant] is very popular and is [worth] 140,000 to
150,000 shares. Mama Kobara* is very kind to me. Mr. Kobara is
good, too.

Recently he bought fourteen acres of land in Kaimukī.† He
plans to build his house there. After that, he plans to build a lot
of houses to rent, he says. He repeatedly says that when Hideko
comes back, he will give a house to her. Both Kobara and Uejio are
rich. Kobara is a great man. Please write a letter of thanks to him
saying that I am greatly indebted to him for his kindness.

Zen'ichi finally came back on the nineteenth, after being away
for two years. Everyone is happy now.

I am afraid that you may not be able to go back to Japan. I am
looking forward to the day when peace comes and you return to
Hawaii. I will write to you again soon.

Take care of the children and yourselves.

P.S. We were invited to the famous Mochizuki Restaurant twice –
on June 14 by the Uejios and on July 11 by the Kobaras.

Date: not dated[11‡]
From: Momoe [Kataoka], Hakalau, Hawai'i
To: Otokichi Ozaki, Tule Lake Relocation Center, California

I was deeply touched by your letter of condolence regarding
Yoshitaka's accidental death. If only my son and his two
companions had not gone on their day off for a boat ride on that
famous Lake Minnetonka. They ran into a storm and lost an oar
due to the high waves. Trying to get them back to shore, Yoshitaka
dove in to retrieve it, but he was swept under. Only five months
ago he had enlisted after finishing his studies at a business school
in Honolulu. He had promised to return safely, but fate can be so
cruel. It will be officially noted that he died in the line of duty.

I had been prepared for his death in combat, but this – it
is such a pity. I realize there are others who experience similar
tragedies (the son of Mizutari Sensei of Kaumana was killed in
New Guinea),§ but this turn of events is just too pitiful. As the

---

* Haru Kobara – Trans.
† A community within the city of Honolulu. – Trans.
‡ The letter was likely written in late June or July 1944. – Trans.
§ Yukitaka "Terry" Mizutari was killed on June 23, 1944. He was the eldest son of Yasuyuki
Mizutari, principal of Kaumana Japanese Language School in Hilo. – Trans.

saying goes, "Yesterday, misfortune for someone else; today, it is my turn."*

Please take good care of yourselves. The war should end soon, so let us wait patiently. You will surely see your parents once again.

A Hilo [bank] official, Mr. Smith, contacted Kazuma several days ago about coming to his office. There was a mistake in the documentation, and Kazuma signed the corrected paper. I am sure you will receive the money from the bank shortly. Please let us know when you have received it. Kazuma will be relieved to hear it.

It has already been forty-seven days since my son's death, but I still feel lost and helpless. A personal experience like this is so heartbreaking.

Date: August 30 [1944][12]
From: Tomoya Ozaki, Honolulu, Hawai'i
To: Otokichi and Hideko Ozaki, Tule Lake Relocation Center, California

How have you been lately? We, three families and Jiji and Baba, are all fine. Kobara's restaurant is always busy. On Sundays, sales amount to $1,200 to $1,300. Uejio also is doing very well. There are eleven people at the Uejio house, including the new bride and us, and they are kind to us. We intend to stay here for the time being, since they say that we can stay here. Please write thank-you letters to the Kobaras and Uejios, telling them that you are grateful for their kindness to us.

Recently I bought twenty-four yards of fabric. I will send it tomorrow. The three coloring books from Haruko are for Yukio, Sachi, and Yuri. I will send some books to Tomoyuki. They should be arriving shortly. These days we cannot buy more than three-and-a-half yards of fabric at a time. Since we cannot get white fabric anymore, I will send instead two *kome baiki*,† which I got from Kobara's restaurant. Nowadays in Honolulu, commodities are becoming scarcer and shopping is getting difficult. I asked them [the Kataokas] to send the typewriter. I will send it to you in the near future.

Kobara's restaurant is closed today. Jiji and Baba are fine.

Take care of the children. Take care of yourselves.

---

* The letter writer is referring to the Japanese saying, "*Kyō wa hito no ue, asu wa waga mi no ue*," 「今日は人の上、明日は我が身の上」 "Today, misfortune for someone else; tomorrow, it is my turn." – Trans.

† Hawaii Japanese slang: a rice bag, 米バイキ. Rice bags were useful to the Japanese in Hawai'i. Made of cotton, they could be bleached and then used to fashion such things as diapers, dishcloths, dresses, or undergarments. – Trans.

P.S. Waiting for the day when peace comes and you return to
Oʻahu. We heard from Mr. Tango that the mother of Toshikazu
Segawa had passed away.

English original
Date: August 29, 1944[13]
From: H. C. Walters, Asst. Vice President, Bank of Hawaii, Hilo,
Hawaiʻi
To: Otokichi Ozaki, Tule Lake Relocation Center, California

Dear Sir:
   We acknowledge receipt of your letter of the 24th requesting
that we withdraw from your Savings Account No. 47198 the sum
of $200.00 and forward it to you.
   As we did not have the savings passbook we contacted your
Attorney-In-Fact, Mr. Kazuma Kataoka, and obtained the book
from him. He informs us, however, that from now on he does
not desire to act for you as Attorney-In-Fact and has left the book
here. We, therefore, will hold the book in our files.
   As far as your old license is concerned, it has expired and we
can allow no withdrawals from the account until you forward to
us the original of the new license No. 14591 which you claim you
now possess.

Yours very truly,
H. C. Walters

English original
Date: September 17, 1944[14]
From: Kazuma Kataoka, Hakalau, Hawaiʻi
To: Otokichi Ozaki, Tule Lake Relocation Center, California

   I withdrew $200.00 from Bank of Hawaii Sept. 16, 1944 in
Block Account so your Savings Book have like this

March 18, 1944 Deposit	$1,500.00
Old License withdrawal	200.00
New " "	200.00
	$1,100.00

   Including I wanted to make clear that yesterday I asked Mr.
Carlsmith & Carlsmith Office. They say I don't have to make a
report to Office of Governor of Hawaiʻi, Foreign Fund Central,
Honolulu.

Yours truly,
Kazuma Kataoka

Date: September 2[?, 1944][15]*
From: Tomoya Ozaki, Honolulu, Hawaii
To: Otokichi and Hideko Ozaki, Tule Lake Internment Camp,
California

How are you doing? Jiji and Baba and the three families are
fine, so don't worry.

The other day I received a letter from Mr. Kataoka of Hakalau,
who suggests that instead of leaving your household goods in
his care indefinitely, if you are willing to sell them, he'd like to
buy them from you. He'd like you to talk it over with Hideko.
Your typewriter was sent to you on September 10. If you need
the sewing machine, we can send it. If you're going to be selling
things, I will buy the *zabuton*. Let me know if you need help in
disposing of the [other] goods. I will borrow your phonograph
records.

I have the ten yards of khaki fabric for you from Mrs. Kobara,
so please write her a thank-you letter. Tell her that I've received the
fabric and am very happy with it.

Send the letter to me, and I will add a few words, and then
mail the letter to her. I will be going shopping to send you a few
things together with the fabric, so if there's anything else you need,
let me know. The knives and forks that we recently sent you were
from Haruko. The *kome baiki* were from Mrs. Kobara.

Everything is expensive nowadays. We are allowed to buy only
three-and-a-half yards of fabric at a time. Apparently, Mrs. Kobara
paid fourteen dollars for the ten yards of khaki fabric. You should
be getting the typewriter and the fabric sometime soon. Look
forward to a shipment.

Take care of the children and yourselves, too.

I stopped writing this letter midway, and the days slipped by
before I could finish it.

Date: September 27 [1944][16]
From: Tomoya Ozaki, Honolulu, Hawai'i
To: Otokichi Ozaki, Tule Lake Relocation Center, California

On the twenty-third, I received your letter of September 10. I

---

* The exact date of this letter is unknown, as it has been partially crossed out. It is known that
Tomoya wrote this letter in September, on one of the twentieth days, and we can surmise from its
context that it was likely in 1944. – Trans.

was glad to note that everybody is doing fine. On our side, Jiji and Baba, and the Kobara, Kosaki, and Uejio families are all fine.

As to the watch you asked for, I asked Mr. Uejio to buy it for you. He says that he had better buy it at a local plantation store that he intends to visit next month. As soon as I get it, I will mail it to you. Mr. Uejio looks quite busy.

Koki Abe went into the Army. Yoji Kobara is scheduled to enlist in the Army soon. Ichiro of the Nadamoto family, who lives in front of Mr. Kosaki, enlisted already on September 4. Mr. Setsuo Isokane also enlisted. I have to send all of them some farewell money.

Thank goodness I am in good health and work every day. Thus, I do not have any real concerns. I rely on Mr. Uejio as usual. Mr. Uejio is now having the inside of his house painted. It will cost about $600, he says.

I will write to you again soon.

Let's hope that peace will come soon.

Today is my day off from Kobara's.

Date: October 11, 1944[17]
From: Otokichi Ozaki, Tule Lake Relocation Center, California
To: Tadasuke Koryu Nakabayashi, Hilo, Hawai'i

Not a single day goes by that I do not think of all of you. Nearly three years have passed since we parted, and I have still not had the opportunity to repay you for the kindness extended to us. No doubt you have been experiencing many changes in Hawai'i.

I understand Jitsuro Fujikawa, one of my former students, was killed in the war in Italy.[*] The other day we went to Mr. Shirasu's barrack with Mr. and Mrs. Tagawa to offer incense for his repose.[†] Eleven of my former students have now sacrificed their young lives under the Stars and Stripes. Who knows when I will be able to visit their homes and bow before their memorial altars?

As I gazed at the photo [of the deceased] that had been sent to Mr. Shirasu, I thought about the Fujikawa family. At the same time a surge of nostalgia swept over me as I saw the faces of old friends in Hilo who had come together [for the funeral]. The craggy lines on your face showed clearly.

I was paroled from Santa Fe Camp in New Mexico and moved with my Hawai'i friends to Jerome Center to join our families.

---

* A member of the 442nd Regimental Combat Team, he was killed during the Rome-to-Arno Campaign in July 1944. – Trans.

† Jukaku Shirasu was a Buddhist priest from the Hilo Hongwanji Mission. Mr. and Mrs. Tagawa are Shizuma and Kazu Tagawa of Hilo. – Trans.

After spending a month there we came to Tule Lake. Though crowded for space, we have adjusted after six months to life in this two-room barrack. The approximately 20,000 people here are waiting to return to Japan.

The children are fine, thank goodness, and they are attending both Japanese and English schools, each for a half-day. Tomoyuki, the eldest, is a third grader at the Eighth National School and is memorizing the Imperial Rescript on Education.* He is in the sixth grade in English school. Yukio, the second son, is a first grader [in Japanese school] and a third grader [in English school]. He has started taking judo lessons twice a week. All the textbooks are the same as those used in Japan.

Since arriving here I have been working at the 79th Block Office as a clerk. Everyone in our block is from Hawai'i. Mr. Tagawa works in the storeroom of the mess hall. As soon as the bell sounds at seven o'clock in the morning, breakfast is served in the mess hall. It amazes me that they manage to feed so many of us three meals a day every day. War is such a waste. There are more than 370 of us in the block. Besides the sixteen dollars a month [for my work], I receive eighteen dollars for clothing expenses (based on the number of family members). What makes me happy is that we can bring our food back from the mess hall to eat in our own room, so I have purchased a small hot plate. Tuna is also available at the [camp] store and is sold for fifty cents a block. We did not bring any household items, however, so my wife is always lamenting the fact that she could have brought everything from home if she had known about the situation. My brother [Kazuki Kosaki] in Honolulu sent us six rice bowls and six teacups, but the children broke half of them, leaving us with just three of each. With a tube of cement glue that I purchased, I have had to piece together the broken dishes several times. Someday I will probably recall such experiences fondly as I share them with you.

Next door to our right, and just a wall away, are our neighbors, Mr. and Mrs. Yoshimi Okumoto and their family.† The other day, Mr. Okumoto received a telegram informing him of his younger brother's passing. Mr. Shirasu was invited to join the rest of us for a memorial service. The barrack is divided into nine sections.

---

* Issued in 1890 by the Ministry of Education in the name of the Meiji Emperor, the document established the guiding principles of education in Japan. It sought to advance Confucianism as the ideological underpinning of imperial rule, placing special emphasis on the virtues of loyalty (*chū*) and filial piety (*kō*). In Japan, all schools received official copies of the rescript and students were required to memorize it as part of their curriculum in ethics. The rescript was rescinded after the war. – Trans.

† Yoshimi Okumoto was principal of the Kukuihaele Japanese Language School in the Waipi'o area of the Big Island. His wife, Tomiyo, also a teacher, and their five children, Yoshito, Toshiko, Kazuto, Shuso, and Keiko, were interned, as well. – Trans.

Rooms A and B are occupied by the Okumoto family, Rooms C and D by us. To our left lives a man from the Mainland. Beyond that there is Rev. Hirayama from Maui and the elderly Tetsuo Tanaka from the Soto Mission.* Mr. Shiba is a waiter in the mess hall.† Mr. Katoda works in the boiler room of the laundry and bathhouse.‡ As long as someone in each family works, he receives sixteen dollars a month and living expenses, as I mentioned earlier. [Following page missing]

English original
Date: October 13, 1944[18]
From: Yoshio Shiwo, New York, New York
To: Otokichi Ozaki, Tule Lake Relocation Center, California

Dear Sir:

I am in receipt of your letter and inquiry, many thanks. We can buy you the following:

Used Rebuilt Singer Electric Sewing Machines. All of these are guaranteed 1 year, and in the best of condition.

There is a 10% buying service, and crating charge of $4.00 each. Tax is included in price.

Cabinet Style.   From $100.00 to 125.00
Desk Style.   From $140.00 to 150.00

We can buy you Electric portables, Singer, but will take at least 2 weeks, as very scarce.

Price from $80.00 to 90.00 plus 3.00 crating.

I have sold a few of the 31-15 Singer tailor sewing machines, in your camp. If you wish to see them you can go to see Mr. Harry Uchida, 3717D Tule Lake. This machine is $120.00 plus 5.00 needles and bobbins.

Thanking you for your inquiry and hoping to be of service to you.

Yours truly,
Yoshio Shiwo

---

* Unni Hirayama, a Buddhist priest from the Lahaina Hongwanji Mission on Maui; Tetsuo Tanaka, a Buddhist priest from the Kawailoa Soto Mission in Waialua, Oʻahu. – Trans.
† Kakuo Shiba, a Shingon Buddhist priest from Paʻauilo on the Big Island. – Trans.
‡ Tetsuei Katoda was principal of the Piʻihonua Japanese Language School near Hilo. – Trans.

Date: October 15 [1944][19]
From: Tomoya Ozaki, Honolulu, Hawai'i
To: Otokichi and Hideko Ozaki, Tule Lake Relocation Center,
California

On the fifteenth, I received letters from Hideko dated the
eighth and from Otokichi dated the eleventh. I am relieved to hear
that Tomoyuki has recovered. All of us, Jiji and Baba included, are
fine, as usual.

Hiromichi, whom you asked about, returned yesterday
morning, the fourteenth. Originally he said that he had to return
immediately, but he was allowed to stay until noon today. Then an
extension was granted until the seventeenth at six o' clock in the
afternoon. He immediately called Nobuko and she came at around
three-thirty. All of us are now enjoying the reunion.

Nobuko has to go to Moloka'i tomorrow. I do not know where
Hiromichi will leave for. I began to work from the fourth of this
month, and I work every day.

The Kobara family received your letter dated the thirteenth,
and they were very pleased. It would be good for me if you were
to write to them that Mrs. Kobara, more than Mr. Kobara, has
been helpful. Besides, when you come back, you many need Mrs.
Kobara's help. Mrs. Kobara is very kind to me, as well.

Date: not dated[20]
From: Tomoya Ozaki, Honolulu
To: Hideko Ozaki, Tule Lake Relocation Center, California

On the twelfth I received your letter of the eighth. I am
happy to know you all are doing well. Please rest assured that the
Kobaras, Kosakis, Uejios, and Jiji and Baba are all fine.

I will soon buy and send to you the fabric that you asked for.
My days off are Wednesdays, but I have to ask someone to do the
shopping [for me]. Therefore, it is somewhat of an inconvenience,
but I will send it as soon as I get it.

I will get the sewing machine and the foot pedal [from
Hakalau] and send it to you. I have not yet retrieved or sold even
one of your things in Hakalau. I now have enough money, so I
don't need to sell any of them.

Kazuma [Kataoka] said that he would soon send Otokichi the
bank deposit certificate showing the proceeds of the sale of the
land. Thus, you will soon receive the bank paper for $1,300, the
remaining balance of the proceeds.

Mrs. Kobara is always kind to me. Please write a thank you

letter to Mrs. Kobara saying that I am very grateful for her kindness. A short note will do, so enclose it in your letter to me. I will hand it to Mrs. Kobara, when Mr. Uejio is away.

I am in good health and work without taking even a day off. I am Mr. Kobara's *yokozuna* among twenty-seven or twenty-eight workers. Since coming to Mr. Uejio's on June 1, I have worked from the early morning to the late evening without taking a break. Since it is my day off today, I am writing four letters -- to you, Kazuma, Mr. Tango, and Bunnosuke Sato.

There are so many things to tell you, but I will write them in the next letter.

Take care of the children. Take care of yourself.

English original
Date: October 20, 1944[21]
From: L. V. Darling, Lambert Brothers Jewelers, New York, New York
To: Otokichi Ozaki, Tule Lake Relocation Center, California

Dear Mr. Ozaki:

In reply to your inquiry of recent date we regret to advise that we do not have any Parker 51 fountain pens on hand.

However, we do have a Schaeffer Triumph set at $21.00 including tax, which we will hold aside until we hear from you.

Trusting we may have the pleasure of serving you again, we are

Very truly yours,
L. V. Darling

English original
Date: October 31, 1944[22]
From: L. V. Darling, Lambert Brothers Jewelers, New York, New York
To: Otokichi Ozaki, Tule Lake Relocation Center, California

Dear Mr. Ozaki:

We wish to acknowledge with thanks receipt of your money order in the amount of $21.00.

We have forwarded the pen and pencil set to you today and feel that the point in the pen is fine and will prove entirely satisfactory.

Thanking you for your valued patronage, we are

Very truly yours,
L. V. Darling

English original
Date: November 14, 1944[23]
From: H. C. Walters, Assistant Vice President, Bank of Hawaii, Hilo, Hawai'i
To: Otokichi Ozaki, Tule Lake Relocation Center, California

Dear Sir:

As requested in your letter of November 7th we enclose our draft payable to your order for $199.60 less exchange. We hold original License No. 14591 in our file.

Very truly yours,
H. C. Walters

Date: November 27 [1944][24]
From: Otokichi Ozaki, Tule Lake Relocation Center, California
To: Mrs. Nakabayashi [wife of Tadasuke Koryu Nakabayashi], Hilo, Hawai'i

I hope you are well. We are in good health, as we greet the winter season. Snow has been falling for the past week, piling up and melting away. It can accumulate up to five-to-six inches. The coldest temperature up to now has been eight degrees [Celcius]. We are gradually becoming accustomed to the cold weather.

Thank you very much for all the unusual and wonderful things sent to us. We are grateful beyond words. Time and again we have imposed on you, and we are so indebted that it moves us to tears. We have done nothing but been willful and self-serving. When will we ever be able to repay you? That is what distresses us.

It has been nearly three years since I left Hilo. Norio-kun must have grown into a nice young man. I hope peace will come as soon as possible so that we can see all of you again.

I have been paying homage to all our former students who died in battle.

My parents in Honolulu are in good health, thank goodness. The other day we were shown photos of the memorial service for those who died in the war and, we became teary-eyed at the sight of the familiar faces of Hilo friends who had helped us for more than twenty years.

There is nothing better than the natural environment of Hawai'i for someone who has been brought up in Hawai'i since childhood. We should pass on this valuable experience, but we do not know when it will happen.

We pray for your family's good health as you prepare to greet a new year. Please give our regards to everyone.

Date: November 29 [1944][25]
From: Mrs. Fujimoto, Hilo, Hawai'i
To: Otokichi Ozaki, Tule Lake Relocation Center, California

I managed to get your address from Fudeko when you wrote to her. It was a great relief to hear that you and your family are all right. Please accept the very small gift of flannel pajamas (two sets) and some towels I am sending you. The pajamas were hand-sewn, so they may not fit well. I sewed one set about eight years ago, when I had intended to return to Japan, so it is quite old, but it has never been worn. I hesitate to send such a meager gift, but please accept my sentiments. It will get colder in the coming days, so please take good care of yourselves. My son is now serving in France. I pray every day that the war will end soon.

Date: December 17 [1944][26]
From: Fudeko Ikeda, Hilo, Hawai'i
To: Otokichi Ozaki, Tule Lake Relocation Center, California

Christmas is coming. The kettles in front of the Kress Store are waiting to be filled by passersby. In spite of the shortage of goods, shops are crowded. They are brightly lit at night.

I can well imagine your feelings about having to spend your third New Year's away from home. We hope the tea cups and dishes we are sending you will arrive intact. How about clothing?

Recently I saw Hideo's photo in the display window at the electric company. I recall he was somewhat of a problem student for you, Mr. Ozaki. Before his induction, I understand he gave a tearful speech at his high school. The smiling face that looked back at me brought tears to my eyes as the impact of his death hit me.

I wonder how Tsutomu is doing. All I pray for is that peace will come soon. I am anxious to see all of you, too. Oh yes, please use the enclosed cash to buy candy or anything else for your children.

Date: January 3 [1945][27]
From: Tomoya Ozaki, Honolulu, Hawai'i
To: Otokichi and Hideko Ozaki, Tule Lake Relocation Center, California

Thank you very much for your letter the other day. I hope all of you have been doing well. I was too busy to write to you sooner. Jiji and Baba and the three families greeted the New Year in good health. Business in Hawai'i is very good, as in the past. I work at Kobara's place. Kobara's business is prospering.

Kosaki finished repairing his house. It cost him about $900. He has bought bags of cement for a concrete slab under the floor. I cannot do it [now], because I have no time. I hope I can do it soon.

I will send the things that came from Hakalau. At the year-end, we pounded *mochi* at Kosaki's house. Both [Hidemichi] and Kazuo could not pound. I pounded with Bāsan's help.

At Christmas I bought gifts worth $16 for Kobara, $13 for Uejio, $77 for Kosaki, $28 for Kataoka, $3.50 for Nakauchi, and $3.25 for Nakamura. All of them are working hard. My wife went to a dentist for treatment. It cost $100. At the year-end I paid $500 for the [sale of the] land; this plus additional costs came to more than $740 in total, but since I have a job, the money wasn't a problem.

On the afternoon of December 21, the child of Dr. [Jun'ichi] Matsumura of Hilo had an operation in Honolulu because of an illness, but the child passed away. Since Dr. Matsumura was staying at Mr. Kawazoe's, Bāsan and I paid a visit to offer our condolences and *kōden* of five dollars.

I returned immediately but Bāsan stayed for a while and heard about the various happenings [in Hilo]. Old Man Mikami of 'Amauulu passed away.* Sakai's wife left him, leaving three children behind.

Hiromichi Kosaki became an instructor and was assigned to the present place. Although you asked us, we cannot send anything like sugar or other foodstuff from Hawai'i. Please send money to Hiromichi and ask him to send you whatever you need.

On November 1, Mr. Hideo Nakauchi was injured on his hand and now is recuperating. Tsutomu is still in Honolulu. He comes once in a while. It would be nice of you to write an *omimai* letter to Mr. Nakauchi in Pāhoa.

I will write to you again soon.

Let's hope that peace will come soon. It is my day off today.

Last, but not least, Bāsan is doing very well.

Take care of the children and yourselves.

Date: January 10, 1945[28]
From: Michi Kajiwara, Hilo, Hawai'i
To: Hideko Ozaki, Tule Lake Relocation Center, California

I'm glad your children are happy with the things I sent them. It doesn't happen often, but whenever we hear that a shipment of toys will be unpacked at Kress Department Store in Hilo, we drop

-----

* Tarobei Mikami, a farmer. – Trans.

everything and dash over. When the doors open at eight o' clock, we stumble in with the crowd and scoop up items at random. It looks shameful but everyone's doing it for the children, and if we worry about appearances, we'll end up with nothing.

The town looked empty last week, but there's a lot more activity now. I'm reminded of my son whenever I see men in uniform. Today was induction day and I recognized a few of Joji's friends. I had mixed feelings as I saw the trucks leaving and the men waving. I can only pray that they'll do their jobs well and return safely. About one hundred men leave with each group, but a third are non-Japanese.

Itsuo's on active duty in France. For Christmas he sent ten dollars to each of his siblings, but they haven't the heart to spend their brother's hard-earned money and are saving it instead. As for my husband, he is so grateful not to have been interned that he has abstained from going to the theater, no matter how good the movie, since the war began. I've gone twice. Joji graduated from business school and will soon be working. Being thin and underweight, he didn't qualify for military service. This gives Itsuo some peace of mind, since he had asked Joji to look after the family while he is away. Since then Joji has surprised me with his mature behavior.

Nobu will graduate from high school in June. He was classified as 1-A when he made eighteen last October, so he'll probably go into military service.

Tamiko is working at Kress Department Store only on Saturdays and until the end of summer. Then she'll go back to school. Last Christmas she bought presents for all of us with some of her earnings.

Toru is in the seventh grade. He seems to have finally adjusted to his new school. He's taken up the clarinet and gives us a jolt now and then with his off-key sounds. I wonder if he'll be able to play well in a year.

We see so many young women in town. It's rare to see men of Itsuo's age (twenty to twenty-five). Young farmers and the sick seem to be the only ones left. The news is that there are many good jobs available in Honolulu, and a high school diploma isn't even necessary.

I plan to visit Mr. and Mrs. Fujikawa soon. They were devastated when their son was killed in action. For a while it was so difficult to even talk to them, but they seem to have finally accepted the fact that Jitsuo is gone.

Date: January 15 [1945]²⁹
From: Keikichi Ochiai,* Crystal City Internment Camp, Texas
To: Otokichi Ozaki, Tule Lake Relocation Center, California

Whoever says whatever, I will never forget about our
tonarigumi.† However, these days I feel lonely because nobody
responds to my calling or shouting. I look back with nostalgia
to the days when we used to lay side by side and call each other
"*tonarigumi*," and to the days when we enjoyed our lives, although
we had many problems. These days are gone like a dream.

Thank you for your letter. I am glad to know that you are fine.
We often talk about you among our family. I always thought that I
should write to you, but delayed until today. Since we are from the
same *tonarigumi*, please forgive me.

As I understand, you are actively engaged in the important
responsibility of clerk. I hope you will do good work for other
people. I work everyday in good health. Since being interned here,
I've been busier than I've ever been.

Mr. Asano works at the school everyday. I will give him your
message as soon as possible. Concerning the production of
babies, our place seems too far behind yours. We had more than
fifty babies last year. This year we've already had ten babies so
far. Yesterday, we had a new record of four babies born in a day.
Among people from Hawai'i, almost all the young teachers had
babies.

Although the population at this center is not as large as that of
yours, the number of students is comparatively large. Presently the
number of students is over 1,000. Most of the teachers are from
Hawai'i. This is encouraging.

We had a *go* tournament in November. I played as an eighth
rank. I started playing this game when I came here. This coming
Saturday and Sunday we will have tournaments again, which I will
definitely join. I will let you know my results. Since I do not have
a *go* board, I cannot practice at home. At the same time, I do not
like to bother other people by visiting them and practicing there.

How is Mr. Katoda of the *tonarigumi* doing? Please convey my
apologies for not writing to him.

It seldom rains and it has not snowed yet. We had frost for two
consecutive days a few days ago. According to the Ochiai weather
station, the temperature in the morning was 40 degrees F and
about 70 degrees F in the afternoon today. These days the weather
here is just like that of Hawai'i. It seems to not to have snowed

---

* See the letter from his wife, Katsuko, to Hideko, p. 178 – Trans.
† Literally, a "neighborhood association," but here the writer uses the term to convey the idea of
a close-knit group of neighbors. – Trans.

here for a while.

My wife always talks about how your wife was kind to her when we were at the [Jerome] Center. Please give our best regards to your wife.

On New Year's Day this year, we missed the good smell of *ozōni,* but we feel happy since we greeted the New Year with the whole family together in good health.

I will write to you again. In the meantime, please take good care of yourself.

Date: January 19 [1945][30]
From: Torazo Ishiyama, Crystal City Internment Camp, Texas
To: Otokichi Ozaki, Tule Lake Relocation Center, California

Thank you very much for your courteous New Year's greeting card. Please forgive me for not responding right away. I hope that we can again maintain our friendship throughout this year.

I think the unity of the internees has loosened, because of this meaningless confinement. I am quite annoyed with the Christian internees, who have neither racial nor national consciousness. They do not understand our feelings toward our mother country, where 100 million people are "all of one mind." They are egotists.

We can live quite a meaningful life even in confinement, as long as you *do your best, very best.*[*] This is because we live together with Nisei people who are growing with us. Luckily, or unluckily, I am putting forth my best effort with my wife. Maybe for this reason, I am quite surprised that the days are flying by very quickly.

I hear from people about the situation at your place, and I envy you. I try my best day and night in the hope that people at this camp will have the same kind of attitude as that of the people at your place. However, there are so many egotistical politicians,[†] who hold to the safety-first principle that up until now nothing has been improved upon. I feel sorry for the children here.

Presently, I teach physics, chemistry, zoology, botany, and mineralogy at the middle school section of the Japanese school here. Besides these, I teach judo two nights a week and gardening one day a week. Thus, I am quite busy. My wife helps at a kindergarten.

In this connection, I have one request. I am troubled because we do not have textbooks for physics, chemistry, and mineralogy.

---

[*] The original letter is written in Japanese; the words italicized here appear in English in the original. – Trans.

[†] I.e., internees. – Trans.

If someone at your place has these textbooks, I would like to borrow them for a while. Since I am a mere laborer without any experience in teaching, it is really a *hard job* to teach without textbooks. However, nobody else dares to take up this job!

[censored] and [censored] families, who came here earlier from Santa Fe are having *Crystal-born** babies one after the other. Aren't they producing in excess babies of inferior quality? Young people are active, but active only on that point.

It is warm today, after a long spell of coldness. If there were no rain, it would be ideal.

A few days ago, Germans went home on board an exchange ship.

P.S. Say hello to *Geo.* Yamashiro (a Nisei who moved from Gila River Center).

Date: January 20 [1945][31]
From: Mino Kiyota, Hilo, Hawai'i
To: Otokichi Ozaki, Tule Lake Relocation Center, California

What a memorable day it is today! I received the New Year's greeting from you, to whom I have not written in a long time.

I wish to congratulate you on your family happily greeting the first day of the New Year, 1945. I have also celebrated the New Year in my mind. I thought I would not be able to get *mochi* this year, but a neighbor friend gave me some. I was quite impressed.

Since I parted from you, this area has changed a lot. Waimea, that small village, has become a big military town, and the roads have been widened and paved. All my friends have gotten married, and I also have become a mother and now spend my days peacefully. I hope you remember me. I'm Kiyota. Your letter is really like a dream. I pray that the day will come soon when we can meet and talk to each other.

In conclusion, I pray that this year be peaceful for you and your family.

Date: January 26 [1945][32]
From: Fudeko [Ikeda], Hilo, Hawai'i
To: Hideko Ozaki, Tule Lake Relocation Center, California

I've read your letter so many times that it's full of creases. The parcel I sent you contained only odds and ends, yet you were so appreciative. It made me cry. I'm happy to report that we're by

---

* I.e., babies born in Crystal City. – Trans.

no means down and out in spirit or in material goods. You can't imagine how happy it makes me feel to put together your care package. After all, I owe you a great debt. I can't thank you enough for the personal guidance you gave this awkward neophyte fresh out of high school. Even as I recall those days and write this letter, tears flow down my cheeks.

There's no Japanese fabric to be found. The servicemen have bought it all. I hope you'll be able to use the scraps I'd been collecting just for fun. I apologize for the condition of some of them. Maybe you can salvage the best pieces for decorative work.

Granny Fujimoto looks younger since she took a permanent and got dentures. Two or three of her sons have gone into military service, so it's quiet at her house. There's hardly a young man to be seen here.

Tsutomu's fine, I guess. His letters are always cheerful. I'm humbled by his attitude. In the midst of a life-and-death situation he doesn't complain about anything and makes jokes instead. How lonely he must be, away from his family.

I don't have a picture of Keiko because she's never been taken to a photo studio. I'll send you one soon. She talks a lot now. She must take after me (chuckle).

I hope you'll write once in a while, Mrs. Ozaki. Hearing from you directly, instead of through your husband, would be so much nicer.

Date: February 15 [1945][33]
From: Fusayo Iwami, Hilo, Hawai'i
To: Otokichi Ozaki, Tule Lake Relocation Center, California

It was impossible to read about your experiences without becoming emotional. I, too, look forward to the day when we can have peace again.

I don't know how to thank you for the beautifully made brooches from Mrs. Ozaki. One can easily see how much time and effort went into making them. My daughter and I will make good use of the pins.

Your continuous personal interest in your former students and your words of comfort regarding my son are greatly appreciated. I never had the opportunity to see Noboru after he left for military service five months ago. Now I can only rely on Buddha's mercy and become a faithful follower of his teachings. According to Noboru's latest letter, he will complete training in March and will probably be sent to the battlefield.

Date: February 22 [1945][34]
From: Seikaku Takezono,[*] Santa Fe Internment Camp, New Mexico
To: Otokichi Ozaki, Tule Lake Relocation Center, California

I understand my family is imposing upon you for assistance. I would be deeply grateful for whatever you can do, since they are all women.

Conditions here are much better than before. The food is suited to our Japanese taste and servings are more than ample. Besides eggs, tofu, and *miso* soup, we have seafood two to three times a week. Meat is readily available.

About forty acres of land behind the camp have been made available to us. We can take daily walks and go hiking for relief from our confining conditions.

The camp newspaper we have now carries the most current news, unlike in the past. Reading about the latest developments is something we look forward to everyday. It gives us great peace of mind.

Date: February 22 [1945][35]
From: Tomoya Ozaki, Honolulu, Hawai'i
To: Otokichi and Hideko Ozaki, Tule Lake Relocation Center, California

Your letter of February 5 arrived here on the afternoon of the thirteenth, and I am glad to note that everyone is in good health except the little boy who caught a slight cold. All of us, including the three families, are fine.

I wanted to buy and send you fabric sooner, but I was kept busy. On the seventeenth, I went to town to buy fabric. There are twelve pieces of fabric, including some that came from Hakalau, ten *kome baiki*, two small bags, four pairs of footwear, and one dictionary. Bāsan made two teapot rests. I made a package of the thirty-one items. I will send it in a few days.

As for the doll that you asked about, Bāsan says that she can do without it and that the grandchildren should have it. She said she would send anything your children want.

By the way, Bāsan is seventy-eight years old, and I am seventy-seven years old now. While I can work this year, it is getting harder for me. I am becoming bent with age, and I do not know if I can continue to work next year. I do not even know about tomorrow.

As for repatriation to Japan, which you mentioned in your

* A Buddist priest from the Wailuku Hongwanji Mission on Maui. – Trans.

letter, I do not think it will happen soon. You had better transfer all the funds from the bank in Hilo to a bank in Tule Lake.

The *kome baiki* that I am sending to you at this time are the ones that Mrs. Kobara gave us. Please write a thank you letter to her. Also, thank her for the money ($100).

I think it is very difficult to go back to Japan. We look forward to you eventually coming back to Hawai'i. Tsutomu is also in Honolulu. He visits us twice a week.

I will write to you again soon.

Take care of the children and yourselves.

Date: February 23 [1945][36]
From: Tomoya Ozaki, Honolulu, Hawai'i
To: Hideko Ozaki, Tule Lake Relocation Center, California

I hesitate to write, but could you kindly sew a pair of pants for me? I am enclosing some khaki fabric for that. The waist is thirty-four inches including the margin for buttons and buttonholes, and the length is thirty-two or thirty-three inches. Please make cuffs.

The pants I ordered in July of last year are not yet made. There are hardly any steamstresses who can sew things like pants in Hawai'i these days. Bāsan will have a dress sewn for three dollars. Twice, I bought five bed sheets, but since the supply of goods is tight, I could not get a bed cover. I use the bed cover that I borrowed from Mrs. Kosaki. When I heard that bed covers had arrived at a shop, I went to buy one, but they were already gone. I placed an order at Musashiya* in August of last year, but it has not come in yet. I hope it will come soon.

Inouye Sensei dropped in a few days ago. He was permitted to come out and moved to Honolulu with his wife, he said.† Yoji Kobara‡ enlisted in the Army on February 8. He invited 150 people to the Mochizuki Restaurant. I also was invited. He will move to the Mainland shortly.

----

* A dry goods store located in Honolulu's Chinatown on River Street. One of the store's earliest proprietors, Koichiro Miyamoto, is credited with creating the first "aloha shirt." -- Trans.

† Kumaki Inouye was the principal of the Chūō Gakuin Japanese language school in Hilo. Like Ozaki, he was picked up on December 7 and interned on the Mainland. – Trans.

‡ Thomas Yoji Kobara, Hideko's half-brother. – Trans.

Date: March 2, 1945[37]
From: Tetsuo Tanaka,* Santa Fe Internment Camp, New Mexico
To: Otokichi and Hideko Ozaki, Tule Lake Relocation Center,
California

I have not written to you since we parted. Although I intended
to write to you, I could not write until today, because I used up
my allocated number of correspondence for my private business.
Please forgive me.

According to letters from my wife, she is in your debt for the
various uncommon generosities of your family. I have no words to
express my appreciation for this.

After two long years of separate living and more than twenty
petitions for us to live together, much like you, with deep emotion
I met my wife and children at the Jerome Center so that we
could live together. However, after ten months, even before I
took a breath as head of the family, we were again forced to live
separately.

Since I think this is my destiny, I have no regrets at all, but
when it snows, I worry if it is cold [in Tule Lake], and a million
thoughts come to mind.

I pray that both of you will kindly take care of my wife while
I am away. Since leaving, she seems to be suffering from morning
sickness. Based on her experiences with my two daughters, I
know that she will suffer. I ask myself, if as a father-to-be, am I
responsible for this? However, I can do nothing from here in Santa
Fe. Fortunately, I hear that the people at your place, especially
your wife, take good care of her, for which I express my deep
appreciation. I ask that you continue to bestow your kindness
upon her.

According to the correspondence from your camp [Tule Lake],
which I received after I arrived at Bismarck, quite a number of
people have been transferred since I left, and some of them are
reported to have come here [to Santa Fe].† However, I have not yet
met any of them. I understand that there are numerous rumors

---

* Tetsuo Tanaka was the priest of the Kawailoa Soto temple in Waialua, Oʻahu. He also taught
Japanese at the temple's language school, along with his wife, Chiyoko. Tanaka, his wife, and their
two daughters, Lucille and Barbara, were interned. – Trans.

† Fort Lincoln Internment Camp in Bismarck, North Dakota initially held Issei and German
internees. In February 1945, authorities began transferring primarily to Santa Fe – but also to Bismarck – Issei and those Nisei internees known as "renunciants;" i.e. Japanese Americans primarily
from Tule Lake, who had renounced their U.S. citizenship under the terms of a new law with simi-
larities to the 1943 Loyalty Questionnaire. Tetsuden Kashima argues that, using both coercion and
the renunciation law, officials sought to rid Tule Lake of its troublemaking elements. See Kashima,
Judgment Without Trial, 168-72. Tanaka may have been sent to Bismarck, and then later to Santa
Fe, by authorities who believed that as a Buddhist priest, he would be helpful in pacifying unruly
internees. On this topic, see Furuya, *Haisho Tenten*. – Trans.

flying around at your place. I hope that since you are wise, you will conduct yourself prudently.

Since I came to this camp, the issue of returning people from Hawai'i to Hawai'i has been tackled, and quite a large number of people from Hawai'i, who are fathers of military service men, may be going back shortly. Following them, the remaining people from Hawai'i may be allowed to go back if they wish. Since the situation involving people from Hawai'i is different from that involving people from the Mainland, a large number of people from Hawai'i now in various camps will be going back to Hawai'i.*

On the other hand, for those who wish to go back to Japan, like me, or for those elderly people, as mentioned in your famous broadcasts, when will the exchange ship to Japan be arranged?

The separation of families is an inconvenience for now, but this will be remedied sooner or later by appealing to the American sentiment of humanism, and we will be able to live together again. Then, I will be able to see you again. When I lived in your center, we lived so closely that we did not discuss matters seriously. Next time we meet, I will tell you a lot of interesting stories.

Here it used to be warm, but now it is becoming cold. Being a returnee [to Santa Fe], I was greeted warmly by old friends and settled into the No. 62 unit. The people in the No. 58 unit are all doing fine.† Mr. Mizutari‡ and Mr. Nakagawa are also going back to Hawai'i.

Looking down from the back of the hospital toward the mess hall of the lower-town,§ I can see barracks under construction. They say they have already finished designing barracks to be built on the sports grounds. There are many kinds of rumors going around, like anywhere else. The only thing that does not change is the scenery of the old town of Santa Fe that can be seen in the distance, with leafless trees standing like brooms amid low-lying clouds.

I pray for your good health.

---

* Despite the many rumors of internees returning to Hawai'i, only six actually made it back before the war's end. They were Kichitaro Kawauchi, an electrician from Pepe'ekeo on the Big Island; Kametaro Maeda, Christian minister from Honolulu; Teiichiro Maehara, Japanese language school principal from Pu'unēnē, Maui; Kyoichi Miyata, a storekeeper from Honolulu; Matsujiro Otani, proprietor of Otani Shokai; and Shigezo Shimoda, Shinto priest and Japanese language school principal from Honolulu. JCCH Internee Database. – Trans.

† Barrack No. 58 is where Ozaki lived while at Santa Fe. – Trans.

‡ Yasuyuki Mizutari, a Japanese language school principal from Hilo, whose son's death in battle is mentioned in the letter from Momoe Kataoka, p. 185 – Trans.

§ Santa Fe was divided into two areas, an upper- and a lower-town. Japanese internees occupied the lower-town. See Soga, *Life Behind Barbed Wire*. – Trans.

Date: March 6, 1945[38]
From: Michi Kajiwara, Hilo, Hawai'i
To: Otokichi and Hideko Ozaki, Tule Lake Relocation Center,
California

Thank you for the beautifully made shell flowers and brooch.
They were so unusual that I decided to show them to my
neighbor. I apologize for having imposed on you, however, and I
ask that you refrain from such gestures hereafter. Sending packages
is a simple matter for me, but it must be a great inconvenience for
you, especially in your situation.

Last month there were a few familiar faces among the
inductees—the barber's son, the noodle shop's son, etc. This
month several young men have completed their physical
examinations and are waiting for the results. The uncertain
situation makes it difficult for the high school students to
concentrate on their studies. I have heard that there are University
of Hawai'i students who have returned to their homes here to wait
for their induction orders. I suppose this means that only the girls
will be left on the college campus. If the war continues, we will
have a shortage of young men. Everyday I pray that there will be
peace soon.

Date: March 27 [1945][39]
From: Haru Kobara, Honolulu, Hawai'i
To: The Family of Otokichi Ozaki, Tule Lake Relocation Center,
California

As they say, "Time flies like an arrow." Three years have passed
since your family moved to the Mainland. During that time
we have not written even one letter, but this was not our true
intention. My husband insists that even if we do not write, our
feelings are conveyed to you. Please forgive us.

I am more than happy to note that all of you are in good health
and live happily. The other day I sent some money to you through
your father [Tomoya], which I hope you have received by this
time.

Thank you very much for your congratulatory and encouraging
words to my son, George Ichiro, when he enlisted in the Army. He
has moved to the Mainland already, and at the same time that I
received your letter, I received a cable from him telling me that he
had safely arrived at his destination. Since he was born a boy, I am
sure that it is a matter of deep satisfaction for him to serve in the
Army. Please pray for his continued luck in arms.

All our family members are spending busy days, but we are all in good health. Your father [Tomoya] is also in good health and works everyday from early morning, but since he is more than seventy years old now, anything may happen at any time. Please take good care of yourselves.

Let's pray for the early arrival of peaceful days and our continued good health, so that we can meet each other soon. Last but not least, please convey our best wishes to Mr. Satoru Morikawa.*

Date: March 29 [1945][40]
From: Tomoya Ozaki, Honolulu, Hawai'i
To: Otokichi and Hideko Ozaki, Tule Lake Relocation Center

On March 27, I received your letter of March 18. I am relieved to hear that Sachi is completely over her cold. I am glad to know that everyone else is doing well.

As for us, Jiji and Baba and all the three families are in good health. The Kobaras received your letter, too. I am enclosing a letter from Mrs. Kobara. On the twenty-seventh, we received a cable from their [Thomas] Yoji saying that he had safely arrived on the Mainland.

Since last year, I have been giving $30 a month each to Kosaki and Uejio as rice money. The year before last, I placed an order to have kimonos made, and I gave all of my salary, except for some pocket money, to Kosaki. As of last year, I decided to give him $30 a month.

I am getting old and cannot work forever. I am now paying a tax of $15.40 a month.

Otokichi and Hideko, please come back to O'ahu for the sake of our country. O'ahu is short of workers.

I will write to you again soon.

Take care of the children. Take care of yourselves.

Date: April 24 [1945][41]
From: Tomoya Ozaki, Honolulu, Hawai'i
To: Hideko Ozaki, Tule Lake Relocation Center, California

I am sorry I have not written to you for a long time. When I received your letter, I wanted to write back to you, but I was so busy. I hope everyone is in good health. Jiji and Baba are fine. The three families are also fine. Mr. Kobara's business is doing better

---

* Satoru Morikawa, also interned, was a baker from Honolulu. – Trans.

and better.

On the twenty-first, I received the shirt and pants that you had kindly sent to me. Thank you very much. They are neither too long nor too short. They fit on my waist well. They are very well made.

The drug that you asked for is very difficult to find and I asked Mr. Uejio to get it. As soon as I get it, I will mail it to you.

Hideko, please write to Mrs. Kobara and thank her for her kindness in taking care of me.

I sent you some fabric the other day. I bought four pieces for the children and two more. All the others came from Hakalau.

Nobuko is getting married this summer. Her intended husband is Mr. Homestead* of Hilo, who has a bachelor's degree in agriculture.

I will write to you again.

Take care of the children and yourselves.

Date: May 30 [1945][42]
From: Tomoya Ozaki, Honolulu, Hawai'i
To: Hideko Ozaki, Tule Lake Relocation Center, California

How have you been lately? Please rest assured that all of us -- the Kobaras, Kosakis, Uejios, and Jiji and Baba -- are in good health. I received and now wear the pants that you made and sent me. They are neither too big nor too small and are just right. I really appreciate them. Thank you very much. I am fine and work everyday without even taking a day off.

In April, the Kobara family held its seventh year anniversary[†] at Mochizuki Restaurant. We attended, along with the Kosakis and Uejios and many others. My wife went to a restaurant for the first time.

Mr. Kobara bought three fee-simple houses on the right side of his present house for $14,000. He says that you can come back at any time. To celebrate this occasion, they invited all of their workers to Mochizuki Restaurant. They are having another event on June 6. If I go, that will be the fifth time. Mr. Kobara's restaurant is very popular.

Nobuko of the Kosaki family is getting married at the beginning of July. The bridegroom is Mr. [Robert] Fukuda of

---

* Nobuko Kosaki married Robert Fukuda of Hilo. Tomoya may have referred to Robert Fukuda as "Mr. Homestead," because he and Nobuko taught and lived at Moloka'i High School, which was surrounded by Hawaiian Homestead lands. Robert Fukuda was an agricultural instructor. – Trans.

† It is not clear what type of commemorative event this is, as Tomoya's use of the term *shichi nenki* 七年記 is ambiguous. It may be a Buddhist memorial service marking the seventh anniversary of a death or, more likely, a celebratory event involving Kobara's restaurant. – Trans.

Hilo.

Bāsan does not have a [black] kimono, and so she had a hard time figuring out what to wear to the funeral of the Matsumura family. So she bought some black material and is having one made, but it is not yet ready. It is supposed to be ready by Nobuko's wedding. She also asked Haruko to make two [Western] dresses last October, but they are not yet ready. Besides these, she has material for two more dresses. Would you please be able to make the dresses, if we send the material along with an old dress as a sample?

Please take care of the children and yourself.

Date: June 1 [1945][43]
From: Mrs. [Haru] Kobara, Honolulu, Hawai'i
To: Otokichi Ozaki and family, Tule Lake Relocation Center, California

These days it is very hot even in Hawai'i. I am afraid that it is much hotter on the continent.

Thank you very much for the beautiful shell-work ornaments that you have kindly sent to us. They are all beautifully done, and I suppose you have personally handcrafted them. Everybody praises your fine craftsmanship. As you suggested, we shared your gifts among the Ozaki family, Uejio family, and ourselves. Everybody was pleased to have them.

I suppose that you have learned or practiced various things since you moved there. I am sure you encountered many hardships while you were learning. The present time may not be a good time, but if you do your best, you will see better times.

Since our children grow day by day, it is important that we are in good health. All of us are doing fine here. Our business is thriving and Grandfather is in good spirits.

Once in a while, you may reminisce about days in Hawai'i. I am keeping my fingers crossed that the day will come soon when we can meet and talk to each other.

If there is anything I can do for you here, please do not hesitate to ask.

Please take care of yourselves. Thank you very much.

Date: June 14 [1945][44]
From: Tomoya Ozaki, Honolulu, Hawai'i
To: Otokichi and Hideko Ozaki, Tule Lake Relocation Center, California

Although I have not heard from you in a while, I hope

everyone is fine. Jiji and Baba and the three families are fine.

Mr. Kobara gave me $100 again and asked me to send it to your children. Since your children are still small, I will send it to Hideko tomorrow. When you receive it, please write a thank-you letter to Mr. Kobara directly.

You told me that it was very difficult to get cotton cloth where you are. I found some here, a piece for each of your four children and for you. I will send them to you within a few days.

Since June 4 was the one-year anniversary of the death of Yoshitaka in Hakalau, I sent them five dollars for flowers. Today I received their thank you letter. In that letter, they wrote that the son of Mr. Bunnosuke Sato in 'Amauulu died in a battle in December of last year.* I will write to Mr. Tango† to confirm this news, and if it is correct, I will send them a letter of condolence and *kōden* of two dollars. As soon as I hear more, I will let you know.

I will write again soon.

Take care of yourselves.

Date: June 28, 1945[45]
From: Ichiro Kasai, Santa Fe Internment Camp, New Mexico
To: Otokichi Ozaki, Tule Lake Relocation Center, California

Thank you very much for your letter. Since leaving here, you continued to move and move and ended up in a place where warm weather is yet to come. Nonetheless, I am glad to hear that all of your family is doing well.

While you were here, we were greatly indebted to you, and for this I wish to express our deep appreciation.

Here, summer is almost around the corner, but still there are heavy sandstorms every afternoon. This is our headache these days.

From the time I was young, I have been poor and accustomed to a life without freedom. Thus, I lead an easy life here, living as if day dreaming, without feeling restricted at all.

However, one day I found that my right *kintama*‡ bulged thrice as large. I was happy, because I would not need to worry about gold any more. I am now in a hospital bed at A Ward on a hilltop.

As they say, "Man's desire has no end." If one thing is satisfied, one wants the next and the next and the next. When I found that I did not need to worry about gold any more, various desires cropped up, and I now am indulging in many fantasies while lying

---

* See his letter, p. 233 -- Trans.
† Rokutaro Tango, a farmer in 'Amauulu. See his letter, p. 233 - Trans.
‡ Slang for the testicles; lit., "gold balls."

in bed holding my gold balls.

Especially regrettable is the fact that I cannot go to see plays and attend lectures. Of course, I missed a good performance on the twenty-fourth, as I was in bed, depressed. I think that this should be my destiny, and I must give up going out. However, my illness is by no means serious, and I will recover soon. Please never take my talk seriously.

Yesterday I received a letter from Mrs. Tagawa. I read it with great reminiscence and fond memories. Under the present tight control and due to my laziness, I do not know when I can write to her. Please convey my best wishes to her.

Here at the center, since Mr. Yama-no-chaya was appointed Entertainment Manager, entertainment activities have become very lively. Plays are often performed. Next month, on the second Saturday, we will have a variety of performances, and on the third Saturday, the Buddhists Federation will sponsor a Bon dance. On the fourth Saturday, a play will be performed. I am trying to get out of bed sooner.

Please forgive my rude writings. Please give my best regards to Mrs. Ozaki and the others.

FAMILY RETURNS TO HAWAI'I, 1945

> The time has come for us to make a clean sweep of our past life behind barbed wire and prepare for a new beginning.
>
> —Otokichi Ozaki, in a letter to Tadasuke Koryu Nakabayashi

WITH THE END of the war in August 1945, came the many months of deliberation by the Ozaki family as to what their next steps would be. There was much talk of the surrender and conditions in Japan. While the Issei pledged loyalty to the U.S. in their pre-arrest interviews, they nevertheless agonized over Japan's crushing defeat. Rumors flew quickly about the devastation in Japan and the suicides among military leaders.

Yet, the Ozakis deliberated as to whether they should move to Japan once they were released. Ozaki's parents and his brother-in-law, Kazuki Kosaki, implored the family to return to Hawai'i, citing that the conditions were much better in Hawai'i. Ozaki's father insisted there was no better place to live than Hawai'i, and that they could buy rice much more easily in Hawai'i than they could in Japan.

In the end, the Ozakis relented. Their last few months of 1945 were spent getting ready to return to Hawai'i, much to the delight of Ozaki's parents. The Ozakis finally returned to Hawai'i in December 1945, and correspondence is filled with friends welcoming them back to the islands and looking forward to seeing them again. Again, future historians are fortunate that Ozaki was such a prolific writer, as he must have corresponded with everyone he knew before returning to Hawai'i. The responses to his letters are included here.

Date: August 12 [1945][1]
From: Tameshige Sueoka,* New York, New York
To: Otokichi Ozaki, Tule Lake Relocation Center, California

I assume you are playing *go* as usual. Since coming out into *shaba*, I have been fortunate to work from morning to night for hourly wages, but I am tired. On top of that, the newspapers are full of pathetic news—naval bombardment, the bombing of Hiroshima, Russia declaring war against Japan, the unconditional surrender of Japan. I cannot read these articles without tears. I think the people at your place were also disappointed.

On the other hand, the days of peace may come sooner. In our city, they are already preparing for the victory celebration. People listen to the radio throughout the night. They say quick-tempered people are already making loud noises at Times Square and Union Square. We have no one to talk to and no courage to listen to the radio, so we feel small and stay at home. I am afraid that our mother country no longer has any ammunition or weapons to fight with.

I understand that cigarettes are in short supply at your place. I bought some cigarettes with the money I made in New York and sent them to you yesterday. Will you give them to the cigarette lovers? Thank you for your help.

Will you tell Mr. Sugasano that I received the golf award certificate he had sent to me? Will you tell him also that I sent the watch he asked for to my brother-in-law?

I understand that Mrs. Umehara's condition is serious. I am sorry about her situation and pray for her recovery.

What with so many priests and teachers [among the internees], you are probably suffering from a shortage of mess hall workers. I suppose that Mr. Nakamura has a headache [and can't work].

No matter the circumstances, let's keep up our pride in being Japanese, and let's stay in good health.

Presently, the city's climate is like that of Hawai'i. Give my best regards to your family.

Date: August 15, 1945[2]
From: Tomoya Ozaki, Honolulu, Hawai'i
To: Otokichi and Hideko Ozaki, Tule Lake Relocation Center, California

How are you doing these days? Jiji and Baba are fine here. The

---

* Originally from Honolulu, Sueoka was interned with Ozaki at Tule Lake and later paroled to New York. – Trans.

war ended yesterday, on the fourteenth; we have been eagerly waiting for this. I am glad to hear this news, because many soldiers are
now saved from death.

We are getting old, and we feel we should not rely on Mr. Kosaki and his family any longer. Since we have lived in Hawai'i for
thirty-eight years, without even once going back to Japan, we wish
to stay in Hawai'i. I humbly beg of you to petition the government authorities to allow you to return to Hawai'i to take care of
us.

I will write to you again soon.

Since we are accustomed to living in Hawai'i, we prefer to live
in Hawai'i.

Take care of the children and yourselves.

From Shobu Ozaki: Come back to Hawai'i. We are waiting for
you. It's the best place to live.

Date: August 24, 1945[3]
From: Yoshio Shiwo, New York, New York
To: Otokichi Ozaki, Tule Lake Relocation Center, California

Thank you for your letter and your remittance of $13.65.
Please excuse the delay in acknowledgement. I bought two bags of
Durham tobacco and now have collected six of them at last.

As you mentioned in your letter, our mother country has suffered through the most deplorable of circumstances in a thousand
years. There are a hundred reasons for the crushing defeat, but
I think the basic problem is that there were no great strategists
or statesmen among the leaders. Men of the Meiji era – Saigō,[*]
Itō,[†] Yamagata,[‡] Kodama,[§] Ōyama,[¶] Togo[**] – were veteran states-

---

[*] Saigō Takamori (1827-77), a samurai from Satsuma (present day Kagoshima), he played a
pivotal role in the overthrow of the Tokugawa government and the establishment of the Meiji Res-
toration in 1868. He then led a revolt by Kagoshima samurai against central government rule in the
Satsuma Rebellion, which ended only after his ritual suicide. Saigō became revered for his selfless
adherence to samurai virtues. – Trans.

[†] Itō Hirobumi (1841-1909) has been called the preeminent statement of Japan's modern era.
He drafted Japan's first constitution and served as prime minister for four terms, guiding the country
in its transformation into a modern nation-state. – Trans.

[‡] Yamagata Aritomo (1838-1922) was one of the most important statemen of the Meiji and
Taisho eras. An imperial loyalist, he led the Chōshū (modern day Yamaguchi) Army that brought
down the Tokugawa, suppressed Saigō's Satsuma Rebellion, built Japan's modern Army, served as
prime minister in its new parliamentary democracy, and became the most influential of the *genrō*,
the group of elder statesmen who ruled from behind the scenes. – Trans.

[§] Kodama Gentarō (1852-1906) was an army general with a distinguished career. He fought
in the war to topple the Tokugawa, the Satsuma Rebellion, the Sino-Japanese War, and the Russo-
Japanese War. He also held several ministerial posts during the Meiji era. – Trans.

[¶] Ōyama Iwao (1842-1916) participated in the civil war that ended Tokugawa rule in 1868 and
was one of the Meiji genrō. Army minister in one of the first cabinets of the modern era, he went
on to command armies in Japan's victories against China (1894-95) and Russia (1904-05). – Trans.

[**] Tōgō Heihachirō (1848-1934) is one of modern Japan's national heroes. He served in the
naval forces during the Tokugawa overthrow and commanded warships in the Sino-Japanese War,

men, who were selfless to a fault. I pray that the country and the people will not revert a thousand years and stoop down to the level of the Chinese and the Mongols. At the very least, I had hoped that it would all end in a draw, but since our comrades have been stripped bare, there is no choice but to wait [who knows how long] for their [recovery] efforts to bear fruit. How disheartening, indeed.

I understand that your wish is to return to Hawai'i, but how about making a trip to the East Coast? Since you are already on the Mainland, I think it would not be a waste of time to see the essence of the materialistic civilization before leaving.

A friend of mine is also coming to New York. Might it not be possible for your family to transfer here, too? I do not know the ages of your children, but I think New York offers them a brighter future than the small world of Hawai'i. This area is very popular with people, except among those who are sick. Making a living here is no problem for the Issei or Nisei.

Using my past experience, I plan to start a U.S.-Japan trade business. I intend to sell my prewar house and spend the next ten years, the rest of my life, using this city as a base and supervising my family and employees. The matter of unrestricted movement of people and goods between the U.S. and Japan will not likely be resolved within a year. This is the greatest stumbling block [for me]. The same applies to our mother country, but we must not lose heart. We must press forward with the courage and resolve of a lone ship in the middle of the vast ocean.

English original
Date: September 3, 1945[4]
From: Richard Hiromichi Kosaki, Fort Snelling,* Minnesota
To: Otokichi Ozaki, Tule Lake Relocation Center, California

Thank you for your letter of August 29. I am glad that you and your family are well and I hope you'll be able to return to Hawaii soon.

You asked about Minoru Shinoda. He is still teaching here at the school and his address is:

M/Sgt. Minoru Shinoda

-----

but Tōgō gained ultimate distinction when, as admiral of Japan's combined fleet, he oversaw the annihilation of Russia's Baltic squadron at the Battle of Tsushima in 1905, the first time in modern history that an Asian nation had ever defeated a Western power. – Trans.

* A U.S. Army base in St. Paul, in 1944 it became the new home to the Military Intelligence Service, when the burgeoning language school was moved from nearby Camp Savage. In all, the program graduated some 6,000 Nikkei linguists who served in the Pacific theater and during the American occupation of Japan.– Trans.

Hq. Co. – Sch. Bn.

Fort Snelling, Minnesota

I would like to visit you and your family at Tule Lake and I may get a chance to do so soon. I'm leaving Fort Snelling on September 10 to go to Fort Mason, California. I understand that Fort Mason is almost right in San Francisco, and I've been told that Tule Lake is not far from San Francisco. In all probability, I will be in California during the end of this month and I will make every effort to visit you at Tule Lake.

I don't know how long I'll be stationed in California but it shouldn't be too long before I'm sent to Japan as part of the Occupation force.

My best wishes to your family and for your continued good health.

Date: September 6 [1945][5]

From: Kazuki Kosaki, Honolulu, Hawai'i

To: Otokichi and Hideko Ozaki, Tule Lake Relocation Center, California

Yesterday I received your letter of August 27. The Second World War seems to have ended. I think that all the people in the world must feel happy now. Although we feel much safer, but we do not feel completely safe, since it is now different from the days when Japan and the United States had a peaceful, friendly relationship. I think the Japanese people in Hawai'i may change.

Not only our grandparents [Tomoya and Shobu], but we also, are quite concerned about you. It is our sincere wish that all of the family comes back to Hawai'i. I think that it may be too undutiful for us to leave the old people behind and go back to Japan by ourselves. I hope you have already understood the feelings of our grandparents through the many letters they have written to you. On top of that, what will happen to your children, who have no Japanese citizenship? If they cannot land in Japan, the problem could become very serious.

Anyway, regardless of the future outcome of the Japan-U.S. relationship, I ask you to come back to Hawai'i at least once. I hope that my parents and all the other members of my family will not separate, but will live together.

As you suggested, I contacted a Caucasian man at the U.S. Department of Justice and asked him to begin proceedings to release your family so that you can return to Hawai'i. He says that he cannot do anything right now, since there have been no instructions from Washington, but as he understands it, many internment facilities are closing down, and people from Hawai'i will be able to return in the not-too-distant future. I asked him to proceed as soon as he gets instructions from Washington. On your side, please be sure to apply with your request to return to Hawai'i.

When we meet again, how happy our parents [Tomoya and Shobu] will feel! I believe that the day when they are reunited with their beloved grandchildren will be the happiest in their lives. I think Grandfather [Tomoya] wrote to you separately.

Hawai'i is the best place to live for those people who are accustomed to a Hawaiian lifestyle.

Now is the time for the weather to change. Please take care of yourselves.

English original
Date: September 14, 1945[6]
From: Otokichi Ozaki, Tule Lake Relocation Center, California
To: B. R. Stauber, W. R. A. Relocation Planning Division, Washington, D.C.

Sir:

I, the undersigned OZAKI, Otokichi, a national of Japan, resident of Hawaii, currently resides at Tule Lake, earnestly desire to return to my home in Hawaii with your approval. I was involuntarily evacuated to the mainland of the United States after the out-break of the present war.

At the out-break of the war I was interned and evacuated to the mainland of the United States on March 30, 1942, after that time to March 1944, I was interned at Alien Internment Camp at Santa Fe, under the jurisdiction of Department of Justice. Then I was paroled to Jerome R. C. to be reunited with my family, and thence to Tule Lake, my present address.

The complete family data desiring to return with me to Hawai'i is attached herein.

I came to Hawaii, when I was twelve years of age, and since that time, I have been a resident of Hawaii all of my life. My former occupation in Hawaii was a Japanese Language School teacher. Nearly fifteen years, under the protection of Constitution of United States, to cooperate with American policy, to educated the spirit of Democracy. I'm proud to have large numbers of my former students, who fight under the Stars and Stripes at all over the front to build freedom for all mankind.[*]

---

[*] What he probably meant here was: For nearly fifteen years as a teacher, protected by the Constitution of the United States, I cooperated with American policy and educated my students in the spirit of democracy. I am proud to have large numbers of my former students, who fight under the

My wife and four children they are all native of Hawaii, and citizen of the U.S. anxious to return to their native land of Hawaii. My old age father and mother, also sisters living in Hawaii, they also, constantly asking me to return as soon as I am able to.

To-day with the war all over, I'm not hesitate to say that I pledge to be a law-abiding resident as prewar life, to cooperate with the United States government and establish permanently world peace to all mankind.

I earnestly request that you consider my application for permission and priority for my family and I to return to the Island of Hawaii. I am anxious to cooperate with the U. S. government in its present program of liquidation of all Relocation Project and resettlement of residents of such project in normal American community. Because of my past experience and long residence in Hawaii, however, I do not feel that it would be possible for my family to resettle successfully in the mainland of the U.S. On the other hand, I feel certain that I am permitted to return to Hawaii, I will be able to support my family without public assistance. My father-in-law, who manage large restaurant at Waikiki, Honolulu, had prepared my job and housing.

I hereby humbly apply to your good office to make favorable arrangement so that my family shall be able to return to Hawaii. My family and I will deeply appreciate if you will give prompt attention and favorable condition to this matter.

I shall be happy to furnish any additional information and look forward to an early reply from you.

Respectfully yours,
Otokichi Ozaki

Date: September 16 [1945][7]
From: Tomoya Ozaki, Honolulu, Hawai'i
To: Otokichi and Hideko Ozaki, Tule Lake Relocation Center, California

Your letter of September 10 arrived in the afternoon of the fifteenth. After reading it, the details became very clear. I will begin the proceeding right away, as you asked. Concerning this, my *aikāne** has been working at a laundry job for a Caucasian employer for ten years. I trust my *aikāne*. He says that he will take care of you as best he can and that he will ask his Caucasian boss to help. Older sister [Kayo] says that she will guarantee you and asks that the [Caucasian] man act as a witness. I will do my best.

Stars and Stripes, all over the front to build freedom for all mankind. – Ed.
  * Hawaiian: friend

Please do your best and come back to Hawai'i.

Although the war is over now, according to the newspaper, the present conditions in Japan are miserable. The newspaper reports that more than thirty top people were arrested and generals committed suicide. I feel terrible for them. Besides, eight million people may die of hunger this winter, the paper says. There could be a lot of people in Japan who have no shelter or clothing this winter. On top of that, if they do not have food, how can they work? I feel very sorry for them.

If Otokichi goes back to Japan, the insurance company says that the $550 insurance premium that we paid will become invalid. The insurance will mature next year. If you come back to Hawai'i and work here, you will be able to buy as much rice as you can. I do not think you can buy even one *sho** of rice in Japan right now. Therefore, all of us are looking forward to the day when you come back to Hawai'i.

This is what happened on my day off, August 29. Beginning in the morning, I did some carpentry work at Mr. Kobara's place. At around seven o'clock, I was asked to join them for dinner, which I did. On my way home, I held out my hand to a dog. And the dog bit my hand. I alone am to blame. I should have rested on my day off. I have worked continuously for the past two years and eight months, without taking any days off, in order to at least earn my food. Now I may need to rest for five or six days. Everybody says that I like working so much that it was *bachi*,† and they are laughing at me. Anyway, I am resting now.

People say that I am enjoying a good vacation, because my injury was not serious. However, because of an infection, I had an operation on my hand on September 2 and then again on September 10. The infection remained, and I had it operated on again on the fifteenth, and I have to go to the hospital everyday. This should be healed within the month.

Since I have worked for two years and eight months and saved some money, I do not need to worry about money, even if I do not work for a month.

If Hideko could write to Mrs. Kobara, I would appreciate it very much. Mrs. Kobara is always good to me. She is a good lady.

Since my right hand is injured, it is difficult to write. The dress and pants have not arrived yet. I hope they will come soon.

Date: September 20, [1945][8]
From: Tomoya Ozaki, Honolulu, Hawai'i
To: Otokichi and Hideko Ozaki, Tule Lake Relocation Center,

* Almost two liters.
† Divine punishment.

California

How are you these days? I am fine. The three families are well.

I had my hand operated on three times because of infection and I am recuperating. It is getting better now, and I think I can work at Kobara's from next Monday. Since it was a minor injury of the hand, I am taking it easy and enjoying the rest.

The dress you sent arrived yesterday. Bāsan is very pleased to find that it is so well made. On wearing it, however, she found it to be a little bigger, the hem a wee bit wider, and the waistline wider than she likes by five or six [inches]. She asked me to ask you to adjust them. I hope you do not mind adjusting them.

It is very nice of you to sew an aloha shirt for me. My measurements are as follows: length, two feet four inches; shoulder width, one foot eight inches; sleeves, seven inches; collar length, one foot, four-and-a-half inches. Since I am bent in the back, please make the front shorter by one inch. As I read this part to Bāsan, she said that I had better ask you to make two with different *hechi*.* Will you make an additional one and keep it until you come back here and then put the different *hechi* on at that time? Sorry for all the trouble.

Many people are doing many favors for us concerning your return to Hawai'i. Hiromichi is coming to town shortly. Your older sister [Hiromichi's mother, Kayo] suggests that you better ask him to be a guarantor. Please discuss this with him. He will be accompanying four officers, however.†

Mr. Tango of 'Amauulu came at seven o' clock on the evening of the twenty-first. He came to Honolulu to offer his condolences to the family of his uncle who passed away. When he visited us at seven that evening, he told us various bits of news. We told him to stay overnight, but he left soon, saying he was very busy.

Yoji's pants have not arrived yet.

Date: September 20 [1945]⁹
From: J. Kaneshiro, Hilo, Hawai'i‡
To: Otokichi Ozaki, Tule Lake Relocation Center, California

The war is over. Now that there's no censorship, I've decided to mail this letter. Just thinking of the suffering you've endured until now brings tears to my eyes. During these past three years I really wanted to keep in touch, but thanks to that "rumor," every letter

---

* Also *hetchi*, a button.
† Richard Hiromichi Kosaki was at this time assigned as part of the Occupation forces bound for Japan. He arrived at the Atsugi Naval Air Facility near Tokyo in November 1945, stopping over in Honolulu en route. – Trans.
‡ Proprietor of the Pana'ewa Soap Factory in Hilo. – Trans.

I wrote (and I always wrote one at Thanksgiving time) was never mailed. The word was that anyone corresponding with Tule Lake internees would be taken into custody. In other words, I feared for my personal safety. Isn't that pathetic? There was never a day, though, that I didn't think of you people. Even as I work now I wonder if I'll ever have a chance to see you again, since the rumor is that all Tule Lake internees will be returning to Japan.

When I met Mr. Okubo today, he let me read your letter. I'm glad you're considering returning to Hawai'i. I hope you will, for the sake of your aging parents and for your friends. Needless to say, this place isn't the same as when you left it. I suppose it's just one of those scourges of war which eventually will jell into some kind of order again. It's not what you see that's distressing so much as what it bodes for our Japanese community. In addition to this sad state of affairs, the Issei, as citizens of a defeated country, have lost their credibility in the eyes of the Nisei. How, and in what direction, then, should the Issei guide the next generation is the obvious problem. This should give you an idea of the situation in Hawai'i.

How are your wife and children doing? My eyes are not as good as before, so reading and writing are a problem.

Date: October 2 [1945][10]
From: Tomoya Ozaki, Honolulu, Hawai'i
To: Otokichi and Hideko Ozaki, Tule Lake Relocation Center, California

On the twenty-sixth, I received two letters dated September 19 and 21. I was happy to note that everyone is doing fine. We are also in good health, as usual.

It was very gracious of Mrs. Kobara. She brought $100 and asked me to send it to Hideko. I will mail it soon. Please accept it. Mrs. Kobara is always kind to us. I think it is better for Hideko to write a letter of thanks to her parents upon receipt of this money. Even though they are her parents, she should write a thank-you letter.

[Thomas] Yoji checked the pants that you sent to us. Since he does not like it, I am sending it back to you. These days the style has changed and pants in fashion now have bulging hips and narrow bottoms. Young people wear tight pants. Will you sew another pair according to the markings I've attached to the pants and send it to us? I hesitate to ask for such a troublesome favor, but please understand the situation and help us.

I think it's best to shorten the pants and let either Tomoyuki or

Yukio wear it. So, I went to buy a new piece of fabric [for a new pair of pants], but I could not find a good one here. As soon as I find a good one, I will buy it and send it to you. So, please adjust the present pants and let our grandsons here wear it. I think it is OK to sew a new pair [for Yoji] after you have returned. Please sew the belt as shown in the drawing. He says the cuffs are one inch wider. He says that he will attach the belt by himself. He complains that the one you sent is different from the drawing he sent. Yoji is quite particular. Sorry to trouble you, but I hope you will fix it according to the drawing on page two. Please do not bother about the [other] ones you have already made. I will send fabric as soon as I find it here.

Shigeo Ota of Pāhoa has not visited us yet. Maybe he is not yet here. The Kobara family treats me very well. Last month, I did not work at all because of the injury on my hand, but they paid me a salary. I am very grateful to them. The Kobara family business is doing very well. I am looking forward to the day when you come back to us.

I will write to you again soon.

Take care of the children and yourselves.

P.S. He says that the belt loops will do if the belt can pass through, although the thinner the better.

Date: October 6 [1945][11]
From: J. Kaneshiro, Hilo, Hawai'i
To: Otokichi Ozaki, Tule Lake Relocation Center, California

It was really great to hear from you so unexpectedly. The feeling was like the Confucian saying about a rare visit from an old friend. As I read your letter aloud to my wife and son, my voice wavered and I became teary-eyed a few times. My wife shed tears, too, but I was surprised when Junichi said in Japanese, "The teacher's hair . . . turned gray? It's because of this evil called war." The emphasis during the war had been to avoid using Japanese, so my son has retained little of what he learned. We, who know only Japanese, have also suffered because of the communication problem. It's such a shame that Junichi understands so little Japanese now, but it can't be helped. The problem is worse for children who are younger. I wish I could at least teach them about our moral and spiritual values, but I cannot learn English quickly enough.

Speaking of values, your comments remind me of that old saying, "Adversity makes a man wise." I'm sure you've gained something from your experiences. With all those families there, you have the chance to hear all sorts of personal stories. Do your best in these difficult times. I intend to do the same.

Date: October 8, 1945[12]
From: Otokichi Ozaki, Tule Lake Relocation Center, California
To: Tadasuke Koryu Nakabayashi, Hilo, Hawaii
Honorable Older Brother;

I received your letter postmarked October 1. Now that the war is over, we must make a fresh start. The time has come for us to make a clean sweep of our past life behind barbed wire and prepare for a new beginning.

It seems that all we can do now is to return to Hawai'i as quickly as we can, become "Japan Jews" and try to help the homeland by sending every single penny possible. There is a poem written by the Emperor Meiji that says, "Though there be highs and lows, the Way of Shikishima* will never change." From this point on, Japan must be strong and must survive as a great nation. It cannot be denied that Japan has been too feudalistic and bureaucratic, too much of a military theocracy, with the mentality of "a frog in a well."[†] At the very least, I can take comfort in knowing that henceforth the farmer, artisan, and merchant will become full-fledged world citizens.[‡]

As we all take to the difficult and thorny road lying ahead, we must begin anew with nothing but the clothes on our backs. Please provide the necessary guidance, and do not forsake us.

Most of us Hawai'i men hope to return to Hawai'i, but no specific plans have been announced. Nevertheless, there is a ten-to-one likelihood that it will become a reality. In the meantime, I find the wild rumors coming from Hawai'i discouraging.

On October first, my nephew Hiromichi Kosaki dropped by as a newly promoted lieutenant on his way to San Francisco. He is scheduled to leave for Japan shortly as an interpreter.

According to a letter from Mr. Koran Murakami in Santa Fe,[§] the Hawai'i men who had wanted to return to Hawai'i have already packed their belongings and are waiting to leave. In his letter from Gila River Center, Arizona, Mr. Yoshimi Okumoto[¶] wrote

---

* Shikishima is a poetic alternative name for Japan. The Way of Shikishima (*shikishima no michi*) is often used to mean "The Way of Japanese Poetry." - Trans.

† The expression is "*I no naka no kawazu, taikai o shirazu,*"「井の中の蛙、大海を知らず．」"A frog in a well does not know of the great ocean." – Trans.

‡ A reference to pre-modern Japan's social hierarchy of samurai-farmer-artisan-merchant, in which the warrior was preeminent. – Trans.

§ Minoru Koran Murakami, see radio scripts "Life Behind Barbed Wire" and "The Death of Mr. Oshima," pp. 65 - 68.

¶ The Japanese language school principal from Waipi'o. See Ozaki's letter dated October 11, 1944, p. 189. – Trans.

that the returning group of people has already been vaccinated against smallpox.

I understand Mr. Shiotani from the Volcano area,* who is in Chicago now, was interviewed in connection with his return to Hawai'i.

It is obvious that the planning for the return of the Hawai'i men is moving along.

At any rate, I think that the 4,000 people in this center who renounced their American citizenship will be the last to be permitted to return. Be that as it may, I look forward to seeing you and the others and shaking everyone's hand within the next six months.

I have come to fully appreciate your heartfelt support during this period, when we internees have been at the core of various rumors. We have learned many valuable lessons during our transient life behind barbed wire.

Since the end of the war, I have been receiving letters from old friends in Hilo. I am grateful that they have not forgotten me. My parents in Honolulu are fine. They have asked that I return as quickly as possible.

I hope to see everyone soon and spend an evening sharing my many experiences.

I want to see the [Japanese school] children, too. Japanese teachers may get a little more respect, when I return to Hawai'i and tell them about my past experiences.

I will write again. Please give my best to your wife.

Date: October 12 [1945][13]
From: Richard Hiromichi Kosaki, Fort Mason, California
To: Otokichi and Hideko Ozaki, Tule Lake Relocation Center, California

Thank you for your hospitality. I enjoyed a real vacation. The Japanese meal I had was a rare treat.

I returned to Fort Mason after two days of training as a censor and am now at Hamilton Airfield waiting to board a plane to Manila. I understand there will be only a two- to three-hour stopover in Hawai'i, but we (five Hawai'i boys) are hoping and praying that it will be extended somehow.

Nights are cold here. It must be cold at Tule Lake, too. I hope Tomo has gotten over his cold. Please take good care of yourselves, at least until you return to Hawai'i.

Writing a letter in Japanese without a dictionary is very difficult. Feel free to make fun of my *kanji* errors and improper

---

* The "Volcano saint." See the radio script, "Life Behind Barbed Wire," pp. 66 - 67.

sentence structure.

Date: October 17, 1945[14]
From: Junto Tsutsui, Pāhoa, Hawai'i*
To: Otokichi Ozaki, Tule Lake Relocation Center, California

On October 13, Monday, I received your letter of October 11, and I read it over many times, learning about your recent news. Since you left Hawai'i, four years have passed. I am sorry for not writing to you for so long, despite your kindness in the past.

As you say, I lived "being small," but I never passed a day without thinking of you. Even when your wife, parents, and children were in Hawai'i, I could not meet them as often as I wished, since trips to Hilo were infrequent and travel control was tight.

Before the war, it was my biggest joy to go to Hilo and visit with you and discuss the current situation and write poetry together. At that time, you used to say three set phrases. They were: "Take a bath," "Drink cold beer," and "Stay overnight," and those came from your kind heart, I believe.

You seldom came to my home because of geographical reasons, and I often went to your home to receive the gentle treatment of you and your wife. However, since the war began, our whole life has turned upside down. I cannot describe our life since then in a page or two.

It was too painful to see you passing by, when you were sent to Hilo from the volcano camp in a military bus. Thus, when the bus passed in front of my house, I intentionally stayed away. After that, I heard briefly about your move to Honolulu and to the continental United States. I assumed that the mental and physical hardships that you went through were much harder than the inconveniences of our life.

After you left, I shouldered a part of the wartime industries as an independent small farmer. I worked from early morning until late at night, unaccustomed to the work of a plowman. In this way, I made a living for my seven-member family.

Since military control has begun to slacken, more and more I am feeling like a human being again. During the past two years, I led an unpleasant life because of groundless rumors. What troubled my mind the most was neither the unaccustomed labor nor the inconvenient economic life, but the education of my children, for whom I had sacrificed myself. Although I was just an inept [education] committee member, I became greatly interested

---

* Junto is the pen name for Junkichi Tsutsui, a farmer from Pāhoa, who, like Ozaki, originated from Kōchi. – Trans.

in the education of my children, because of the good influence of you and others, and it caused me to think that I should be providing my children with a good education. As you know, [the war years] were the most crucial for the education of my children, and my worries as a father were really acute.*

If I write about these things, I will write endlessly. Since we will be able to talk about the past when we meet again, I will write about my recent situation.

According to your letter, you are preparing to soon come back to Hawai'i. I pray that day will come even sooner. However difficult the procedures are, please do your best, so that we may meet again and live together forever. For this I pray day and night.

People in Hawai'i were lucky. All of us were not sent to remote places on the Mainland, unlike our fellow countrymen on the West Coast. The fact that we did not need to go was evidenced by the events that happened in later years. Out of our meager salaries, we, including you and I, made an effort to raise good citizens. Nisei servicemen responded to our efforts; our efforts were rewarded.

According to your letter, your life has been happier than expected. I can see many reasons for that. First of all, you have lived with intellectual people. Especially, I think, with your talents you have discharged your responsibilities as block manager, and with your special diplomacy, you have consoled many people. At any rate, it seems to me that you are destined to play the role of caretaker wherever you are. I hope we will soon be able to talk about our past experiences.

Due to my full day's labor, I am always too *moloā*† to write even a daily diary. I have not written so much as a letter to friends or acquaintances. Nonetheless, they are always on my mind. I think about them more than anyone else. Even to Mr. Kunizo, who is already back in Honolulu, I wrote to only once since the war began. I have become really lazy.

I should have written to you, but I did not, using the present control situation as an excuse. Please forgive me. Please write to me about your feelings and thoughts, if time permits. I will look forward to it with pleasure. Even though my handwriting is terrible and my writing is poor, I would like to tell you the recent news about our friends and myself. But, I have lost so many friends, so please understand that today I will write about my family.

Mother-in-law: Sixty-three years old. In good health. She gets up early in the morning and is busy making *bentō*.‡ Maybe due to

---

* Tsutsui is referring to the nearly wholesale incarceration of Hawai'i's Japanese language teachers and the effect this had on education. – Trans.
† Tsutsui writes "*moroha*," a Japanese rendering of the Hawaiian word for lazy. – Trans.
‡ Boxed lunches

her age, she always complains that she is bad at this and that. She always worries about you. She waits for your early return.

Myself: I leased two acres of farmland here and work another two acres in Puna. I am literally a poor peasant. Since I cannot buy a truck, I took off the back seat of that car and drive it around. I mainly raise sweet potatoes and *gobō*.* I sold about 40,000 pounds of sweet potatoes of various kinds.

Besides that, I take care of twenty-six acres of the sweet potato farms of other people and of my mother-in-law. Because there is a labor shortage, I do everything for them, from spreading bone meal [fertilizer] to spraying insecticide. I am amazed that I have such formidable energy.

Eldest son Kojun: Graduated from high school last June. (Irregular form of graduation.) Presently employed at a sugar plantation. He works in the fields from early morning and is doing *tsuraiken*.†

Eldest daughter Fusae: Third grade in high school. She will graduate in June of next year.

Second daughter Mitsue: Ninth grade at 'Ōla'a Junior High School.

Second son Seijun: Sixth grade at Kurtistown School.

Third son Eijun: Second grade at the same school.

Wife: Dimwitted. She gets scolded from the morning. Still alive.

I will stop writing about us. It is endless.

[On a separate sheet]

If there is anything I can do for you, let me know. Since peace has returned, I can be of some help to you. If you need any information from our side, let me know. I am running an independent business, so I can spare time, anytime for you. We can mail goods to you, too. Are you not troubled by money matters? Don't hesitate to let me know.

Date: October 21 [1945][15]
From: Kenzo Maehara,‡ Santa Fe Internment Camp, New Mexico
To: Otokichi Ozaki, Tule Lake Internment Camp, California
. . . . These are my reactions to the dawn of peace.

---

* Burdock
† A derivative of the term *kachiken*, to cut sugar cane, from the language spoken by Japanese immigrants on the sugar plantations. This suggests that *tsuraiken* is the most onerous of the cane-cutting tasks. – Trans.
‡ A photography studio owner from Hilo. – Trans.

In the vast ocean
I am but a trifling drop of water
Still the state of my homeland
Tears my heart apart.

大海の
水一滴に
似し我れも
祖国の姿
胸裂くる思ひ。

I was born into this era
Counting my blessings
But having lived to this day –
All was for naught, in vain.

此御代に
生れ来し
幸数へしに
生きて甲斐なき
今日あらんとは。

In the end the sun descends
Beneath the ocean depths
Yet I continue plodding
Through the century's darkest days.

日は遂に
海のかなたに
落ちにけり
世紀の暗を
歩み続けん。

Peace has finally arrived
And I succumb
To the summer heat.

平和遂に来れり
夏痩せにけり。

Date: November 10 [1945][16]
From: Tomoya Ozaki, Honolulu, Hawai'i
To: Otokichi and Hideko Ozaki, Tule Lake Relocation Center,
California

How have you been these days? We are in good health and doing fine.

By the way, according to a newspaper today, many people
are returning to Honolulu by the ship arriving on the com-
ing fifteenth. According to the paper, among my acquaintances
from Hilo are: Saito Sensei, [Kenzo] Maehara, Kango Kawasaki,
Minoru Murakami, [Gakuji] Ishibashi, Matsuo Marutani, Shinji
Tokushiro, Katsujiro Kagawa, Masato Kyosaki, [Kenji] Shiigi,
Tomoji Matsumura, Yaroku Tanaka, Takaichi Saiki, and [Atsuo]
Sakimizuru.* I wanted to let you know this.

* Saito Sensei is Haruto Saito, a teacher at Dokuritsu Gakkō; Kenzo Maehara, a photographer,
see his poems in the preceding letter; Kango Kawasaki, a law office employee; Minoru Murakami,
chief of the *Nippu Jiji* office in Hilo; Gakuji Ishibashi, the proprietor of a dry goods store; David
Matsuo Marutani; Shinji Tokushiro, president of the *Hawaii Mainichi* newspaper; Katsujiro Kagawa, general manager of Hata and Co.; Masato Kyosaki, general manager of Kyosaki Brothers; Kenji
Shiigi, a storekeeper; Tomoji Matsumura, a storekeeper; Yaroku Tanaka, General manager of the *Volcano Times*; Takaichi Saiki, assistant general manager of Bank of Hawaii in Hilo and the spokesman
for the internees while they were in Missoula; Atsuo Sakimizuru, a hat maker. Information about

I think you are coming back on the next ship. As soon as you receive this letter, please let the Kobara parents know that you are scheduled to return to Hawai'i soon and may ask for their assistance. I think it is better for you to inform the three families including the Kosaki and Uejio families, too.

Please take care of yourselves.

P.S. I think you had better stay in Honolulu, when you return to Hawai'i. I am expecting that you will drop by Honolulu, even though you will be returning to the Big Island. However, you may not find a good job on the Big Island. If you find something good on another island, you could go there. So, please drop by Honolulu first. I am looking forward to your coming back to Hawai'i as soon as possible.

I am in good health and work very hard everyday as usual. Since last year, my job has been to wash table rags, peel potatoes, and make castella cakes. Until August, I was making more than 500 pounds [of cake] a week, but lately I make only 340 to 350 pounds. I have to wash sixty table rags when it is busy. I pick up more and throw out the ones that are stained with oil. Today, I worked from morning until night.

I will write again.[*]

Date: November 13 [1945][17]
From: Mrs. Nakauchi, Honolulu, Hawai'i
To: Otokichi Ozaki, Tule Lake Relocation Center, California

Thank you for writing to us so often. Please forgive me for not replying sooner but my eyesight is beginning to trouble me. I understand you've come down with colds. Please be very careful. How wonderful that Hiromichi has been promoted to second lieutenant. I understand he left for Guam last month and will head on to Japan. Tsutomu, too, was sent to Japan in May after returning last year. He visited you several times, and I'm most grateful for the hospitality he received. Hideo is in Italy, but we haven't heard from him in a month. He may be on his way home by ship. I'm happy to know that your parents, who are in Honolulu, are well. We're all eager to see you again. I thought of sending you a Christmas gift but couldn't find anything suitable. Please use the small cash gift I've enclosed to buy candy and such for your children.

Date: November 29 [1945][18]
From: Mitsuko, Chicago, Illinois

---

the Hilo internees is from the JCCH Internee Database. – Trans.

    * This letter may be the last letter Tomoya wrote to Otokichi and Hideko. The Ozaki family left Tule Lake on December 2, 1945. They arrived in Honolulu on December 10. – Trans.

To: Otokichi and Hideko Ozaki, Tule Lake Relocation Center, California

I read your letter with mixed feelings of joy and regret. Anyway, I am glad to know that both of you are in good health. I am at a loss as to what I should tell you first, and am just reading your letter repeatedly.

I regret to know that you are leaving tomorrow. I feel miserable to realizing that we did not know that both of us lived on the same continent for a long time. I can only imagine how hard your life has been.

After spending eleven months in the Poston Camp,* I came out into the free world through the kind offices of my friends in Chicago. Even while in the camp, I had almost the same degree of freedom as that of the outside people, for which I am truly grateful.

I never dreamed that your family was in a camp. How much better I would have felt if I could have known. I do not know what I shall do now that you are leaving. I feel really regretful.

How hard it must have been for Mrs. Ozaki, taking care of four people in a noisy camp in an unaccustomed climate. How happy we would have been if we could have written to each other during the past years. When I cope with my nasty sons, I always remember Tomoyuki-san. He was a clever boy. I have fond memories of your home. That house may be gone by now, I am afraid. How often did I visit your home!

I heard that Mr. Arakawa was in Chicago, but my children are small, and I cannot go out to see him yet. I think that your life in camp was hard, but these are the trials of life that those who did not go through camp life could never experience. I am sure that this will contribute to your future activities.

It was strange that you, Mr. Ozaki, a Nikkei teacher, were put into the camp while the schoolmaster was paroled. Anyway, I am glad to know that you will go back to our Hawai'i since you could not get tickets to Japan.

It is getting cold here in Chicago. The snow melted and rainy days continue. That may be why many people get colds here. If I could walk over to a post office, I would like to send a cable telling you how I feel, but I cannot bring out a seven-year-old boy and a two-year-old boy right now. Please understand that I cannot do anything and forgive me. Hereafter I will write to you often.

Since my brother was in the Fort Snelling barracks, I used

---

* Poston Incarceration Center on the Colorado River Indian Reservation in southwestern Arizona. – Trans.

to meet him on furlough day. Now he is in Japan. My husband works in the defense industry. About one week ago, I wondered to myself about the kind of work that you were supposed to be doing in Hilo. Again, when I looked at a picture taken at Aka Hall, I received a letter from a younger sister asking me, "Did you see Mr. and Mrs. Ozaki?" I felt that the way of the mind is very mysterious.

Since I never thought that you were interned, I imagined that you came to the Mainland on business. Then I thought that since we could see each other soon, what should I treat you to, and I would go downtown with Mrs. Ozaki . . . I expected a dream.

Compared with the life of people in Japan, our hardship is not so serious. Let's go forward with good spirits. I keep my fingers crossed that I will visit Hawai'i someday.

I congratulate you on the new start of your family and pray for good luck.

P.S. I just could not resist. I am going now to the post office to send you a cable. Do you hear my voice?

Date: December 15 [1945][19]
From: Yoshio Shinoda, Hilo Hawai'i*
To: Otokichi Ozaki, Honolulu, Hawai'i

Thank you for your letter. Welcome back. Since all of you came back safely, I am sure that not only your parents but also all your relatives were pleased to see you. I sympathize with you for the hardship you went through in the past four years.

I have met almost all the people who came back to this island. I told them that you had come back to Honolulu. I hope you will visit us when you get a rest and are settled at your place. We cannot write in our letters all the anecdotes we each had since we parted. I look forward to the day when I can see you and enjoy our reunion. Please give my best wishes to Mrs. Ozaki and others.

The enclosed check represents the gift to Mrs. Ozaki from the Hilo Women's Club upon their dissolution. Mrs. Fujii, chairwoman (Bank of Hawaii), gathered other gifts and asked Mr. Masao Kimura to remit them to you. However, Mr. Kimura forgot about this for a long time. Later he found the check in his desk and brought it to me.

Since you, Mr. Yamakawa,[†] and others were already scheduled to come back to Hawai'i, I held it and waited for you here. Herein

---

* Principal of Dokuritsu Gakkō - Trans.
† Yoshinobu Yamakawa was principal of the Waiākea Uka Japanese Language School on the Big Island. – Trans.

enclosed is the check for Mrs. Ozaki, which I hope you will please accept.

Date: December 18 [1945][20]
From: Rokutaro Tango, 'Amauulu, Hawai'i
To: Otokichi Ozaki, Honolulu, Hawai'i

I was extremely pleased to receive your letter informing me that you had arrived safely in Honolulu. Since you were confined at the center for four long years, I am sure you have found that many things have changed in Hawai'i. You have probably seen that some things have become more pleasant, while others have become more deplorable. We cannot do anything about that, but I believe firmly that things will steadily improve as many people return and bring their new ideas.

Rev. and Mrs. Kokuzo told me many things about you. Although I do not need to mention again that you are a man of your word, I am always grateful that you are so. I have many things to write to you, but I cannot write even one millionth of what I am thinking about. Since I am such a diligent letter writer (?),* it is agony—like being cut on my body—for me to write letters.

My mother would like to ask you and your wife to visit and stay in our home for a few days, before you get settled and start a new life. She says that you know that we cannot entertain well, as other people do. I understand that her wishes are to welcome you from the bottom of her heart, so I also humbly ask you to visit us. My wife suggests that you come on December 27 or 28, after Christmas, and stay with us through the New Year days, if possible. She says that the sole purpose of her hard labor will be for you to enjoy this time. Since Nobuhiko's birthday is January 3, she asks you to come before that day.

I will write to you soon again.

Date: December 20 [1945][21]
From: Bunnosuke Sato, 'Amauulu, Hawai'i
To: Otokichi and Hideko Ozaki, Honolulu, Hawai'i

Thank you very much for your letter. I am very pleased to note that you arrived in Honolulu on the morning of the tenth, after you lived such an uncomfortable life and endured hardships for four years. I can imagine how happy your parents and sisters were.

---

* The actual phrase is 「筆まめ(?)なので」, with the question mark being used for sarcasm. – Trans.

I am sorry for my long delay in responding to you. As a matter of fact, comrades of the late Takeo were discharged from military service and have returned. They explained how Takeo was killed in battle. Everyone told me different stories. Every time I heard their talk about the sorrowful situation in which Takeo was killed, I felt as though my body was being stung with needles.˙

The soldiers with whom Takeo had gone to the front from ʻAmauulu came back one by one. I will tell you about them. Mr. Yoshiaki Yahata was injured and recuperated in ʻAmauulu for two months, but because he has not recovered from his injury, he went to the Mainland. Mr. Sanji Watanabe was discharged from the military service and came back to ʻAmauulu, but because of his business he is now in Honolulu. Mr. Tokuichi Kubota† was promoted to first lieutenant and came back for a while, but he went to the Mainland for his studies.

Mr. Otosaku Hirayama‡ was also discharged from the military service, but because of his business, he is also now in Honolulu. Both Mr. Mitsuo Tachibana§ and Mr. Yoshitaka Toyama¶ are said to have arrived in Honolulu. Both soldiers returned in glory and their families are happy, but we feel a kind of despair, which cannot be expressed. However, if we look up or down, there are countless people who are either happier or unhappier than we (don't you think?).

I have so many things to tell you and so many things to hear from you. I hope you will visit us someday. I told the [ʻAmauulu] camp residents that you had safely come back to Honolulu. They also look forward to you visiting them.

Last but not least, please give my best regards to your parents. Wishing you and Mrs. Ozaki good health.

Date: December 24 [1945][22]
From: A former internee,** Hilo, Hawaiʻi
To: Otokichi Ozaki, Honolulu, Hawaiʻi

Have you settled in a bit? Since returning [to Hilo], I realize

---

* Bunnosuke Sato's son, Takeo (b. 1922), a member of the 442nd Regimental Combat Team, and was killed in action in December 1944 in the aftermath of the Vosges Mountains Campaign to rescue the "Lost Battalion," one of the fiercest battles that the U.S. waged in the Europe. Prior to his induction in 1943, Takeo Sato worked as a carpenter for the Hilo Sugar Company. See http://honoringtheniseiveteran.org/KIA's/ALL_KIAS/Sato%20Takeo.pdf – Trans.

† Son of Sakuichi Kubota, a farmer in ʻAmauulu. – Trans.

‡ Son of Naokichi Hirayama, a farmer in ʻAmauulu. – Trans.

§ Son of Shingo Tachibana, a farmer in ʻAmauulu. – Trans.

¶ Son of Tokushiro Toyama, a farmer in ʻAmauulu. – Trans.

** There is no signature on this letter. The writer and his wife were likely interned with the Ozakis at Jerome or Tule Lake, and based on the letter's tone and the informality of the language, we can surmise that they were close friends. – Trans.

that this recent vacation was a bit too long. Hilo, which had become quite deserted [during the war], is still feeling its after effects – airplanes flying above from morning until night, the sound of cars running all around – it's enough to make me dizzy. For now, I spend my days quietly and meekly like a borrowed cat, living mindlessly from morning until night. At any rate, since we've missed the chance to take part in the current economic boom, there's no sense in struggling. If I'm going to fool around, I might as well really enjoy myself.

Tomorrow is Christmas. And, although this year will be ending within five or six days, I live in a happy-go-lucky fashion. Since I'm bumming off at a friend's house, I don't have to worry about rent, and I have no intention of pounding *mochi*, since there is no *mochi* rice in the market. I feel like I'm leading the life of a millionaire.

The blue sky is high and clear. Cottony white clouds float here and there. All the trees are green. Even the grass in the yard is refreshingly green. I'm not cold in my aloha shirt. Friends have given me a dozen bottles of whisky and a case of beer. *Aikāne* one after another invite me to their homes. I feel like humming, "Hawai'i is a good place, come and visit at least once."*

I was so happy when Mr. Koryu [Nakabayashi] invited me to dinner last night. We talked a lot. He served me two small bottles of valuable *sake* – Kokusui—for which I was grateful. It was a taste I hadn't had in four years.

Many *aikāne* visit me and say, "You endured such hardship for so long." But I feel somewhat embarrassed, since I used to play *go* and lead an easy life in camp. Nonetheless, because their words come from their heart, I feel the layers of fatigue, accumulated over the years, falling off slowly and steadily. I am grateful for their words.

On the other hand, there are also those who look upon the internees with disapproval. When I hear this kind of talk, it disturbs me greatly, but what can I do, since that is their perspective. That's why it seems that those who came back from Santa Fe also maintain their silence and appear to be more troubled than we are. It is understandable. After seventy-five days or so, I guess they will begin to slowly get about.

The company for which I had worked before asked me to come back, but I declined. I believe it is not yet the time for an Issei to come up to the stage so brazenly, given the present wartime conditions. I think that it might be safer to look for a job as, say,

---

*"*Hawai yoi toko, ichido wa oide.*" This is a parody of the "Kusatsu bushi," a traditional folk song about one of Japan's most famous hot springs, the Kusatsu Onsen in Gumma prefecture. – Trans.

a gardener,* and I may go out to Honolulu, if there are opportunities there. If you hear of something, please let me know. I am in a bind, since I have no house here in Hilo. I'm a lazy fellow,† as you know, so I've been asking around the Waiākea area about any good plumbing jobs.‡

I'd forgotten to mention this, but thank you very much for the kindness you showed me for so long. I am sorry that we parted before I could repay my indebtedness to you. Please forgive me for the sake of our *aikāne yoshimi*.§

Please give my best to Mrs. Ozaki. My wife also sends her regards. Please come to Hilo soon.

If you happen to have Mr. Matsui's address, please send it to me.

---

* The letter writer uses the slang term *niwa-haki* 庭掃き, lit. to sweep the grass. – Trans.
† *Runpen* ルンペン, i.e., the lumpen masses
‡ The letter writer uses the slang term *tekkan* 鉄管, lit. a steel pipe. – Trans.
§ *Aikāne* (Hawaiian) friends; *yoshimi* 誼み friendship

EPILOGUE: POSTWAR LIFE

DESPITE THE SETBACK of four years "lost" to internment, Ozaki's life flourished upon his return to the islands. Whereas he had been a much respected and revered teacher before the war, postwar he rekindled his journalism career, this time at the *Hawaii Times** in Honolulu. The media-type activities he engaged in during the war foreshadowed the leadership he would assume in the community after the war. He ardently promoted Japanese film and magazines in Hawai'i. He not only served on the board of a local Japanese radio station, but also broadcast his internment experiences on radio, the scripts of which are included in this book. He remained active in poetry clubs and published several works of poetry. He was also a generous donor to many causes, both in Japan and in Hawai'i.

This final short chapter of the book chronicles Ozaki's life from his return home, through his death on December 3, 1983.[1]

Postwar Career

On February 1, 1949, Ozaki joined the *Hawaii Times*, the publishing firm of the daily Japanese newspaper in Honolulu. He was assigned to the advertising department and ascended rapidly through the ranks. In July 1957, he was appointed director of the advertising department; in May 1963, he was promoted to managing director; and in May 1967, he was promoted to executive vice president and general manager. His significant achievements included continuing a six percent dividend to shareholders, giving employees annual leaves that had not been realized before, introducing company-sponsored medical and life insurance plans, and introducing the Japanese Market Report to the paper, with the cooperation of Yamaichi Securities, Daiwa Securities, Nikko Securities, and Nomura Securities.

Ozaki also served on boards of other companies while he managed *The Hawaii Times*. In January 1963, he was appointed to the Board of KOHO, at that time Hawai'i's only Japanese radio station. KOHO started broadcasting on December 29, 1959, but fell on hard times, terminating the operations due to internal conflicts. At the time, *The Hawaii Times* acquired the station's majority shares, and KOHO came under the control

---

* Formerly the *Nippu Jiji*, the bilingual newspaper ran from November 1942 until March 1985.

of *The Hawaii Times*.

In January 1967, he was appointed to the Board of Directors of Hawai Nihonjin Kyōsaikai (Hawai'i Japanese Mutual Aid Association). This non-profit organization was founded in February 1934 by Jiro Watanabe to help Japanese assist one another in Hawai'i. Its major undertaking was to provide monetary assistance to the families of deceased members. It apparently was quite successful, as its capital fund was some $522,466, which was a significant amount in those days. It distributed $355,000 to the families of 600 deceased members by March 30, 1971. After the founder's retirement, it was decided to cease its existence at the general meeting held in March 1971.

On February 1, 1969, Ozaki retired from all held positions and retired from business.

Community Activities

Ozaki was very active in the community after the war, as he had been in Hilo prior to his internment. He served as chairman of the Waikiki Aloha Kai (Waikiki Aloha Association) from 1950 to 1951, and vice chairman from 1959 to 1960. In January 1957, he was appointed to the Board of Trustees of Kuakini Hospital and Home.*

From 1950 through 1954, he was engaged as a commentator on various radio programs. Ozaki spoke about his experiences as an internee, and commented on Japanese movies and other forms of entertainment, believing that it was important to pass on the legacy of Japanese culture. He was featured on programs on KGMB, KHON, KAHU, and KGU. He also broadcast programs on Japanese entertainment on KOHO, every Sunday at seven in the morning from September 1955 through May 1970.

To further promote Japanese entertainment in the islands, he published columns in Japanese newspapers from September 1955 through May 1970. He had a weekly column in *The Hawaii Times* called "Eiga Orai" (Movie News), and a weekly series in the *Hawaii Hōchi*† from 1971 to December 1973, entitled "Eiga, Geino, Terebi Orai" (Movie, TV &

---

* Today Kuakini Medical Center. Known as Japanese Hospital when it was constructed in 1917, the hospital's Board of Trustees was comprised of Nikkei, earning it the distinction of being the only hospital in America to be occupied by the U.S. Army during World War II. Kuakini Home, the forerunner of today's Hale Pulama Mau senior care facility, began as a care home for elderly Issei men, many of whom were unmarried plantation retirees. – Trans.

† Established in 1912 by Fred Kinzaburo Makino (1877-1953), the *Hōchi* and Soga's *Nippu Jiji*, later *The Hawaii Times*, became the dominant journalistic voices for the Japanese community in Hawai'i. With the closure of *The Hawaii Times* in 1985, the *Hawaii Hōchi* became the only Japanese language daily left in the islands. – Trans.

Entertainment News).

Ozaki served as a liaison between various Japanese entertainment companies and their Hawai'i audiences. On August 21, 1966, he was appointed counselor-advisor of *Shufu no tomo* Hawai'i Tomonokai (*Shufu no tomo* Magazine Subscribers Club, Hawai'i chapter). The Hawai'i chapter had 150 members and collected a five-dollar annual fee. *Shufu no tomo* (Friend of Housewives) is a monthly magazine for women based in Japan. It had gained a substantial following and reputation in Hawai'i for over fifty years. The Hawai'i chapter was founded on August 21, 1966 to promote mutual friendship among the readers and to enrich women's daily lives. The club was engaged in cultural activities such as Japanese and Chinese cooking, lectures, and craft exhibitions. Particularly for Japanese and Chinese cooking, *Shufu no tomo* headquarters in Tokyo offered tremendous support and often sent Japan's top-ranking chefs to display their culinary skills, not only in Honolulu, but in Hilo and Lihue, Kauai. Free cooking classes attracted large crowds of club members, as well as the general public. His correspondence from this time includes many handwritten letters from *Shufu no tomo* headquarters, as well as Shochiku Films of America. In January 1968, he was appointed to the Movie-Making Subcommittee of the 100th Anniversary of Japanese Immigration to Hawai'i Committee.

Literary Activities

Before the war, Ozaki had been an active member of Gin-u Shisha, a *tanka* poetry club in Hilo. He continued his poetry writing after the war, beginning in 1948, as a member of the Cho-on Shisha (Sound of the Sea Poetry Society), a *tanka* club in Honolulu. In 1950, he edited and published a *tanka* collection entitled *Chinmoku no Tō* (Tower of Silence) by Zanka Iwatani, at the request of Iwatani and his family. In 1957, he edited and published *Keiho Kashū* (Keiho's Poetry Collection) by the late Yasutaro Soga, by request of Soga's wife.

Another project was editing and publishing *Hawai Jijo* (Things Hawaiian), a book written in Japanese to correctly introduce things Hawaiian to the Japanese public. It was revised and republished in 1958, 1964, and 1967. He was also a member of the Honolulu Japanese Press Club, beginning in 1969.

Commendations

In November 1945, he received a letter of appreciation and a commemorative gift from former internees of the Tule Lake Relocation Center,

California, for his devotion to Hawai'i internees and their families as Block Master, as well as his daily broadcast of camp news and liaison duties with the authorities.

On January 3, 1951, he received a letter of appreciation from Nishimori Ryoi, principal of Ikegawa-machi Intermediate School, in Agawa district, Kōchi, his hometown, for his donation of school supplies.

On September 7, 1953, he received a letter of commendation from Murata Yachiho, of the Office of the Secretary of the Prime Minister, for his donation to the rebuilding fund of Oshima Intermediate School in Oshima, Yamaguchi prefecture.

On February 11, 1963, he received a letter of commendation and a commemorative gift from Consul General Kenji Yoshida for his assignment of liaison agent before the war and for his active involvement in developing the Japanese community.

On May 27, 1964, he received a letter of commendation and a commemorative gift from the Hawai Nikkeijin Rengo Kyōkai (Hawai'i United Japanese Association) for writing a book entiled, *Hawai Shodai-jidai no Nihonjin no Geinō* (Japanese Immigrants' Entertainment during the Issei Period) as part of the programs of the seventy-fifth anniversary of government-contracted Japanese immigration to Hawai'i.

On June 13, 1968, on the occasion of the one hundredth anniversary of Japanese immigration to Hawai'i, he received a letter of commendation and a commemorative gift from the Foreign Minister of Japan, Takeo Miki, for his devotion to the advancement of Japanese overseas and strengthening the U.S.-Japan relationship.

In 1968, he received a letter of appreciation from the Hawai'i Cancer Society for his cooperation in fundraising efforts by the Japanese Women's Society.

On April 12, 1969, he received a letter of appreciation and a commemorative gift from the Chief Priest of Ise Jingu (Ise Shrine) for his donation to the Ise Shrine 60th Rebuilding Fund.

On May 1, 1969, he received a letter of appreciation and a commemorative gift from Sister Mary Higa, head of Airen-en Orphanage in Yonabara, Shimajiri District, Okinawa, for his fundraising efforts.

On August 25, 1975, on the tenth anniversary of the founding of *Shufu no tomo* Hawai'i Tomonokai, he received a letter of commendation from Kazuo Ishikawa, president of *Shufu no tomo* Hawai'i Tomonokai and a commemorative plaque from Takeo Isoshima, chairman of the Hawai'i chapter for his devotion to the club since its founding.

On November 1, 1975, he received a letter of appreciation from Susumu Yoshigami, general chairman of the Welcome Reception Committee hosted by Japanese and Japanese American communities for his service as a committee member for the imperial visit to Hawai'i.

In the autumn of 1977, Ozaki was bestowed the Sixth Class Order of the Sacred Treasure by the Japanese government for his active role in the Japanese community.

Ozaki eventually became a naturalized citizen of the United States. He passed away in Honolulu on December 3, 1983 at the age of seventy-nine.

GUIDE TO THE OTOKICHI OZAKI COLLECTION

By Jane Kurahara

Ozaki, Otokichi, 1904 – 1983
Papers, 1927 – 1988
Japanese Cultural Center of Hawaiʻi (JCCH) Resource Center Archival
Collection 1
7 linear feet

Abstract:

The Ozaki papers cover the internment experience of the Otokichi Ozaki family of Hilo, Hawaiʻi, during World War II, as well as postwar reflections on internment and Mr. Ozaki's interests in other areas such as the movies, song lyrics, and poetry. Included in the collection are personal correspondence, lists of various internment camp internees, internment camps newspaper issues, poetry, song lyrics, radio scripts, reflection notes, news articles, as well as some internment photos and sketches.

One of the strengths of the collection is the more than 350 *tanka* poems written by Mr. Ozaki during internment; they contribute an insider's perspective during a key period in American history. Another is the set of Mrs. Ozaki's letters received throughout the time the couple were separated (1941-1944). Yet another is the radio script series (beginning in 1950), which seems to be based on diaries Mr. Ozaki may have kept.

The majority of items are in Japanese. A growing number of papers are being translated into English. The papers are in fragile condition. As much as possible, researchers will work with photocopies of the original materials.

The collection is located at the JCCH Resource Center.

Restrictions:

There are no access restrictions on the materials, and the collection is open to all members of the public in accordance with state law. However, the researcher assumes full responsibility for conforming with the laws of libel, privacy, and copyright, which may be involved in the use of this collection.

Summary of Biography:

Otokichi Ozaki was born in Ikegawa town, Kōchi prefecture, Japan, on November 5, 1904, and came to the island of Hawai'i at the age of twelve to join his parents. He attended boarding school for English and completed his Japanese education at Hilo Dokuritsu Japanese School. He worked at *The Hawaii Mainichi* newspaper from 1920 to 1923, then taught at Hilo Dokuritsu Japanese School from 1923 to1941. He married Hideko Kobara, a Nisei, who was educated in Japan, and had four children, Earl, Carl, Alice, and Lily. Hideko also taught at Hilo Dokuritsu Japanese School.

Mr. Ozaki was arrested on December 7, 1941, and was subsequently detained at the following eight internment camps during the period December 1941 to December 1945: Kīlauea Military Camp; Sand Island; Angel Island in San Francisco; Fort Sill, Oklahoma; Camp Livingston, Louisiana; Santa Fe, New Mexico; Jerome, Arkansas; and Tule Lake, California. He and his family were reunited in Jerome and Tule Lake. He was Block Manager of Block 79 at Tule Lake and coordinated the return home of the Hawai'i group at Tule Lake in 1945.

After returning to Hawai'i, he managed his father-in-law's Blue Ocean Inn before working for *The Hawaii Times* newspaper from 1947 to 1977.

He wrote under his pen name, Muin Ozaki. At age nineteen, he was the youngest charter member of the Gin-u Shisha (Silvery Rain Poetry Society). After the war he joined the Cho-on Shisha (Sound of the Sea) *tanka* club and also helped edit two *tanka* anthologies for Zanka Iwatani and Keiho Soga. He also did radio programs on stations KGMB, KGU, KHON, KOHO, and KULA on O'ahu. A series of radio scripts included in the collection recounts his internment experience. In the late 1970s, he received the Sixth Class Order of the Sacred Treasure from the emperor of Japan. Mr. Ozaki died on December 3, 1983, at the age of seventy-nine.

Scope and Content:

The collection includes a variety of documents which reflect the activities of Mr. Otokichi Ozaki and his family from 1927 to1988. The collection is especially strong in relating the personal experience of one family to the internment of Japanese in the U.S. during World War II. Approximately 300 pieces of correspondence, most of which were incoming correspondence to Mr. Ozaki while he was interned, were meticulously kept by Mr. Ozaki. Before the family was reunited, most of the incoming correspondence was from Mrs. Ozaki. Other correspondents included his sons, relatives, friends, and other internees. Also included is correspondence about business transactions and official notices and replies.

In addition, Mr. Ozaki expressed his perspective and response to internment in the forms of over 350 *tanka* poems, which are included. These appear to cover the period from December 7, 1941, when he was taken from his home, to about 1942 when he reached Oklahoma. About forty poems have been translated into English poetic language with the assistance of poets Frances Kakukgawa and Jean Toyama.

Lists of internees in various camps include those in Missoula, Montana and Santa Fe, New Mexico. Issues of various camp newspapers, including the *Santa Fe Times* from 1943 to 1944, a *Tule Lake Special Edition* on voluntary repatriation in 1945, and a *Los Bagu Times* New Year Special Edition in 1943, have been kept. There are several folders of sketches and photos of internment camp life.

Mr. Ozaki's postwar reflection notes, radio scripts, and news articles recounting the internment are included. He did radio programs on KGU, KHON, KULA, and KGMB. News articles from a variety of papers, including the *Hawaii Hochi, Hawaii Times, Hawaii Herald*, and *Nichi Bei Times* are included. The news articles cover a variety of subjects, but primarily internment. They are mostly postwar articles within the years of 1943 up to 1988. In addition, news articles, song lyrics, and movie flyers reflect Mr. Ozaki's other postwar interests. There are also articles about Mr. Ozaki receiving the Emperor's Award, the Sixth Class Order of the Sacred Treasure, on November 3, 1977. One folder holds the notes on the celebration held in his honor.

There are very few materials from the period prior to 1941 and the period after Mr. Ozaki's death in 1983. Family records include graduation diplomas, certificates, report cards, and ID cards. Family memorabilia include movie flyers, a visit to an Okinawan orphanage, information about the anthurium, the Ozaki Red, and organizations to which Mr. Ozaki belonged.

See also the papers of Gladys Naitoh.*

---

* The Gladys S. Naitoh Collection of the Japanese Cultural Center of Hawai'i. The collection is comprised of papers related to the internment of the Naitoh family, Kyojo, a Buddhist priest from Kōloa, Kaua'i, his wife, Naoe, and their daughter, Gladys Suzuyo.

Acquisition:
Presented by Earl Ozaki (deceased), in 1996, 1998, and 1999.

Processing:
Processed by Jane Kurahara, Resource Center volunteer, March – December 1999.

JCCH Resource Center Archival Collection 1:
Box 1—Series: Correspondence, 1942 - 1944
    Folder 1: Letters from home (Hawai'i) to Mr. Otokichi Ozaki, February 1942 to December 1942.
    Folder 2: Correspondence to Mr. Ozaki, January - December 1943, while he was living in the following internment camps: Sand Island, Fort Sill, Camp Livingston, and Santa Fe.
    Folder 3: Letter from Mr. Ozaki to Mrs. Nakabayashi, 4/19/43, shows censorship; letter from a teacher asking for Mr. Ozaki's help, not dated, no signature; letter from a student to Mr. Ozaki, 11/14/43.
    Folder 4: Thomasine Allen's letter recounting her wartime experience, 12/9/43.
    Folder 5: Correspondence from Mrs. Ozaki to Mr. Ozaki, January – April 1943.
    Folder 6: Correspondence from Mrs. Ozaki to Mr. Ozaki, May – December 1943.
    Folder 7: Correspondence, January 4, 1944 – March 12, 1944.
    Folder 8: Correspondence, March 14 – October 1944, including Mr. Ozaki's letters to his parents in Hawai'i.
    Folder 9: Correspondence, November – December 1944.

Box 2—Series: Correspondence, 1944 – 1955.
    Folder 1: Letter re: repatriation from Spanish Embassy, 1944; Mr. Ozaki's letter to Mr. Norio Sumida, 12/30/44, censored.
    Folder 2: Incoming correspondence for Mr. Totaro Matsui, 1944 – 1945; report card for son, Richard Matsui.
    Folder 3: Letter from Mr. Sato, Camp 'Amaulu, Hawai'i, 1945, regarding *katta gumi*;* draft of a thank you letter written after the Hawai'i

---

* Japan-won-the-war groups. In the aftermath of the war, a very small minority of Oah'u Issei, having confined themselves to Japanese vernaculars for war news, tenaciously held on to the belief that Japan had been victorious. The zeal of the *katta gumi* often brought them into conflict with returning internees and other prewar leaders, who saw the *katta gumi* stance as hurtful to the overall

group returned to Hawai'i at the end of 1945.

Box 3—Series: Correspondence, 1944 – 1946, 1950, 1963
    Folder 1: Correspondence for Mr. Ozaki, January – July 1945, while he was interned at Tule Lake.
    Folder 2: Correspondence for Mr. Ozaki, August – October 1945, including Mr. Ozaki's letter to Mr. Nakabayashi.
    Folder 3: Correspondence for Mr. Ozaki, November – December 1945.
    Folder 4: Correspondence for Mr. Ozaki, 1946.
    Folder 5: Letter from Dr. Yoshina, 5/14/50; letter from University of Hawai'i, 2/4/63.

Box 4—Series: Radio Scripts/Plays
    Folder 1: Radio scripts 1943?
    Folder 2: Radio scripts, not dated
    Folder 3: Radio play script, 1947? : "1,000-stitch belt made in America."
    Folder 4: Radio script (handwritten) and translation, 1949, "Life in Sand Island"
    Folder 5: Radio scripts (handwritten) and translation 10/16/49 on KHON, "Life Behind Barbed Wire."
    Folder 6: Radio script (handwritten) and translation, 10/16/49/ Introduction, on KHON.
    Folder 7: Radio script (handwritten) and translation 10/31/49, #3.
    Folder 8: Radio scripts and English descriptions (handwritten), 1950.
        #5: "Memories of Four Years Behind Barbed Wire (Bodily Search)."
        #6: "Bodily Search," part 2.
        #7: "Memories of Internment Camp."
        #F: "Monologue on Cigarettes."
    Folder 9: Radio script, 2/9/52, on KGU.
    Folder 10: Radio script, 3/15/52, on KGU.
    Folder 11: Radio script, 3/22/52, on KULA.
    Folder 12: Radio script, 3/29/52, on KULA.
    Folder 13: Radio script (handwritten) and translation, not dated #4.

reputation of the Japanese community. See Yukiko Kimura, *Issei: Japanese Immigrants in Hawaii* (Honolulu: University of Hawai'i Press Press, 1988), 243-51.

Folder 14: Radio script, date? .

Folder 15: Radio script (handwritten) and English description, date? .
   #12: "Internees and Numbers."

Folder 16: Radio scripts (handwritten), date? .
   #16: "Life Behind Barbed Wire" (13ᵗʰ KGMB broadcast).

Folder 17: Radio scripts.
   #8: "Cucumber Pickles."
   #9: "Heart of Lincoln."
   #10: "Enlightened by the Teaching of Buddha."
   #1: "Life Behind Barbed Wire."

Folder 18: Play script by Mr. Ozaki; play performed at McKinley High School Auditorium.

Box 5—Series: Sketches/Photos

Folder 1: Photographs of "Silvery Rain" poetry collection participants, January 1925.

Folder 2: 1942 photocopies of sketches of internment camps, including Lordsburg Internment Camp, Kīlauea Military Detention Camp; Sam Houston Internment Camp.

Folder 3: ? grade class, Jerome Center, 1943, photo; New Year's card, January.

Folder 4: Santa Fe Camp group photo, December 1943.

Folder 5: Photos from Mr. Totaro Matsui's file; one is partially identified.

Folder 6: Group photo including Mr. Ozaki; no date or location.

Folder 7: Yokozuna Hana Kuroyama; photos of scenes from "*Futari no* idea."

Folder 8: Negative of wedding couple: Otokichi Ozaki and Hideko Kobara.

Folder 9: Photocopies of internment camp life in Ozaki family, Tule Lake camps, 1943, 1944, 1945.

Box 6: Series: Other Writings

Folder 1: Handwritten notes, letters: 1942, 9/14/43, 1945.

Folder 2: Handwritten notes on relocation camp, [1944?], the German [1942?].

Folder 3: Notes for Mother's Day speech.

Folder 4: Chronology—internment camp and dates.

Folder 5: Miscellaneous notes on 1) mothers; 2) growing plans; 3) *obon.*

Folder 6: Reflections on December 7, 1941 [Fort Sill, Oklahoma] and assorted notes.

Folder 7: Reflections by Muneo Komura.

Folder 8: Handwritten notes on brief history of the Japanese immigrants in Hawai'i, not dated

Folder 9: Handwritten notes, numbered pages 1-41 about the internment, food, and other matters, not dated

Folder 10: Notes, self-reflections, not dated

Folder 11: Miscellaneous notes—no sequence or relationship to each other.

Folder 12: Part 1, "Diary" during internment; draft of "essay"; note pad of statements in Japanese by Mr. Ozaki.

Folder 13: Part II, "Diary" during internment; draft of "essay"; note pad of statements in Japanese by Mr. Ozaki.

Folder 14: Part III, "Diary" during internment; other draft of "essay"; note pad of Japanese statements by Mr. Ozaki.

Box 7—Series: Family Records and Memorabilia

Folder 1: Family records: assorted ID cards, Hideko Kobara's graduation diploma, scroll of appreciation, 1929, 1932, 1942, 1944.

Folder 2: Family records: passports for Hideko Ozaki; membership certificate Hawai'i Nihonjin Kyosaikai for Hideko Ozaki, 3/1/38; two-time certificates from Sumitomo Bank, 7/35/34; Talmage letters.

Folder 3: Certificates of achievement, Hilo Japanese School, Tomoyuki Ozaki, 1939, 1940, 1941.

Folder 4: Eye record for Mr. Ozaki, 4/18/44; immunization certificate for Lily Yuri Ozaki (daughter).

Folder 5: Report card, Earl Ozaki, 1945; graduation diplomas for Yukio and Yuri Ozaki, 1945; Judo certificate for Yukio Ozaki, 1945; certificate of appreciation for Mr. Ozaki, 1945, photos of children.

Folder 6: 1945 certificate of completion for Sachi Ozaki, second grade, first half.

Folder 7: Memorabilia (photos, magazine photos) of Okinawa visit to Christian orphanage [1973 – 1977?].

Folder 8: Nippon Theater Movie Flyers, 5/2/76 – 7/25/78, including written contributions by Mr. Ozaki.

Folder 9: Internee reunion at Natsunoya including memorabilia, 11/13/77, (photos, list of attendees, news clippings, and notes).

Folder 10: Mr. Ozaki's receipt of Sixth Class Order of the Sacred Treasure from the Emperor of Japan, 1/24/78; news article about ceremony.

Folder 11: Mr. Ozaki's notes on teachings—saddest thing in the world is to have nothing to do; writing about *giri* (duty).

Folder 12: Waikiki Aloha Kai membership roster.

Box 8—Series: News Media in Internment Camp

Folder 1: Santa Fe Camp News, 6/17/ - 9/15/43.

Folder 2: *Los Bagu Times* New Year Special Edition, 1943.

Folder 3: 9/14/43 article from the *New York Times* that Mr. Ozaki translated re: populations in various camps.

Folder 4: Copies of *Santa Fe Times*, Friday, 7/2/43 – 12/9/43.

Folder 5: Copy of *Santa Fe Times*, 1/12 – 4/11/44.

Folder 6: "The Tule Lake" Special Edition—Japanese language version of announcement about voluntary repatriation to Japan, 11/26/45, and special edition in the English language.

Folder 7: Military Proclamation in Japanese; orders for internees; salary; medical coverage; days off, not dated

Folder 8: Copy of newsletter published for camp residents, June 18 – September ? ; copy of *Santa Fe Times*, May 3, 11, 19, 1944.

Box 9—Series: Poetry/Other Poetry Activities, Including Song Lyrics

Folder 1: Handwritten poems by Mr. Ozaki (?); other poems by Japanese citizens, Big Island Poetry Club, varied dates: 1925, 1931, 1932, 1935.

Folder 2: Personal copies of collections: 1) Silvery Rain [1926?]; collection of poems with rain as a theme, 23 contributors; 2) collection of song lyrics by Otokichi (Muin) Ozaki, 1927 - 1940.

Folder 3: Otokichi (Muin) Ozaki, tanka poetry, 1941 – 1943? .

Folder 4: Fair Department Store Song Contest poster of winners, including Mr. Ozaki; poster includes song lyrics, 1947? .

Folder 5: Clippings of poems by poetry club members, 1982, in *Hawaii Hochi* and *Hawaii Times*; articles about Honolulu poetry club, selected poems from Japan.

Folder 6: Program materials, 9/27 – 9/29/83, *Poets Behind Barbed Wire*.

Folder 7: Sheets numbered #1 to #8, duplicates of *tanka* poetry in other folders; next five unnumbered sheets—new materials to be reviewed for translation.

Folder 8: Selected *tanka* poems (40) in *romaji*, literal translation, and poetic renderings by Frances Kakugawa.

Folder 9: Other poetry activities: notes—verse for song; poem by Michiko _____ for husband who died in war.

Folder 10: Poems written by Jiro Nakano plus unidentified writer or writers.

Folder 11: Plate lunch poem.

Folder 12: Poems—chronological order? .

Folder 13: Song lyrics in which Mr. Ozaki does a variation of a song to include Tule Lake and birds, not dated

Folder 14: Song lyrics.

Folder 15: *Tanka* poetry, Kīlauea Military Camp [probably Mr. Ozaki's earliest poems during internment]

Folder 16: Original writing – 4th Poetry Reading, August 1942.

Box 10—Series: Internment Camp Organization and Operations

Folder 1: Totaro Matsui's papers: December 9, 1941 – October 19. 1945: statistics on each boat distribution [8/10/44], Camp Livingston internees to be transferred to Missoula, Montana; Camp Livingston internees to be transferred to Santa Fe, New Mexico; to Kooskia, Idaho; to Kenedy, Texas; 10/15/43 Missoula list of officers and workers; instructions for repatriation; alien Detention Station form, Missoula, 7/1/43; 10/18/43 typewritten list of officers; information about Missoula Camp requested by Mr. Kashima 12/14/43; list of internees who wish to be repatriated alone, 12/23/43; written requests of Consul of Spain 12/16/43; list of officers 1/15/44; list of internees to be repatriated with families 12/23/43; Hasebe letter requesting release 3/14/44; list of internees from Missoula assigned to Santa Fe 4/3/44; Referential data on Hawai'i internees 5/1/44; Recapitulation and list of Santa Fe internees 5/6/44; list to be reunited, Crystal City 11/22/44; list to go to Crystal City 12/2/44; Repatriation dates—Mrs. Tatsuko Matsui; memo about individuals wishing to return to Hawai'i 10/19/45; instructions (Crystal City) to "Hawaiian Group" 10/22/45; dividends from Japanese canteen to outgoing persons 10/23/45; list titled "Hawaiian Group"; Form, Consent—Internment in Family Internment Camp, AC-DC-2 12/17/43—account in Japanese language of interview with a Spanish consul.

Folder 2: 1942 documents.

Folder 3: Lists of baggage acknowledged received, 12/24/42.

Folder 4: Evacuee organized governments in the Tule Lake Center,

Newell, CA, May 27, 1942 – September 19, 1945, typewritten; 2 carbon copies.

Folder 5: November 1, 1943 Santa Fe Internment Camp, list of people by sections A-Z.

Folder 6: Receipts [1944, 1945]; notices [1944]; instructions in Japanese for those leaving relocation centers [1943]; Jerome Center instructions for short-term leave; certification re: Ozaki family repatriation [3/30/43]; notice informing Mrs. Ozaki of move to Tule Lake; list of trip number leaving Jerome 5/8/44; instructions for train monitor and coach captains; housing form 2 – unidentified camp.

Folder 7: Business letters [March, 1944 – February, 1946].

Folder 8: Instructions, bill of lading, lists of names, correspondence related to return of island residents from Tule Lake Camp to Hawai'i [1945]; addresses for Hawai'i returnees Block 79 [11/19/45]; notes and notice of meeting to discuss return to Hawai'i; Matson Line Immigration Check passes, family member cards, cabin card.

Folder 9: Notes describing camp community buildings

Box 11—Series: Compensation

Folder 1: Written information about Mr. Ozaki, family, and finances provided for compensation claim [1977 – 1978?]; follow-up letter.

Box 12—Series: News Articles, 1943 – 1976

Folder 1: Internment news photos [1943]; other clippings 1949, 1976, 1979, list of internees, 1941; "My Baggage and Me," by Mr. Ozaki; "Loss of Life Under Protective Confinement" by Mr. Ozaki.

Folder 2: News articles (Japanese) 1944, 1945; "My Former Student," by Mr. Ozaki.

Folder 3: News clippings, 1948, New Year article by Mr. Chikuma on Drama Group at Camp.

Folder 4: Musical score, "Aloha Boogie," lyrics by Mr. Ozaki; clippings [1950] and translation.

Folder 5: [1951?] Musical score, "*Yume Miru* Hawaii," lyrics by Muin Ozaki, 7/7/51; article about lyrics by Mr. Ozaki for "Hawaii Nisei *Butai*" and unrelated article.

Folder 6: Varied news clippings between 11/55 and 1/74 about movies, entertainment, TV, Waga kai, Waga uta; New Year's special issue [1974], interview with actress Hideko Takamine.

Folder 7: Clippings related to Ozaki family, varying dates 1957, 1976;

obituary of Otokichi Ozaki 12/15/83; articles by Mr. Ozaki.

Folder 8: Article on story of Niʻihau incident [1962]; *Fujin no Tomo* [1/20/65].

Folder 9: "Ozaki Red" – anthurium article, *Shufu no Tomo*, December, 1970.

Folder 10: Copies of Mr. Ozaki's essays printed in *Hawaii Times* [1972, 1973, 1976, 1977, 1978, 1983].

Folder 11: Assorted news clippings [1973, 1975, 1976, 1980].

Folder 12: Clippings from *Hawaii Hochi*, four Japanese-style of Chinese character writing, Series 1-86, not dated; one of clippings dated 11/17/76.

Folder 13: Memories of an internee by Muin Ozaki [12/1/76] published by *Hawaii Times* [1/1/77]; *Hawaii Times* news clipping on internment [2/20/76]; magazine article on internment by Muin Ozaki [7/1/76].

Folder 14: News clippings on Manzanar [1976]; Kanyaku Imin last survivor; why Pearl Harbor was bombed.

Folder 15: *Hawaii Times* "Burning Weeds" by Mr. Ozaki comparing freedom of today to internment years; Series 1-10 (#6 missing) about Japanese American soldiers in World War II [8/2/76 – 10/11/76].

Folder 16: King Kalakaua article by Masaji Marumoto, 11/21/76; an article about Princess Kaiulani; and an unrelated article.

Box 13—Series: News articles, 1977 – 1988

Folder 1: Clippings: *Hawaii Hochi* 3/1/77; "Secrets of Emperor Meiji and King Kalakaua"; *Hawaii Hochi*, January – February 1978, 9-part article on Princess Kaiulani's life.

Folder 2: News clippings on assorted subjects of personal interest [1977 – 1978].

Folder 3: News clippings on a variety of subjects—internment, entertainment, Katsu Goto, poetry club [1977, 1980].

Folder 4: 11/2/77 copies of *Hawaii Times* and *Hawaii Hochi* articles on Mr. Ozaki's Emperor's Award, 1977.

Folder 5: Clippings from *Hawaii Hochi*, *Nichi Bei Times* of 1977, 1978, 1979, 1981, 1982 about internment.

Folder 6: Article by Yoshiaki Ito, "Eradication of the Melon Fly on Kume Island by the Mass Releases of Sterile Insects" [1979?].

Folder 7: Clippings from *Hawaii Hochi*, originally printed in *Yomiuri Shinbun* of Japan covering events from Pearl Harbor to _____; book *Kibei* by Max Templeman, 1979.

Folder 8: *Hawaii Hochi* news clippings, May 1979, expressing views of U.S. Senators Daniel Inouye and S. I. Hayakawa regarding compensation for internees.

Folder 9: News clippings [1979] about Japanese poetry club on Big Island.

Folder 10: Internment recollections—news articles in *Hawaii Hochi*, 1981, 1982.

Folder 11: News clippings about Reverend Seikaku Takezono; other articles including Mr. Ozaki dates concerning internment, statement presented at Seattle hearings on internment [1981].

Folder 12: Varied news articles [1981 – 1983], *Hawaii Hochi*, *Hawaii Times*, *Hawaii Herald*.

Folder 13: Assorted clippings from *Hawaii Hochi* on internment, 5/30/81 – 9/26/81.

Folder 14: *Nichi Bei Times* clippings on internment 8/13/81 – 12/12/81.

Folder 15: News clipping on "Hole Hole Bushi" and Harry Urata, 9/19/81.

Folder 16: News clippings on internment experience [1981]; news clippings—Earl Nishimura's response to former State Supreme Court Justice Marumoto's speech and the latter's reply [1982].

Folder 17: *Hawaii Hochi*, 8/20/82, "Reminiscences of Internment," by Nishikawa Tooru.

Folder 18: *Hawaii Hochi* articles of 1983 on remembrances of internment camp.

Folder 19: News clippings from *Nichi Bei Times*, 1983, on evacuation and redress.

Folder 20: *Hawaii Hochi* special edition of four sections on internment of Hawaii residents of Japanese ancestry, 10/25/88.

Appendix A

WHEN JANE KURAHARA began volunteering at the Japanese Cultural Center of Hawai'i in 1994, much of the Ozaki Collection had been gathered, but it was in disarray. Supporters of the Japanese Cultural Center of Hawai'i had initiated the acquisition of the collection well before she discovered it. "Hideto Kono [a prominent figure in the Japanese-American community in Hawai'i] did a lot to connect this place [the Resource Center at the JCCH] with the community," says Kurahara. "George Akita [professor emeritus of history at the University of Hawai'i] probably convinced the Ozaki family to give the collection to the JCCH."

For a while, nothing was done with the collection, but sometime after Kurahara began volunteering, an Archival Workshop was held by Marie Dolores (Dolly) Strazar of the Hawai'i State Foundation. "We met at the YWCA and came back all enthusiastic," reminisced Kurahara. "But then we didn't know what to do with the collection, so we called Dolly and she said, 'Just bring me the collection and let's get started.'" She then told the JCCH volunteers to put the collection into archival folders and archival boxes. "But we don't have any," was the response. "Then write a grant," said Dolly. So Kurahara applied for a grant with the Hawai'i Council for Humanities. The Ozaki Project was awarded a $5,000 preservation grant.

"With the money we were able to get supplies and to get Shige [Yoshitake] to translate Ozaki's poetry," says Kurahara. "There were about 300 poems but Shige said a lot were duplicates so we ended up with about forty. Then we asked a published poet, Fran Kakugawa, to render the translations poetically."

Kurahara first decided to focus on the Ozaki Collection when Florence Sugimoto, another JCCH volunteer, began to translate the letters Mrs. Ozaki wrote to her husband. "She showed them to me and I was touched. Mrs. Ozaki was left with four young children, and these letters showed the human side of the story, not just the internment side," says Kurahara.

Working on the Ozaki Collection helped the Resource Center focus on preserving its entire internment collection. Out of the experience, Tatsumi Hayashi and Kihei Hirai, at the time new JCCH volunteers, were moved to translate the Issei story on internment. This gave birth to Hirai's translation and publication of Yasutaro Soga's *Life Behind Barbed Wire*, and Tatsumi Hayashi's forthcoming translation of Kumaji Furuya's *Haisho Tenten*.

Word continued to spread about the Ozaki Collection, because once the collection was preserved, the Resource Center had to create a brochure on it and send it to libraries and museums around the state. Word even spread to Japan, where one professor, whose research focused on creative writing in internment camps, stopped by the JCCH to examine the collection. Parts of the collection were used by the state Department of Education to teach students about internment. Donna Mills, the Hawaiian studies resource teacher, also stopped by to use the collection. Also, a handbook entitled, "World War II: Hawaii Internees' Experiences Resource Folder," was compiled and disseminated to every public school in Hawai'i. Public school teachers are currently writing lesson plans to accompany the handbook. In May 2009, the lessons were completed and can be found online at http://www.hawaiiinternment.org.

"The human story grabbed everybody's heart. It became a labor of love," explains Kurahara. "It could have happened to anybody and is still happening in different forms. So if we could all learn from it, this world will be a better place."

Appendix B

Interview with Tatsumi Hayashi
Translator of Otokichi Ozaki's radio scripts and camp news, Ozaki's personal history, and the letters of Tomoya Ozaki

TATSUMI HAYASHI SAYS he had no special training in English that qualified him to become a translator. He learned the fundamentals of English in school, the way most Japanese do, but became especially proficient in it through his lifelong love of music.

"In high school I became enthusiastic about jazz by African-Americans," Hayashi says. "I discovered 'East Coast' jazz, performed by African-Americans, as opposed to West Coast 'cool' jazz, performed by white people." He asked his mother to pay for a subscription to *Downbeat* magazine, a true "hard jazz" lover's publication, in contrast to "soft jazz" magazines like *Metronome*, that included articles on pop music. In this way, he was forced to read English so he could understand the articles about his favorite jazz artists.

Hayashi was fortunate to have a Royal typewriter at home, so he diligently copied and retyped stories from *Downbeat*. "I tried to collect as many LPs as possible," he recalls. He diligently covered his albums with sheets of paper, on which he had typed information relating to that jazz artist. "I have about 400 LPs at my home in Tokyo, some of which are originals, recorded in mono, worth $500 each," he says. "But I'll never sell them."

His proficiency in English took another leap in college, when he was a senior writing a report on Franklin Delano Roosevelt's New Deal. "I convinced the professor that I had to see the United States in order to write the report," he chuckles. "At that time I had connections to the Mitsui Steamship Company, so in 1957 I went on a months-long trip around the world." On the first leg, he headed westbound to the Philippines where the ship picked up raw sugar, which was to be delivered to Domino Sugar Company in New York.

While the ship was docked in New York, he snuck out at night, and struck out on his own onto the streets and subways of New York City in search of jazz clubs he had read about in *Downbeat*. With a little bit of broken English, a mind filled with images of jazz club fronts that he had seen in magazine photos, and a lot of luck, he stumbled onto famed East Coast jazz clubs that featured the likes of Sonny Rawlings, John Coltrane, and Dizzy Gillespie. "I was the only Asian in the club in those days," he recalls. "Dizzy Gillespie took a particular interest in me because there I was, I must have looked fifteen years old, the only Asian in the club, and could barely speak English." Other artists he met were less open, like Miles Davis and Thelonious Monk.

These experiences fueled Hayashi's desire to go into international business. He did write the paper on FDR, and upon graduation from college in 1958, joined Japan Airlines, and stayed with the company for forty years. Out of those forty years, he spent several years in Tokyo, ten in Fukuoka, and the rest in international cities, including New York City, Frankfurt, and Honolulu. His last post, his third stay in Honolulu, led him to retire in Hawai'i at the age of sixty-two.

In January 1998, the year after he retired, he shared a table at a social function with Hideto Kono, a prominent figure in the Japanese American community in Hawai'i. "Hideto asked me what I was doing, and I said,

'Golf,' so he asked if I could work at the JCCH to do translation," Hayashi says. "So I was put in touch with Jane Kurahara, who was then leading the Otokichi Ozaki project, and that's how I got started translating these documents."

Unsure at first if he had the know-how to translate the documents, he says the hardest part was reading Ozaki's handwriting, since Ozaki had written the scripts and news for himself, hastily scribbling notes, rather than taking the time to write everything out neatly and carefully. It was difficult work, since many of the pages were out of order and upside down. Hayashi had to make heads-or-tails of the documents by piecing together the last lines of certain pages and the first lines of others.

Cultural differences between Japan and the U.S. also made some passages difficult to translate. For example, Hayashi says, in America, it's customary to begin speeches with a joke. In Japan, many speakers begin with a self-deprecating excuse for why the speech won't be very good or why the speaker isn't prepared. "If you tried to translate this literally, it wouldn't make sense," Hayashi points out. Nevertheless, Hayashi used his good sense to take the Japanese writing and translate it as accurately as possible while making the English relevant and comprehensible to a modern-day audience.

He has since gone on to work on the translation for the manuscript, *Haisho Tenten*, soon to be published by JCCH. He has also written Japanese subtitles for a documentary on the USS *Ward*, a destroyer in Pearl Harbor, believed to have fired the first shots in the 1941 conflict, when it sank a Japanese midget submarine just before the air attack on Pearl Harbor began. He is also working on an exhibit at the Pacific Aviation Museum.

Appendix C

Interview with Florence Sugimoto
Translator of Otokichi Ozaki's radio scripts and camp news and the letters from Hideko Ozaki to Otokichi Ozaki

FLORENCE SUGIMOTO'S FATHER was an Issei and came to Hawai'i as a young man of seventeen. Her mother was born in Hawai'i but went back to Japan, and returned when she was in her teens.

Sugimoto was the youngest of six children, born and raised in Kalihi, where there "weren't many Japanese families around us." The most important influence on her interest in Japanese was her father, who used to take Sugimoto and her siblings to see Japanese movies three or four times a week. "After dinner, we would go to the theatre, watch the ending of the first showing first, then watch the first part of the second showing," she says. "This way, we learned how to put things together." Her father also took on female roles in local Japanese plays, which furthered her interest in Japanese drama.

Another influence was her sisters, who were very good Japanese school students. Her sisters used to tell her stories they read in Japanese school, which sparked her interest in Japan. She used to go to the Japanese school library and take out books. "We still have the book about the story of the forty-seven *rōnin** that we took out," she says. "We couldn't return it to the school, because the war broke out and the school closed down."

Sugimoto was also a student of *odori* (Bando school), or Japanese dance. Because of *odori*, she and other students entertained Japanese POWs held at Sand Island after the war. Once, the POWs held a thank-you party for the dancers. "I was so impressed with the *manjū*† they had made," she recalls. "We even exchanged letters with them for a few years after they left." She was very young at the time, only nine years old when war broke out in Hawai'i.

After the war, her family used to make care packages to send back to her father's hometown in Hiroshima. In return, her family received many thank-you letters, which Sugimoto would read with the help of her sisters. "I got lots of practice translating the letters," she says. "I even translated in my head watching movies." Her father often played music, and Sugimoto would listen to it over and over, scribbling down the lyrics to learn and translate them. "That's how we grew up and spent our time."

At Farrington High School in Honolulu, Sugimoto took two years of Japanese. Her teacher was the wife of the Reverend Furuta of Makiki Christian Church. "I was kind of an outcast in high school because of my interest in Japanese things," she says. "I was considered an oddball, because

---

* Based on an incident in 1703, in which former retainers of the lord of Akō avenge their master's death by assassinating a vassal of the Tokugawa shogun, whom they believed had insulted their liege and caused his destruction. In punishment, all the *rōnin* (masterless samurai) were ordered to commit ritual suicide. Renown as one of the greatest examples of loyalty and samurai ethics, the incident has been depicted in plays and film, most famously as the tale *Chūshingura* by Takeda Izumo. See its translation by Donald Keene, *Chūshingura: The Treasury of Loyal Retainers* (New York: Columbia University Press, 1971).

† Japanese sweets

after the war Japanese culture was shunned." At that time she wanted to go to Japan to teach English. She knew Japanese so well that when she entered the University of Hawaiʻi, she passed the exam to go into second-year Japanese. At the university, she had a part-time job in the sociology department conducting studies for the journal, *Sociological Process in Hawaiʻi*. Her job was to translate Japanese newspaper articles. "The hardest part was understanding the *kanji* and putting it all together."

After receiving her bachelor's degree in education, she taught at Honomu Elementary School ten miles outside of Hilo for one year, then worked at ʻEwa, Kaʻewai, and Puʻuhale elementary schools. After she got tenure, she went to Japan to teach English to military dependents for the U.S. Department of Defense. She was assigned to Sagamihara outside army base Camp Zama in Kanagawa prefecture from 1962 to 1964. While she was stationed there she also volunteered to teach English at a Japanese junior high school outside of Zama town.

She returned to Puʻuhale Elementary School after her two-year stint, then went back to teach for the Air Force outside Yokota in Saitama prefecture from 1965 to 1966. In addition to working for the Air Force, Sugimoto took a part-time job teaching English to seven or eight students for Mitsui Bussan, an industrial conglomerate. At this time, her sister, whose husband was in the military, was living in "a huge house" in Kanto-mura near Fuchu Air Base. Finally, her father said to come home to Hawaiʻi. "There weren't many teachers in my circle who went to Japan."

She began volunteering at the Resource Center of JCCH in 1996, which aptly fit her interest as she could borrow books and carry out investigations. She became interested in internment, because she had classmates who had been interned. The first volunteer translator for the Ozaki project, she was asked to work on the letters, specifically between Otokichi Ozaki and his wife.

What struck her most about the letters was the level of emotion. "I know where she's (Mrs. Ozaki) coming from," she said. "Her family was very much like my family." Indeed, Mr. Ozaki and Sugimoto's father were of the same generation. Her father used to go to the *Hawaii Times* building, where Mr. Ozaki worked, and was active in the United Japanese Society, the Hiroshima Kenjin-kai, or prefectural organization, and the Otake Chiho Kenjin Kai, the organization of his hometown, Otake-machi.

Because of this, she says, she feels close to the Ozaki family. "I am sensitive to feelings, and picked up on the feelings that Mrs. Ozaki conveyed to her husband. Her hardship was conveyed not so much in what was said, but how it was said." Sugimoto explains: "In the Japanese language, you beat around the bush and have to read between the lines. The choice of words is very important. Frustration is very evident; for example, the fact that her son wasn't doing very well in school. As a writer she's just an ordinary housewife. But as I read her letters, I got teary-eyed."

In one letter, she wrote to her husband that she had gained weight, perhaps trying to reassure him that all was well. (In Japanese culture, gaining weight used to be a sign of well-being. But in camp, gaining weight is not necessarily good, as this could mean it was due to inactivity.) She clearly wanted to have her husband around, explains Sugimoto. Among internee families, a lot of children rebelled because their father wasn't around. In the mess hall, kids would run off with their friends rather than eat with their families. "I felt her frustration of being stuck with four children."

Appendix D

Interview with Shige Yoshitake
Translator of Otokichi Ozaki's poetry

IN POETRY, IT'S hard to determine what the person was really thinking," says Shige Yoshitake. "If you want to go to the real meaning, you have to go to the count, but Ozaki's poems were free-style."

Yoshitake began his education in the Japanese language at Waipahu Japanese School. "I went to a country Japanese school for eight years. Our family moved to Kaua'i (Waimea) after that, and there were no Japanese schools in Waimea that had classes beyond eighth grade." To continue his education in the Japanese language, his parents bought him a magazine, *Shonen Kurabu* (Youth Club). His father also got him *Chuichi Kanbun*, or seventh grade correspondence classes in Chinese characters. "Nobody taught me," says Yoshitake. "I had to read and figure it out." His father also subscribed to the Japanese language newspapers *Hawaii Hochi* and *Nippu Jiji*, which Yoshitake read. "That's how I started out."

Throughout high school he gradually lost the habit, but upon graduation, he enrolled at the University of Hawai'i at Mānoa and studied Mandarin with a business major. He chose Mandarin because Japan had invaded China and in business you needed a foreign language to graduate. "There was no sense taking French or German." "That's how I started out and how I learned *kanji*." Thus, because of Chinese, he "got back into it." After the war broke out, he spoke Japanese only in the home. He was drafted in the army, and went to Military Intelligence School, where he had six months of intensive training in Japanese. Again, he lost his ability to speak Japanese after the war, when he embarked on his career, but gradually people brought him newspapers and magazines from Japan so he regained his skills.

He retired in 1981 after working for the state of Hawai'i, and in 1983 volunteered at the Waikīkī Aquarium. In 1988, he began helping at Kapi'olani Community College, where he developed historical walking tours of downtown Honolulu, the pre-1940 University of Hawai'i campus, and the Kaimukī neighborhood in Honolulu.

In 1994, he started volunteering at the JCCH to work on the storyline and exhibit committees. At the time, the Resource Center started to be developed, with Clara Okamura heading up the organization. "At the time there was no true work for translators," he said. "I translated book titles and shelved books." Then Jane Kurahara began assisting Okamura, and Kurahara gradually took on more and more of the work.

Suddenly, all kinds of internment things started to come in. *Poets Behind Barbed Wire* (a collection of internees' poems, including Ozaki's, published by Bamboo Ridge Press) was donated to the Resource Center. Earl Ozaki, Otokichi's son, brought his father's materials in to the Resource Center, because there was publicity about Ozaki's writing. One of the items brought in was 200 poems written on a single sheet of paper. Earl Ozaki brought in more and more and no one knew what to do with it all.

Kurahara got a small grant so they could buy boxes, acid-free paper, and folders to organize the materials, recalls Yoshitake. As part of that grant, there were small stipends available for Florence Sugimoto and Yoshitake to do translation work. Yoshitake was named lead translator and was assigned the poems. Later, Tatsumi Hayashi joined the group and translated the radio scripts and camp news.

Translating the poetry was difficult because different sheets of paper had the same poems on them. After much work, the correct sequence of the poems was sorted out. The poetry starts on December 7 with Ozaki's arrest, then proceeds to Kīlauea Military Camp, the Honolulu Immigration Station, and Sand Island. "I tried to find a sequence based on where he was. There were thousands of poems, but they were not all one hundred percent different. It was a mess." Some he simply couldn't translate. "Some of the words he used I wasn't too familiar with."

Appendix E

Interview with Kiyoshi Tsuchiya
Former resident of 'Amauulu Plantation Camp 1

A PPENDIX E IS a record of an interview with Kiyoshi Tsuchiya, a former resident of 'Amauulu Camp 1 in Hilo, Hawai'i, where Ozaki was living when Pearl Harbor was attacked. When he returned after his internment, he and his family moved to Honolulu.

Name: Kiyoshi Tsuchiya
Date of Birth: November 9, 1927
Place of Birth: Hilo, Hawaii
Occupation: Retired Auto Parts Manager
Hobbies: Listening to audio tapes, radio and TV news

What was the name and location of the Plantation camp?
Amauulu Camp 1, Hilo (across Okura's present home)

About how many people lived in this camp?
Approximately 190.

Describe the setting and climate of this camp (what did it look like?).
There was one small store (Tsuchiya Store), one gym built by the Plantation and a community hall used by all denominations for church services. Japanese families lived in the same area, so did the Filipinos. Six of the Portuguese families lived in one part of the camp and another, perhaps four, lived in another part.

The houses were built by the Plantation for the workers. Houses were wooden structures on post and pillar about 6-7 feet off the ground and consisted of 2 or 3 bedrooms, a large living room, a spacious kitchen, and a porch. The houses all stained red so they looked alike. Families that could afford it, renovated their houses, adding bedrooms, bathing area, etc. There were gravel lanes between rows of houses, wide enough for maybe one car. Of course, in a big rainstorm, the gravel would be washed away and the Plantation would deliver gravel and grade again.

Toilets were outhouses, built by the Plantation over a pipeline with water running—water may have run into Wailuku River. Beginning around 1942, families who could afford it, began installing "flush" toilets in their homes.

Bathhouses were community ones, segregated by nationalities—each had female and male *furo* or wooden tubs: wash outside the tub and soak in the hot water. Families who were responsible for heating the water for the bath were paid by the rest of the families. Payment received had to also cover the cost to purchase lumber to heat the water.

The water line was installed by the Plantation and because it was surface water, when it rained, the water turned brown and was not fit to drink unless boiled. But we were fortunate in that we did not need catchment tanks.

Laundry was hung on a clothes line stretched across a small yard area, under the house, or porch.

What nationalities were present on this camp? Were any nationalities dominant?
As stated before, there were Japanese, Filipino, and Portuguese, but the Japanese were dominant.

Were any jobs on the plantation camp only given to certain nationalities?
It seems that most of the Portuguese were the truck drivers and equipment operators. Field work and some office jobs were given to Japanese and Filipinos.

Was there any friction or racism between the different nationalities present?
Not certain but I think everyone lived harmoniously and helped each other.

What were the different jobs on the plantation camp?
Residents worked in all areas of the Plantation as truck drivers and operators of heavy equipment, mechanics, mill workers, field workers, and office workers.

Did plantation workers usually marry within the camp? (If yes, please explain why.)

Not sure, some may have.

Did people usually marry within their race? (If yes, please explain why.)

Most Japanese marriages were arranged among the Japanese. Not sure about others. Most of the Filipino men were bachelors. That may be the reason why there were very few intermarriages among the Japanese at that time. There was an instance where a Japanese girl married a Portuguese boy and her family became very upset about it so the couple moved to the mainland. Intermarriage was not accepted by the first-generation Japanese.

Did people in the camps go to school? What level of education and where?

The older siblings attended through eighth grade because they had to work to help with family finances. Children began to attend high school from about 1935; after the war, some attended college mostly in Honolulu, a few went to the mainland. Most third generation children began to attend some post high school institutions.

Was college an option for people in these camps?

A few second generation children went to college but it was only if families could afford it or they were motivated to attend college. Some served in the military and attended college on the G. I. Bill.

What type of food was eaten in the camp?

I believe we all ate our own ethnic foods, but everyone ate rice. Portuguese families ate a lot of pork because they went hunting. The Japanese diet consisted of a lot of vegetable dishes cooked with home grown chicken.

What did people on the camps do for fun in their free time (games, hobbies)?

The Plantation organized sports leagues at each camp to compete with each other. They also provided transportation. Organized sports were baseball, volleyball and basketball. Of course, we swam in the Wailuku River, too. Girls generally were sent to sewing school during the summer.

What forms of transportation were used?

The Plantation truck would go around to pick up workers. Students walked to school. In 1932, our family was the only one to own a car, purchased secondhand from a Portuguese family.

Did any of the camps have gardens (vegetable)?

Each family had its own vegetable garden next to their houses so there was hardly any yard area. The Plantation also provided space next to the camp for families to use for their vegetable garden.

NOTES

Abbreviations:
AR = Archival Resource
B = Box
F = Folder
n.d. = not dated
- - - - - - - - - -

Message from a Daughter
1. Jiro Nakano and Kay Nakano, eds. and trans., *Poets Behind Barbed Wire: Tanka Poems by Keiho Soga, Taisanboku Mori, Sojin Takei, and Muin Ozaki* (Honolulu: Bamboo Ridge Press, 1983), 15. Translation used with permission.
2. Federal Bureau of Investigation, "Otokichi Ozaki, Registration Act," report prepared by Dale A. Curtis, Honolulu, Hawaiʻi, January 27, 1942, File No. 97-238, AR1, B14, F4.

Preface
1. Yasutaro (Keiho) Soga, *Life Behind Barbed Wire: The World War II Internment Memoirs of a Hawaiʻi Issei*, trans. by Kihei Hirai (Honolulu: University of Hawaiʻi Press, 2008); Soga Yasutaro, *Tessaku Seikatsu* (Honolulu: The Hawaii Times, 1948).
2. Suikei Furuya, *Haisho Tenten* (Honolulu: The Hawaii Times, 1964).
3. *Interview with Otokichi Ozaki*, directed by Bishop Museum, 1 hr., videocassette (Honolulu: Bishop Museum, 1978).
4. *Hawai nenkan: Jinmei jūshoroku, 1941* [The Hawaii Japanese Annual and Directory] (Honolulu: Nippu Jiji Co., 1941).

Introduction
1. Otokichi Ozaki, Radio Script, 1950, AR1, B4, F8, #5.
2. Patsy Sumie Saiki, *Ganbare! An Example of Japanese Spirit* (Honolulu: Mutual Publishing, 1982).
3. Saiki, 94.

Otokichi Ozaki's Internment History

1.   Otokichi Ozaki, "Internment History," n.d., AR1, B6-1, F14.

Chapter 1

1.   Nobuko Kosaki Fukuda, "A History of the Kosaki Family" (bound photocopy, 1993), 11.
2.   Hope Uejio Shimabukuro, "Biography of Haruo Ozaki Uejio" (photocopy, undated).
3.   Eiichiro Azuma, *Between Two Empires: Race, History, and Transnationalism in Japanese America* (New York: Oxford University Press, 2005), 30.
4.   Fukuda, 11.
5.   Lily Ozaki Arasato, interview by editor, April 19, 2007, Honolulu, Hawaii.
6.   Otokichi Ozaki, "Personal History, July 10, 1976," trans. Tatsumi Hayashi, (photocopy, 2001).
7.   Arasato interview.
8.   Bernice Yamagata Hirai, interview by editor, March 10, 2008, Honolulu, Hawaii.
9.   Shiho S. Nunes, email correspondence from Susan Nunes Fadley, daughter of Mrs. Nunes, to Lily Ozaki Arasato, to editor, March 18, 2011.
10. Shiho S. Nunes, letter to Lily Arasato, July 2011.
11. Ozaki, "Personal History, July 10, 1976."
12. Kiyoshi Tsuchiya, interview by unknown.
13. Elaine Hayashi Takato, interview by editor, October 4, 2007, Honolulu, Hawaii.
14. Patricia Hayashi Matsuda, interview by editor, October 4, 2007, Honolulu, Hawaii.
15. Herbert Segawa, "Mr. Otokichi Ozaki," (photocopy, 2008).
16. Lily Ozaki Arasato, "Hideko (Kobara) Ozaki," (photocopy).
17. Richard Kosaki, interview by editor, April 19, 2007, Honolulu, Hawaii.
18. Kosaki, interview.

Chapter 2

1.   Federal Bureau of Investigation, *Otokichi Ozaki, Registration Act*, prepared by Dale A. Curtis, Honolulu, Hawai'i, January 27, 1942, File No. 97-238, AR1, B14, F4.

2. Gary Y. Okihiro, *Cane Fires: The Anti-Japanese Movement in Hawaii, 1865-1945* (Philadelphia: Temple University Press, 1991), 210.

3. Tetsuden Kashima, *Judgment without Trial: Japanese American Imprisonment during World War II* (Seattle and London: University of Washington Press, 2003), 68.

4. Ibid., 78.

5. Federal Bureau of Investigation, *Otokichi Ozaki, Registration Act*, prepared by Dan M. Douglas, Honolulu, Hawaiʻi, November 1, 1941, File No. 97-238 GLP, AR1, B14, F1.

6. John Edgar Hoover, Federal Bureau of Investigation, to L. M. C. Smith, Special Defense Unit, memorandum, Washington, D. C., December 6, 1941, AR1, B14, F2.

7. Otokichi Ozaki, Radio Script, 1950, AR1, B4, F8, #5.

8. *Poets Behind Barbed Wire*, 16. Translation used with permission.

9. Otokichi Ozaki, Radio Script, 1950, AR1, B4, F8, #6.

10. Otokichi Ozaki, Radio Script, October 16, 1949, AR1, B4, F5, #1.

11. Otokichi Ozaki, Radio Script, n.d., AR1, B4, F15, #13.

12. Otokichi Ozaki, Radio Script, n.d. AR1, B4, F16, #14.

13. Translator's note, AR1, B9, F1.

14. Translated poetry, AR1, B9, F1.

15. Otokichi Ozaki, Radio Script, n.d., AR1, B4, F13, #7.

16. Otokichi Ozaki, Radio Script, n.d. AR1, B4, F13, #5.

17. Translated poetry, AR1, B9, F1.

18. Otokichi Ozaki, Radio Script, October 31, 1949, AR1, B4, F7, #3.

19. *Poets Behind Barbed Wire*, 20. Translation used with permission.

20. Otokichi Ozaki, Radio Script, 1950, AR1, B4, F8, #F.

21. Otokichi Ozaki, Radio Script, 1949, AR1, B4, F4, #2.

22. Otokichi Ozaki, Radio Script, n.d., AR1, B4, F15, #12.

Chapter 3

1. Otokichi Ozaki, Radio Script, n.d., AR1 B4, F13, #5.

2. Office of Japanese Detainees, Missoula, Montana, December 23, 1943, AR1, B10, F1.

3. U.S. Department of Justice Immigration and Naturalization Service, Missoula, Montana, October 18, 1943, AR1, B10, F1.

4. *Report of Internee Meeting with the Consul of Spain, Capt. A.R. Martin*, Missoula, Montana, December 17, 1943, AR1, B10, F1.

5. Document, n.d., AR1, B10, F1.

6. Charles Hasebe, to the Commanding General, Office of the Military

Governor Honolulu, Territory of Hawai'i, March 14, 1944, AR1, B10, F1.

7. Otokichi Ozaki, Radio Script, 1950, AR1, B4, F13, #B.
8. Otokichi Ozaki, Radio Script, 1950, AR1, B4, F13, #A.
9. Otokichi Ozaki, Radio Script, n.d., AR1 B4, F13, #7.
10. Otokichi Ozaki, Radio Script, n.d., AR1, B4, F8, #7.
11. David M. Marutani to Otokichi Ozaki, May 1 [1943], AR1, B1, F2, KH3-012 (AR1-BOX 6), #12.
12. Shoichi Asami to Otokichi Ozaki, June 24, 1943, AR1, B1, F2 KH-AR1-B1F1 #19.
13. Kametaro Maeda to Otokichi Ozaki, August 4, 1943, AR1, B1, F2, No. 25-2.
14. Otokichi Ozaki, *Santa Fe Internment Camp News*, c. July 1943, AR1, B6-2, F12, KH3-002.
15. Otokichi Ozaki, *Santa Fe Internment Camp News*, c. July 1943, AR1, B6-2, F12, KH3-003.
16. Otokichi Ozaki, *Santa Fe Internment Camp News*, c. July 1943, AR1, B6-2, F12, KH3-004.
17. Otokichi Ozaki, *Santa Fe Internment Camp News*, c. July 1943, AR1, B6-2, F12, KH3-004.
18. Otokichi Ozaki, *Santa Fe Internment Camp News*, c. July 1943, AR1, B6-2, F12, KH3-004.
19. Otokichi Ozaki, *Santa Fe Internment Camp News*, c. July 1943, AR1, B6-2, F12 KH3-005.
20. Otokichi Ozaki, *Santa Fe Internment Camp News*, c. July 1943, AR1, B6-2, F12, KH3-006.
21. Otokichi Ozaki, *Santa Fe Internment Camp News*, c. July 1943, AR1, B6-2, F12, KH3-006.
22. Otokichi Ozaki, *Santa Fe Internment Camp News*, c. July 1943, AR1, B6-2, F12, KH3-006.

Chapter 4
1. Kosaki, interview.
2. Kayo Kosaki to Otokichi Ozaki, February 25, 1942, AR1, B1, F1.
3. Hideko Ozaki to Otokichi Ozaki, May 6, 1942, AR1, B1, F1.
4. Hideko Ozaki to Otokichi Ozaki, May 20, 1942, AR1, B1, F1.
5. Hideko Ozaki to Otokichi Ozaki, June 3, 1942, AR1, B1, F1.
6. Hideko Ozaki to Otokichi Ozaki, July 6 [1942], AR1, B1, F1.
7. Shiho Shinoda Nunes to Otokichi Ozaki, July 7, 1942, AR1, B1, F1.

8. Earl Tomoyuki Ozaki to Otokichi Ozaki, July 16, 1942, AR1, B1, F1.

9. Tom T. Okino to Otokichi Ozaki, July 28, 1942, AR1, B1, F1.

10. Hideko Ozaki to Otokichi Ozaki, August 3 [1942], AR1, B1, F1.

11. Earl Tomoyuki Ozaki to Otokichi Ozaki, August 7 [1942], AR1, B1, F1.

12. Nobuko Kosaki to Otokichi Ozaki, August 12, 1942, AR1, B1, F1.

13. Earl Tomoyuki Ozaki to Otokichi Ozaki, n.d., AR1, B1, F1.

14. Kayo Kosaki to Otokichi Ozaki, August 25, 1942, AR1, B1, F1.

15. Hideko Ozaki to Otokichi Ozaki, August 30 [1942], AR1, B1, F1.

16. Hideko Ozaki to Otokichi Ozaki, September 4 [1942], AR1, B1, F1.

17. Hideko Ozaki to Otokichi Ozaki, October 15, 1942, AR1, B1, F1.

18. Nobuko Kosaki to Otokichi Ozaki, October 29, 1942, AR1, B1, F1.

19. Hideko Ozaki to Otokichi Ozaki, November 20 [1942], AR1, B1, F1.

20. Kazuki Kosaki to Otokichi Ozaki, November 24, 1942, AR1, B1, F1.

21. Kumataro Yoshioka to Otokichi Ozaki, December 1, 1942, AR1, B1, F1, 15A KHK-AR1-B1F1 #42.

22. Kazuki Kosaki to Otokichi Ozaki, January 13, 1943, AR1, B1, F2, KH-59 AR1 B1 F4.

23. Edward J. Ennis, Department of Justice, Alien Enemy Control Unit, to Otokichi Ozaki, January 20, 1943, AR1, B1, F2.

24. Kazuki and Kayo Ozaki to Otokichi Ozaki, February 17 [1943], AR1, B1, F2.

25. E. B. Whitaker, War Relocation Authority, to Hideko Ozaki, n.d., AR1, B1, F2.

26. Tomoya Ozaki to [Hideko Ozaki], March 1 [1943], AR1, B1, F7, KH-41 #17.

27. Tomoya Ozaki to Otokichi Ozaki, March 22, 1943, AR1, B1, F2, KH3-009.

28. Tomoya Ozaki to Otokichi Ozaki, April 28 [1943], AR1, B1, F2, KKH-AR1 B1 F1 #14.

29. Kazuki Kosaki to Hideko Ozaki, May 7 [1943], AR1, B1, F2, KH3-013 #15.

30. Edward J. Ennis, Department of Justice, Alien Enemy Control Unit, to Otokichi Ozaki, July 13, 1943, AR1, B1, F2.

31. Tadasuke Nakabayashi to Otokichi Ozaki, November 14, 1943, AR1, B1, F2, KH AR1-B1 F2 #38.

32. Kazuki Kosaki to Otokichi Ozaki, December 3, 1943, AR1, B1, F2, KH-AR1 B1 F2 #35.

33. Kazuki Kosaki to Hideko Ozaki, December 3, 1943, AR1, B1, F2,

KH AR1-B1 F2 #36.

34. J. Lloyd Webb, Jerome Relocation Center, to Hideko Ozaki, December 11, 1943, AR1, B1, F2.

35. Tomoya Ozaki to Otokichi Ozaki, January 5, 1944, AR1, B1, F7, KH-49 #2.

36. Kazuki Kosaki to Otokichi Ozaki, January 6 [1944], AR1, B1, F7.

37. Kazuki Kosaki to Otokichi Ozaki, January 16 [1944], AR1, B1, F7, KH-52 #6B.

38. Tomoya Ozaki to Hideko Ozaki, March 8, 1944, AR1, B1, F7, KH-42B #18.

Chapter 5

1. Hideko Ozaki to Otokichi Ozaki, March 10 [1943], AR1, B1, F5.

2. Hideko Ozaki to Otokichi Ozaki, April 13, 1943, AR1, B1, F5.

3. Hideko Ozaki to Otokichi Ozaki, April 27, 1943, AR1, B1, F5.

4. Hideko Ozaki to Otokichi Ozaki, May 11, 1943, AR1, B1, F6.

5. Hideko Ozaki to Otokichi Ozaki, May 31 [1943], AR1, B1, F6.

6. Tomoyuki Ozaki to Otokichi Ozaki, June 3 [1943], AR1, B1, F6.

7. Hideko Ozaki to Otokichi Ozaki, June 10, 1943, AR1, B1, F6.

8. Hideko Ozaki to Otokichi Ozaki, July 2 [1943], AR1, B1, F6.

9. Hideko Ozaki to Otokichi Ozaki, July 10 [1943], AR1, B1, F6.

10. Hideko Ozaki to Otokichi Ozaki, July 21 [1943], AR1, B1, F6.

11. Hideko Ozaki to Otokichi Ozaki, July 29 [1943], AR1, B1, F6.

12. Hideko Ozaki to Otokichi Ozaki, August 5 [1943], AR1, B1, F6.

13. Paul A. Taylor, Jerome Relocation Center, to Hideko Ozaki, August 7, 1943, AR1, B10, F6.

14. Hideko Ozaki to Otokichi Ozaki, August 10 [1943], AR1, B1, F6.

15. Hideko Ozaki to Otokichi Ozaki, August 20 [1943], AR1, B1, F6.

16. Hideko Ozaki to Otokichi Ozaki, n.d., AR1, B1, F6.

17. Hideko Ozaki to Otokichi Ozaki, October 23 [1943], AR1, B1, F6.

18. Hideko Ozaki to Otokichi Ozaki, November 22 [1943], AR1, B1, F6.

19. Hideko Ozaki to Otokichi Ozaki, November 25 [1943], AR1, B1, F6.

20. Hideko Ozaki to Otokichi Ozaki, November 26 [1943], AR1, B1, F6.

21. Hideko Ozaki to Otokichi Ozaki, December 6 [1943], AR1, B1, F6.

22. Hideko Ozaki to Otokichi Ozaki, December 27 [1943], AR1, B1, F6.

23. Hideko Ozaki to Otokichi Ozaki, December 30 [1943], AR1, B1, F6.

24. Hideko Ozaki to Otokichi Ozaki, January 7, 1944, AR1, B1, F7.

25. Hideko Ozaki to Otokichi Ozaki, January 17 [1944], AR1, B1, F7.

26. Hideko Ozaki to Otokichi Ozaki, January 21 [1944], AR1, B1, F7.

27. Hideko Ozaki to Otokichi Ozaki, January 25 [1944], AR1, B1, F7, #9.
28. Hideko Ozaki to Otokichi Ozaki, January 29 [1944], AR1, B1, F7, #10.
29. Hideko Ozaki to Otokichi Ozaki, February 23 [1944], AR1, B1, F7.
30. Hideko Ozaki to Otokichi Ozaki, March 1 [1944], AR1, B1, F7.
31. Tsutomu Nakauchi to Tomoyuki Ozaki, February 18, 1944, AR1, B1, F2.
32. Hideo Nakauchi to Hideko Ozaki, 1944, AR1, B1, F2, KH AR1-B1 F2 #41.
33. Hideo Nakauchi to Tomoyuki Ozaki, March 20, 1944, AR1, B1, F8.
34. Mrs. Nakauchi to Hideko Ozaki, March 17 [1944], AR1, B1, F2, KH-58.
35. Bob Toyama to Hideko Ozaki, October 14, 1943, AR1, B1, F2.
36. S. Kubota to Hideko Ozaki, April 4, 1944, AR1 B1 F2.

Chapter 6

1. Thomas B. Lyle, War Relocation Authority, to Otokichi Ozaki, April 5, 1944, AR1, B1, F8.
2. Katsuko Ochiai to Hideko Ozaki, April 14, 1944, AR1, B1, F8.
3. Otokichi Ozaki to Kazuki and Kayo Kosaki, n.d., AR1, B1, F8.
4. Otokichi Ozaki to Kazuki and Kayo Kosaki, April 19 [1944], AR1, B1, F8.
5. Otokichi Ozaki postscript to April 19 letter to Kazuki and Kayo Kosaki, April 26 [1944], AR1, B1, F8.
6. Tomoyuki Ozaki to Tomoya and Shobu Ozaki, April 22, 1945, AR1, B3, F1.
7. Kazuma Kataoka to Tomoya Ozaki, May 12 [1944], AR1, B1, F8, KH-45.
8. J. Lloyd Webb, Jerome Relocation Center, to Hideko Ozaki, June 6, 1944, AR1, B1, F8.
9. H. C. Walters, Bank of Hawaii, to Otokichi Ozaki, June 29, 1944, AR1, B1, F8.
10. Tomoya Ozaki to Otokichi and Hideko Ozaki, July 20 [1944], AR1, B1, F2, KH-AR1 B1 F2 No. 21.
11. Momoe [Kataoka] to Otokichi Ozaki, n.d., AR1, B3, F1.
12. Tomoya Ozaki to Otokichi and Hideko Ozaki, August 30 [1944], AR1, B1, F2, KH-AR1 B1 F2 No. 24.
13. H. C. Walters, Bank of Hawaii, to Otokichi Ozaki, August 29, 1944,

AR1, B1, F8.

14. Kazuma Kataoka to Otokichi Ozaki, September 17, 1944, AR1, B1, F8.

15. Tomoya Ozaki to Otokichi and Hideko Ozaki, September 2[?, 1944], AR1, B3, F2.

16. Tomoya Ozaki to Otokichi and Hideko Ozaki, September 27 [1944], AR1, B3, F2, KH-08.

17. Otokichi Ozaki to Mr. and Mrs. Koryu Nakabayashi, October 11, 1944, AR1, B1, F8, KH-55.

18. Yoshio Shiwo to Otokichi Ozaki, October 13, 1944, AR1, B1, F8.

19. Tomoya Ozaki to Otokichi and Hideko Ozaki, October 15 [1944], AR1, B1, F8, KH AR1-B1 F8-7.

20. Tomoya Ozaki to Hideko Ozaki, n.d., AR1, B1, F8, KH AR1-B1 F8-5.

21. L. V. Darling to Otokichi Ozaki, October 20, 1944, AR1, B1, F8.

22. L. V. Darling to Otokichi Ozaki, October 31, 1944, AR1, B1, F8.

23. H. C. Walters, Bank of Hawaii, to Otokichi Ozaki, November 14, 1944, AR1, B1, F9.

24. Otokichi Ozaki to Mrs. Nakabayashi, November 27 [1944], AR1, B1, F9, KH-53.

25. Mrs. Fujimoto to Otokichi Ozaki, November 29 [1944], AR1, B1, F9.

26. Fudeko Ikeda to Otokichi Ozaki, December 17 [1944], AR1, B1, F9.

27. Tomoya Ozaki to Otokichi Ozaki, January 3 [1945], AR1, B3, F1.

28. Michi Kajiwara to Hideko Ozaki, January 10, 1945, AR1, B3, F1.

29. Keikichi Ochiai to Otokichi Ozaki, January 15 [1945], AR1, B3, F1, KH-28.

30. Torazo Ishiyama to Otokichi Ozaki, January 19 [1945], AR1, B3, F1, KH-26.

31. Mino Kiyota to Otokichi Ozaki, January 20 [1945], AR1, B3, F1, KH-48.

32. Fudeko [Ikeda]to Hideko Ozaki, January 26 [1945], AR1, B3, F1, KH-15.

33. Fusayo Iwami to Otokichi Ozaki, February 15 [1945], AR1, B3, F1.

34. Seikaku Takezono to Otokichi Ozaki, February 22 [1945], AR1, B3, F1.

35. Tomoya Ozaki to Otokichi and Hideko Ozaki, February 22 [1945], AR1, B3, F1, KH-56.

36. Tomoya Ozaki to Hideko Ozaki, February 23 [1945], AR1, B3, F1,

KH-33.

37. Tetsuo Tanaka to Otokichi and Hideko Ozaki, March 2, 1945, AR1, B3, F1, KH-22.

38. Michi Kajiwara to Otokichi and Hideko Ozaki, March 6, 1945, AR1, B3, F1.

39. Haru Kobara to the family of Otokichi Ozaki, March 27 [1945], AR1, B1, F8, KH-43.

40. Tomoya Ozaki to Otokichi and Hideko Ozaki, March 29 [1945], AR1, B1, F8, KH-44.

41. Tomoya Ozaki to Hideko Ozaki, April 24 [1945], AR1, B3, F1, KH-04.

42. Tomoya Ozaki to Hideko Ozaki, May 30 [1945], AR1, B1, F2, KH3-015 #16.

43. Mrs. [Haru] Kobara to Otokichi Ozaki and family, June 1 [1945], AR1, B3, F1, KH-06.

44. Tomoya Ozaki to Otokichi and Hideko Ozaki, June 14 [1945], AR1, B3, F1, KH-05.

45. Ichiro Kasai to Otokichi Ozaki, June 28, 1945, AR1, B3, F1, KH-08.

Chapter 7

1. Tameshige Sueoka to Otokichi Ozaki, August 12 [1945], AR1, B3, F2, KH-21.

2. Tomoya Ozaki to Otokichi and Hideko Ozaki, August 15, 1945, AR1, B3, F2, KH-30.

3. Yoshio Shiwo to Otokichi Ozaki, August 24, 1945, AR1, B3, F2, KH-29.

4. Hiromichi Kosaki to Otokichi Ozaki, September 3, 1945, AR1, B3, F2.

5. Kazuki Kosaki to Otokichi and Hideko Ozaki, September 6 [1945], AR1, B3, F2, KH-10.

6. Otokichi Ozaki to B. R. Stauber, September 14, 1945, AR1, B14, F23.

7. Tomoya Ozaki to Otokichi and Hideko Ozaki, September 16 [1945], AR1, B3, F2, KH-13.

8. Tomoya Ozaki to Otokichi and Hideko Ozaki, September 20 [1945], AR1, B3, F2, KH-12.

9. J. Kaneshiro to Otokichi Ozaki, September 20 [1945], AR1, B3, F2.

10. Tomoya Ozaki to Otokichi and Hideko Ozaki, October 2 [1945], AR1, B3, F2, KH-11.

11. J. Kaneshiro to Otokichi Ozaki, October 6 [1945], AR1, B3, F2, #1.
12. Otokichi Ozaki to Koryu Nakabayashi, October 8, 1945, AR1, B3, F2, KH-54.
13. Hiromichi Kosaki to Otokichi and Hideko Ozaki, October 12 [1945], AR1, B3, F2.
14. Junto Tsutsui to Otokichi Ozaki, October 17, 1945, AR1, B3, F2.
15. Kenzo Maehara to Otokichi Ozaki, October 21 [1945], AR1, B3, F2, KH-23.
16. Tomoya Ozaki to Otokichi and Hideko Ozaki, November 10 [1945], AR1, B3, F3, KH-1.
17. Mrs. Nakauchi to Otokichi Ozaki, November 13 [1945], AR1, B3, F3.
18. Mitsuko to Otokichi and Hideko Ozaki, November 29 [1945], AR1, B3, F3, KH-15.
19. Yoshio Shinoda to Otokichi Ozaki, December 15 [1945], AR1, B3, F3, KH AR1-B3 F3-11.
20. Rokutaro Tango to Otokichi Ozaki, December 18 [1945], AR1, B3, F3, KH2-007, AR1-B3-F2.
21. Bunnosuke Sato to Otokichi and Hideko Ozaki, December 20 [1945], AR1, B3, F3, KH2-009 AR1-B3-F3.
22. Unknown to Otokichi Ozaki, December 24 [1945], AR1, B3, F3, KH AR1-B3 F3-10.

Epilogue

1. All of his postwar activities were taken from the "Personal History of Otokichi Ozaki," based on his own writing on July 10, 1976, and translated by Tatsumi Hayashi.

BIBLIOGRAPHY

Books

Azuma, Eiichiro. *Between Two Empires: Race, History, and Transnationalism in Japanese America.* New Y ork: Oxford University Press, 2005.

Chang, Gordon, ed. *Morning Glory, Evening Shadow: Yamato Ichihashi and His Internment Writings,* 1942-1945. Stanford: Stanford University Press, 1997.

Fiset, Louis, ed. *Imprisoned Apart: The World War II Correspondence of an Issei Couple.* Seattle: University of Washington Press, 1997.

Furuya, Suikei. *Haisho Tenten.* Honolulu: The Hawaii Times, 1964.

Hawai nenkan: Jinmei jūshoroku, 1941. Honolulu: Nippu Jiji Co., 1941.

Hazama, Dorothy Ochiai and Jane Okamoto Komeiji. *Okagesama de: The Japanese in Hawaii, 1885-1985.* Honolulu: The Bess Press, Inc., 1986.

Hirabayashi, Lane Ryo. *The Politics of Fieldwork: Research in an American Concentration Camp.* Tucson: University of Arizona Press, 1997.

Kawakami, Barbara F. *Japanese Immigrant Clothing in Hawaii, 1885-1941.* Honolulu: University of Hawaii Press, 1993.

Keene, Donald, trans. *Chūshingura: The Treasury of Loyal Retainers.* New York: Columbia University Press, 1971.

Kimura, Yukiko. *Issei: Japanese Immigrants in Hawaii.* Honolulu: University of Hawai'i Press, 1988.

Kotani, Roland. *The Japanese in Hawaii: A Century of Struggle.* Honolulu: The Hawaii Hochi, Ltd., 1985.

Moon, Thomas N. *The Deadliest Colonel.* New York: Vantage Press, 1975.

Nakamura, Richard I. and Gloria R. Kobayashi. *The History of the Waiakea Pirates Athletic Club and the Yashijima Story (Waiakea Town).* Hilo: Waiakea Pirates Athletic Club, 1999.

Nishimoto, Richard S. *Inside an American Concentration Camp: Japanese American Resistance at Poston, Arizona.* Edited by Lane Ryo Hirabayashi. Tucson: University of Arizona Press, 1995.

Nunes, Shiho S. and Sara Nunes-Atabaki. *The Shishu Ladies of Hilo: Japanese Embroidery in Hawai'i.* Honolulu: University of Hawai'i Press, 1999.

The Pacific War and Peace: Americans of Japanese Ancestry in Military Intelligence Service 1941 to 1952. San Francisco: Military Intelligence Service Association of Northern California, 1991.

Saiki, Patsy Sumie. *Ganbare! An Example of Japanese Spirit.* Honolulu: Mutual Publishing, 1982.

Soga, Yasutaro. *Gojūnenkan no hawai kaikō.* Osaka: Osaka kōsoku insatsu kabushiki kaisha, 1953.

_____. *Life Behind Barbed Wire: The World War II Internment Memoirs of a Hawai'i Issei.* Translated by Kihei Hirai. Honolulu: University of Hawai'i Press, 2008.

_____. *Tessaku Seikatsu.* Honolulu: The Hawaii Times, 1948.

Soga, Keiho, Taisanboku Mori, Sojin Takei, and Muin Ozaki. *Poets Behind Barbed Wire.* Edited and translated by Jiro Nakano and Kay Nakano. Honolulu: Bamboo Ridge Press, 1983.

Online sources

"Killed in Action: The Complete List," on the Honoring the Nisei Veterans website, http://honoringtheniseiveteran.org/KIA's/ALL_KIAS/Sato%20Takeo.pdf (Takeo Sato page discontinued).

Miller, J. Scott. "Early Voice Recordings of Japanese Storytelling." *Oral Tradition,* 11, no. 2 (1996): 301-19. http://journal.oraltradition.org/files/articles/11ii/10_miller.pdf.

Unpublished manuscripts

Arasato, Lily Ozaki. "Hideko (Kobara) Ozaki." Photocopied.

Fukuda, Nobuko Kosaki. "A History of the Kosaki Family." 1993. Photocopied and bound.

Ozaki, Otokichi. "Personal History, 10 July 1976." Translated by Tatsumi Hayashi. 2001. Photocopied.

Segawa, Herbert. "Mr. Otokichi Ozaki." 2008. Photocopied.

Shimabukuro, Hope Uejio. "Biography of Haruo Ozaki Uejio." Undated. Photocopied.

Interviews

Arasato, Lily Ozaki. 2007. Interview by editor. Honolulu, Hawai'i, 19 April.

Hayashi, Tatsumi. 2008. Interview by editor. Honolulu, Hawai'i, 3 December.

Hirai, Bernice Yamagata. 2008. Interview by editor. Honolulu, Hawai'i, 10 March.

Kosaki, Richard. 2007. Interview by editor. Honolulu, Hawai'i, 19 April.

Kurahara, Jane. 2008. Interview by editor. Honolulu, Hawaiʻi, 4 December.

Matsuda, Patricia Hayashi. 2007. Interview by editor. Honolulu, Hawaiʻi, 4 October.

Sugimoto, Florence. 2007. Interview by editor. Honolulu, Hawaiʻi, 20 July.

Takato, Elaine Hayashi. 2007. Interview by editor. Honolulu, Hawaiʻi, 4 October.

Tsuchiya, Kiyoshi. Interview by unknown. Place and date unknown.

Yoshitake, Shige. 2007. Interview by editor. Honolulu, Hawaiʻi, 20 July.

Videocassettes

Interview with Otokichi Ozaki. Directed by the Bishop Museum. Honolulu: Bishop Museum, 1978. Videocassette, 60 min.

Manuscript Collection

Ozaki, Otokichi. Papers. Japanese Cultural Center of Hawaiʻi Resource Center, Archival Collection 1, Honolulu, Hawaiʻi.

INDEX

Production Notes for Honda / Family Torn Apart

Design and composition by Shu Zong Chen and Suann Chen of
FreelanceDreams LLC with text in Garamond and display in CgGothic.

ABOUT THE EDITOR

Gail Honda is a communication instructor at Hawai'i Pacific University and holds a Ph.D. in Japanese history from the University of Chicago. She is president of Global Optima, Inc., a writing, editing, and training company.